To Nick
Best Wishes
at W and L

Earl Weaver

IT'S WHAT YOU LEARN
AFTER
YOU KNOW IT ALL
THAT COUNTS

Also by Berry Stainback

A VERY DIFFERENT LOVE STORY

JOE, YOU COULDA MADE US PROUD
(with Joe Pepitone)

It's What You Learn After You Know It All That Counts

By
Earl Weaver

with
Berry Stainback

DOUBLEDAY & COMPANY, INC.

GARDEN CITY, NEW YORK

1982

Library of Congress Cataloging in Publication Data

Weaver, Earl, 1930-
    It's what you learn after you know it all that counts.

    1. Weaver, Earl, 1930-   . 2. Baseball—United
States—Managers—Biography. I. Stainback, Berry.
II. Title.
    GV865.W38A34   796.357'092'4 [B]   AACR2

DESIGN BY RAYMOND DAVIDSON

ISBN: 0-385-17650-3
Library of Congress Catalog Card Number 81-43301

This book is dedicated to my mother and dad and all the members of our closeknit family . . . particularly my children Michael, Rhonda, Terry, and Kim, who understood the absence of a father due to his chosen profession; and above all to my wife, Marianna, who through her love and understanding made me realize that most goals are easily attained.

IT'S WHAT YOU LEARN
AFTER
YOU KNOW IT ALL
THAT COUNTS

PREFACE

Writers have often found Earl Weaver to be a most complex and controversial individual. Certainly he has always spoken his mind with a kind of the-truth-shall-set-them-free gusto, and he suffers fools ungladly. Weaver has snapped at uninformed members of the media, railed at unenlightened members of the umpiring profession, charged American League President Lee MacPhail with ignorance of the rules of baseball, battled bosses who were reluctant to pay him a reasonable salary, and loudly challenged players who were not performing up to their capabilities.

Aggressiveness and positive thinking are keystones of Earl Weaver.

When he was named manager of the Baltimore Orioles midway through the 1968 season—a short, pudgy, gravel-voiced veteran of twenty years in the minor leagues—Weaver says, "I had a talk with myself. I felt the team was good enough to win and that the players would respect me. Some would like me and others would not when I had to sit them down. But I told myself that all my decisions would be *right*. They couldn't all be, of course, and I'm not so hard-headed that I haven't profited from wrong decisions. But I always make the decision convinced it will be right and go from there."

Like Pete Rose, as a player Weaver extended himself to the maximum. His abiding regret is that his own playing abilities were not of major-league caliber. But as a manager he is nonpariel. Going into the 1981 season Weaver's major-league winning percentage of .599 was second only to Joe McCarthy's .614, and experts maintain that, overall, Marse Joe's ball clubs had more talented personnel. Weaver has been able to adjust and win with every kind of ball club—young teams, old teams, power teams, running teams—because he makes exquisite use of every individual on his twenty-five-man roster.

In the past twenty-five years, Weaver's teams have finished first or second nineteen times. How he has managed to win so often is the theme of this book. But before Earl begins to tell his story, I want to "show" the man behind that astounding record as he performed his duties during a home-and-away series against the Yankees. Though the series occurred early in the 1981 season, each game between the rivals was played amidst the aura and intensity of World Series competition. Earl Weaver was, of course, aggressive and positive.

The first series would be in Baltimore, and Weaver arose as usual before 8 A.M. at his three-bedroom home in suburban Perry Hall. He donned old jeans and a polo shirt, then made instant coffee and brought in the newspapers. His slender, attractive wife, Marianna, joined him at the kitchen table. She hurriedly drank her coffee and Earl kissed her on the cheek and said, "Good luck" as Marianna went off to an early golf date. Then Earl ran through the sports sections and swiftly filled in the crossword puzzle while consuming three cups of coffee and inhaling three Raleigh cigarettes. He smokes constantly and refuses to be photographed while indulging in "this filthy habit," not wanting to influence youngsters. The kitchen, in which he does as much cooking as Marianna, is replete with gadgets he has acquired for Raleigh coupons. A stack of them was growing in a container on the counter, and I asked what else he might get with the coupons? Earl smiled and said, "A brass coffin."

He walked out the back door to the tool shed beyond his in-ground swimming pool, taking the long, quick strides that are characteristic of the man. When he has laid out a job for himself, Earl does everything at full speed, as if his energies cannot be contained. This morning he was going to work on his garden, which sits on the rise above the pool. The plot was only 25′ × 35′, but Earl had made use of every inch of his soil. He had planted tomatoes, peppers, eggplant, zucchini, onions, radishes, lettuce, cauliflower, broccoli, and stringbeans, and all of the plants appeared to be thriving.

But Earl was not satisfied. He wanted his garden to be a pennant winner and he began performing a task one might not expect of the finest manager in baseball history. Oriole coach Cal Ripken had given Earl a five-gallon bucket of cow flop, the contents of which he began mixing with water in a garbage can. The odor that emerged as he stirred with a shovel sent me scurrying up wind, but Earl was not deterred.

"Pat Santarone got me into gardening when we were in Elmira, New York, together in the sixties," said Earl, whose recommendation of Santarone brought the groundskeeper to Baltimore. "Pat claims cowshit will triple the size of your vegetables, and he has the best garden I've ever seen."

Earl, whose voice sounds like it is filtered through gravel, let out a raspy cackle. "Billy Martin and I used to have contests to see who could grow the biggest tomatoes. In September of 1980 Oakland came in and I presented Billy with a tomato the size of a melon! When I carried it over to Billy he reached out and touched it as if it was a stage prop. 'Match that, Billy!' I said. Earl cackled again, his expressive eyes agleam with mirth. "Then I had to tell him that Santarone had grown that tomato using cowshit. It's wondrous stuff."

When the manure had been diluted to the point where it could be poured through a watering-can nozzle, Earl submerged the can until it was full. He pulled it out and his gloveless hand was wet to the wrist. "Maybe this'll help my arthritis," he said, smiling. He dipped, hauled, and poured the fertilizer for more than an hour, all the while planning his five-minute pregame show he had to write and record for WFBR radio. Then he showered, did his show, and played it back to check the time with a stopwatch.

"Last season, when I started doing this I was terrible," he said. "But like anything else, the more you do something the better you become. Now I'm semi-professional and improving. Once I started leaving in the 'thems' and 'thoses,' the show read smoother."

On "Manager's Corner" Earl discussed the doubleheader loss in Detroit the day before, saying the first-place O's had not "played that bad a baseball," but wildness among his pitchers had hurt. "Our team batting average had gone up from around .210 to .270 in the past few weeks, and we'd been getting our hits at the right time. So things had to level off and some of the breaks had to start going against us." He went on to talk about the thinness of his bullpen for that night's game. "If we can get seven or eight innings out of Jim Palmer, it would really help us for the final two games of the series. There is no such thing as a crucial series this early in the year, but both teams know how important these games are." The fact was that the team that won the season's series between the Yankees and Orioles would likely win the division. Call these games quasi crucial.

Weaver then cooked a lunch of leftover ham, fresh beets that he and Marianna had canned the previous year, and succulent deep-fried corn. As Earl doesn't have room to grow corn, he gets it by the bushel from a nearby farmer friend and stores it in one of his two freezers. The meal was so delicious we did not leave many vittles for Marianna. But she returned from golfing too excited to eat much.

Earl glowed as Marianna described the two good rounds she had shot, interrupting her only to seek clarification or to praise. Earl loves his wife and he loves a winner, and when they are one and the same he is ecstatic. They are both very competitive golfers who play daily throughout the winter in Hialeah, Florida, where they have a beautiful home abutting the country club course. His first marriage was a sudden and depressing casualty of his nomadic baseball career. Meeting Marianna, whom he married in 1964, saved his sanity, he feels. "She's the best thing that ever happened to me," he said flatly as he cleaned up the pots from the stove. "From the beginning she boosted my confidence."

"That's because I always felt Earl could do anything he set out to do," Marianna said.

She had a light snack, then joined Earl in the bedroom for his daily one-hour afternoon nap before he leaves for the ball park. "It refreshes me for the game," he said. "And I can really use it after a workout like today's."

At 3 P.M. we set off for Memorial Stadium, a twenty-five-minute drive, in the 1981 Toyota Celica Supra that Weaver's radio-show sponsor provided for the season. Thinking about the tired arms on his pitching staff, Earl said, "I'm glad I didn't go along with Palmer's request to move to the bullpen ten days ago. After Jimmy got knocked out of a game in Toronto, he told the writers: 'I've pitched over thirty-five hundred innings in the majors, and I just can't go nine anymore. I think I should go to the bullpen. Or maybe I should retire.'"

Earl laughed, saying, "After fifteen years with Palmer, I'm never surprised by anything he says. But I didn't know about his postgame comments until the next morning. The writers started calling me at seven-thirty asking if Palmer was going to the bullpen. I said I didn't know anything about that. I certainly had no such plans, but I hadn't talked to Jim. His record was 1-and-1 and he hadn't pitched that badly.

"It turned out his quotes had gone out on the wire services, though, and my phone kept ringing and ringing. I finally started getting mad, because I didn't know what to tell the writers—except to call Palmer himself. The trouble is that Palmer goes to model underwear in the mornings and he goes to the movies in the afternoons. Nobody could reach him."

That evening, Palmer arrived at the ball park soon after Weaver, who asked, "What the hell's the problem, Jim?"

"What problem?"

"I understand you're telling everyone you can't go nine innings anymore."

"Oh, I can go nine. But the other starters are pitching better than me, so I volunteered to go to the bullpen. I'll do anything you want to help the club. But I think I should retire."

"Retire?" Weaver said. "Jim, you're too smart to do that."

"I know it," Palmer said.

Earl laughed and shook his head. "Jimmy's such a competitor. He went out and beat the Twins 6–3 in his next start. His arm isn't resilient enough for the bullpen anyway, and once Steve Stone went on the disabled list there was no way I could've put Jim in the pen even if I wanted to." Earl lit a cigarette. "But Jimmy's always making some comment that, in context or out, gets into the papers. Then the writers call me as if *I* know something. Last winter in Florida, I got a dozen calls on Palmer one day. There was a big story in the New York *Post* in which

Palmer said he was contemplating retirement, that he was really hurting. I got right on the phone to our general manager, Hank Peters, to find out what the hell was going on. Hank told me Palmer was pitching every day from a special mound they'd built under the stands in Baltimore."

Weaver turned into the "official parking" gate at the stadium and parked by the main entrance. He strode through it like a king entering his castle, his neatly barbered silvery hair undulating to his steps as he zipped through a series of labyrinthian passageways to the Oriole clubhouse and on into his corner office. It was austere: a desk, three chairs, a TV set, a dressing cubicle crammed with uniform number 4, and a refrigerator stocked with beer and soft drinks. No photos or decorations on the walls, nothing that speaks of his success over the years.

Weaver changed into his uniform, then sat at his desk and put on his glasses. He seldom wears them except when he studies the famous "stat" sheets he uses in making out his lineup. He picked up the sheets, which contained the batting records of each Yankee player against each Oriole pitcher. The Orioles chart every pitch thrown by their staff, recording not only the type of pitch and its location—in, out, high, low—but where those pitches that were hit landed. Thus, the Oriole pitchers know how to work on each batter. Weaver, and usually pitching coach Ray Miller, goes over the opposing lineup with his starting pitcher and catchers before each game.

"I understand Morales has been saying he hits the shit out of Ron Guidry [the Yankee starter]," Earl said, speaking of his right-handed pinch-hitting ace José Morales. In 6 major-league seasons, Morales had led his league in pinch hits 4 times, which was why the O's had signed him as a free agent that winter. Morales was hitting .364 in 22 at-bats this season.

"Let's see what he's done against Guidry," Earl said, running his finger down the stats steet. "He's 4-for-14 lifetime. That's right at .300." His finger moved up to Benny Ayala, another strong right-handed hitter. "Benny's 4-for-8 against Guidry lifetime. I don't know how. Benny's not really a fastball hitter, he's a breaking-ball hitter."

Earl lit a cigarette and thought a moment. "I ought to DH Morales and play Ayala in left, moving Roenicke to center." Gary

Roenicke was batting .376 in 37 games and was excellent defensively in center field. The regular there, Al Bumbry, had a pulled hamstring muscle, but said he could start. "I can't play Ayala and Kenny Singleton in the same outfield with Palmer pitching," Earl said.

"Why?" I asked.

"Because Palmer won't pitch!" He laughed.

Ayala is merely adequate defensively. Singleton has a fine arm but slow feet. Still, if that was the only starting lineup that Earl felt the O's could win with—he would play it and Palmer would pitch.

Ralph Rowe, the Orioles' batting instructor, came into the office and Earl greeted him. Rowe had been working with the players who had come out early for extra batting practice: Mark Belanger, Terry Crowley, Doug DeCinces, Rick Dempsey, and Dan Graham.

"There's a tremendous spirit on this club," Weaver said. "Everyone's taking extra BP. Jimmy Williams [who had replaced Frank Robinson on the coaching staff after he signed to manage the Giants] has a sore arm from throwing so much BP." The phone rang and Earl said, "That'll be Russo. Take it at my desk, Ralph."

Rowe picked up the receiver and made notes on the Yankee pitching patterns, as related by advance man Jimmy Russo, who had been scouting the Yankees for eight games. "We'll give the players Jimmy's information," Earl explained, "what the Yankee pitchers have been throwing in various situations."

Weaver went through the 3 × 5 cards he had on each Yankee player. The cards contained all the inside information on how to pitch to and defense the hitters, as well as complete scouting reports on the pitchers and their patterns. Combining these with the computer print-out stats and Russo's perceptions gives Weaver a lot of insights on how to make best use of his players. Earl Weaver is the manager who introduced the use of statistics into the dugout. Earl actually tapes his stats and copies of his and the opposing lineups to the dugout wall for ready reference during games. Having witnessed the efficacy of this procedure, Frank Robinson took it with him to San Francisco. Why every major-league manager doesn't adopt the system is a mystery, be-

cause most would pinch hit for a lifetime .229 hitter like Mark
Belanger against an awesome pitcher such as Nolan Ryan. Not
Weaver, whose stats tell him that Belanger's career average
against Ryan is .300.

"When Ralph's done," Earl said to me, "I'll take the hitters
from Russo. If he's got anything new, I'll add it to my cards. I
doubt that he'll make me change anything at this point. But I
need his report on catcher Barry Foote. The Yankees got Barry
from the National League to fill in for Rick Cerone. We have no
stats on Foote."

Rowe finished and Earl sat at the desk and cradled the phone
against his left ear with his shoulder. He listened to Russo's reports while reading his cards to see if changes should be made.
Foote turned out to be a highball hitter with power, who "looks
bad swinging at sliders."

"Let's skip Reggie Jackson," Earl told Russo at one point.
"Reggie hit .146 against us last season, only 6 hits. I know four
of them were homers, Jimmy, but you're gonna make 4 mistakes
against him over a season, that's a cinch. I know he gets anxious
up there. If he keeps his bat on his shoulder, we'll walk him."

Russo went on for a few more minutes and as he finished, Earl
said, mimicking the O's superscout: " 'Pitch him up and in—but
make it good.' For chrissake, Jimmy, you said that about fifteen
guys! He cackled. "Say, are you home now? You put in a garden
this year? Look, Rip just got me a bucket of cowshit for fertilizer. What do you mean you want a bucket of cowshit? You already got enough bullshit for three gardens!"

Earl then proceeded to write out his lineup, but three names
into it he suddenly tore up the card. He threw it and the green
pen into the wastebasket. "I'm not gonna make out a lineup with
that *former* nine-game-winning-streak pen. We lost two with it
yesterday." He unzipped a small plastic case, dumped out a
number of red, green, black, and blue pens and selected a blue
one. He printed his lineup, starting Bumbry and using Ayala—a
.214 average on the season but .500 lifetime against Guidry—as
the designated hitter in the fifth spot in the order. Then he wrote
in "DeCinces," followed by "Roenicke," saying, "I'm batting a
.216 hitter [Doug DeCinces] ahead of the hottest bat in the
league [Gary Roenicke]. Some people think I'm nuts, but they

don't know that DeCinces's got better career stats against Guidry than Roenicke." Morales was on the bench for pinch-hitting duties if needed.

He wasn't needed. Bumbry opened the game with a single, stole second, and scored on Rich Dauer's sacrifice fly. Ayala went 3-for-3 with 2 RBIs. DeCinces hit a 2-run homer in the second and a 3-run shot in the fifth, giving him 4 in the last 3 games. Palmer pitched a complete game, allowing only 5 hits and 1 run as the Orioles won 10–1. Good lineup, Earl.

In addition, Belanger hit his first home run at Memorial Stadium in almost five years—a ball that caromed off the left-field foul pole—and the 43,000 spectators in attendance cheered him back out of the dugout for a wave. The .181 hitter and impeccable fielder tipped his cap and smiled. Fans also insisted that DeCinces step back out for some adulation after his second home run. When Ultimatefan Bill Hagy began leading cheers atop the O's dugout, several players leaned out to admire his antics. The players and fans in Baltimore seemed to have a sweet sympatico going.

"Paul Richards said it many years ago," Earl told the press afterward: " 'You're never as good as you look when you win. And you're never as bad as you look when you lose.' " It was the Orioles' eleventh win in their last 14 games and maintained their hold on first place in the American League East.

Someone asked about Palmer's performance and Earl said, "The smartest move I ever made was keeping my ace out of the bullpen. We needed that complete game and Jim gave it to us, as he has so many times. On nights like this—hell on most nights —he makes it look so damned easy. With that fluid motion of his, there's no reason why he can't pitch five more years. He'll still have his bad days and get in the dumps and maybe say he wants to go to the bullpen. But the man remains a master. Nobody has a better idea of what he wants to do going into a game and then goes out and executes it."

Weaver answered the sportswriters' questions for more than twenty minutes, showered, and then headed out of the clubhouse. Palmer, exiting the trainer's room, hollered, "You did wonders tonight, Earl!"

"Thanks, Jim," Earl said, without slowing. "Who's pitching

tomorrow?" He laughed, loving the constant jibbing he engages in with the now-thirty-five-year-old kid who had won his two hundred and forty-fourth game that night. The three-time Cy Young Award winner was a certain future member of the Baseball Hall of Fame, and as outspoken and combative as his manager. Their screaming matches are both legendary and unique in the annals of baseball, yet at the core of their relationship appears to be an almost father-son regard based on mutual admiration and respect.

Earl Weaver has an abiding love for all of his players. They are, after all, what he always wanted to be. When he couldn't make the majors as a player, he did so as a manager. His baseball credo is: Strong arms and long, long balls. His favorite strategy is the three-run homer, but finding people who can hit the ball over Memorial Stadium's distant fences has been his most difficult task. Those aspects of the game over which he has more control—pitching and defense—have been consistently excellent. He has been successful by getting out of the talent at his disposal all that was there—and in some instances more than was there.

But in order to do this, Weaver realized early on that he could not be close to his players, he could not be their friend. Friendship can only tug the heart and blur one's judgment—and managerial skills start with the ability to evaluate talent.

"You have to keep your distance from your players no matter how much you like them," Earl says. "You're the person who decides all the worst things in their lives. You're the one who has to pinch hit for them, pinch run for them, bench them, trade them, fire them. You know the day will come when you've got to look every one of them in the eye—these guys who have given their all for you, who have won all those ball games that have helped you keep your job—and tell them: 'I'm sorry. You can't do the job anymore.' It rips your heart, but it goes with the manager's office. You can't help loving them, yet you can't afford to."

"Earl has said a hundred times," one of his former, longtime coaches confided, "'I only wish my heart were as hard as another part of my anatomy. It would make this job a helluva lot easier.' But I never saw him falter when he had to make those painful personnel decisions. Winning always came first."

And winners overlook no detail, making certain their players don't either. The minutely organized Oriole system that Weaver installed years ago was designed to insure precision. But there had been a screwup in the scheduled meeting to go over the hitters prior to that night's game. Russo's report had run long, through the meeting time. So Weaver himself ran around and gathered Palmer, pitching coach Ray Miller, and catcher Dan Graham into his office. Rick Dempsey, he learned, was still out on the field. No problem. Earl hurried out and found Dempsey standing just off the dugout doing a television interview.

"Rick, let's go!" Earl hollered, turned, and went back to his office, expecting Dempsey to come in as soon as he finished.

"But we sat there waiting and waiting," Earl said later. "So I ran back out there. I'll be damned if Dempsey wasn't doing *another* TV interview. I went right over when he was on camera and hollered, 'Dempsey, I said *let's go!*'

"Rick got very upset. 'Damnit, you embarrassed me on TV!' he said.

" 'I don't care if you're embarrassed,' I told him. 'We have a meeting and you were told once. The meeting's more important than any damn TV show.' "

They shouted at each other on the way into Weaver's office, and once inside shouted some more. Dempsey thought the meeting was scheduled for fifteen minutes after batting practice. But confusion over the schedule was of no moment, as far as Weaver was concerned, once he had personally called Dempsey to the meeting. At the end of it, Dempsey was no longer talking to his manager. A writer who was unaware of the contretemps asked Dempsey a question about Weaver, and the catcher said a dirty word and nothing more.

Later, en route home, Earl said he wasn't planning to say anything to Benny Ayala about his violation that night "of the cardinal rule of baserunning—he did not watch the runner in front of him." Ayala had singled with runners on first and second, driving in Ken Singleton. And thinking Eddie Murray would advance to third with 2 outs, Ayala ran head down to second only to find Murray there. Then Ayala fell back on his Oriole training, which calls for the hung-up runner to occupy the fielders long enough for the man on second to advance a base. He did, the

Yankee execution missing a play on Murray at third and allowing Ayala to reach second after all.

"Physical errors I can abide," Earl said. "Mental errors I call to the attention of the culprit. But Benny is an excellent base runner. In fact, if I didn't need him to pinch hit, I'd [pinch] run him. I've never seen him mess up on the bases before, so I know that was just a lapse and that he knows it too. This was one of those nights where even our mistakes worked out right."

Earl was home minutes after midnight, had two gin and tonics with Marianna, then went to bed thinking about the next game against the Yankees. The O's had lost the pennant the previous year due to a slow start, and he had to keep them primed now.

After Weaver had gone through his mail at the park that afternoon, he glanced at the "press notes" the Oriole PR department had left on his desk. The two hits the night before by second baseman Rich Dauer had raised his average to .309, and the notes said he had made only one error in his last 99 games.

"You can't be any better on concentration than Rich," Weaver said. "A few years ago he played eighty-six straight games without making an error. He made one and then had seventy *more* errorless games. *That's* concentration. He charges every ball and gets to 'em before the short hop, then goes down on one knee to make the stop. That's what almost every second baseman did in the old days, but he's the only one today. That's one reason why there are so many careless errors these days."

A visitor wondered why Dauer had not won a Gold Glove in 1980, and Weaver said, "That's voted by the players and Dauer's not flashy. He doesn't have a lot of speed and he doesn't do things spectacularly. But he's got very good range. Rich makes all the plays—and never carelessly. He makes sure he steps on second and he always guns the ball to first. The Yankees had a double play last night, but Willie Randolph didn't get anything on his throw and our runner beat it. We don't give away nothing at second base."

Dauer had made a mistake in that game, too. With a Yankee runner on first and only one out, Dauer fielded a groundball hit right at him. Instead of going to second for a double play, Dauer threw to first and started running in, thinking there were three outs. Fortunately for the Orioles, the next batter flied out.

"When Dauer came in," Earl said, "the players in the dugout waited to see what I was gonna do. I went over to Dauer, who had played on two National Championship teams at USC, and said, 'Rich, I'm sorry. But we don't have those cards with "One Out," "Two Out," and "Three Out" on them like they hold up in college.' He laughed and then his teammates got on him."

Weaver phoned Minnie Mendoza, the manager of the O's farm club in Miami to see if he had ever seen the rookie pitcher New York was starting. Mendoza had not seen Gene Nelson and the Orioles had scant information on him. But they knew Nelson liked to change speeds and that his fastball was less than overwhelming.

Earl started left-hand-hitting Terry Crowley at DH, John Lowenstein in left field, and Dan Graham behind the plate. Including Bumbry in center and switch-hitters Ken Singleton and Eddie Murray, the rookie right-hander would have to face six lefties. Crowley was hitless in his last 9 at-bats and had yet to hit a home run in '81, though he had batted .288 with 12 home runs in '80.

"Terry should be our man tonight," Earl said. "He's a good off-speed hitter. He's also due to bust out. Rowe and Cal Ripken worked with him yesterday and showed Crowley videotapes that revealed he's been overstriding."

After posting his lineup on the dugout wall, along with the Yankees' lineup and stats, Weaver sat for his nightly pregame session with the newspaper writers, radio reporters, and television personnel.

An attractive young woman, who was obviously on her first sports assignment, interviewed Weaver in the dugout off-camera to acquire some background information on players she would question later. Earl talked about several of his players, then asked, "You gonna do Rich Dauer?" The reporter nodded. "Well I'll give you a good question." He took her pad and wrote: "You have been quoted as saying that USC coach Rod Dedeaux is a better baseball man than Earl Weaver. Why do you say that?"

Later, when he spotted the young woman leading Dauer before the camera, Weaver popped to his feet and drifted over to observe the interview. The girl asked the question, Dauer broke up, and Earl cackled.

"Dempsey still hasn't spoken to me, except in meetings," Earl said, resuming his seat in the dugout. "He's mad at me, but he's madder at himself because he's not hitting. Rick can't help showing his emotions. Now last night he hit a ball right on the nose, a hard line drive to left that was caught. That's the *worst* thing in the world to him—to hit a ball hard and make out. Rick can't stand that, and he lets you know it. The only thing he can't stand even more is striking out. He gets so angry you'd think he might explode into little pieces."

Weaver shook his head. "I remember a game we won in which Dempsey was 0-for-4, but felt he should have been credited with one hit. He went berserk hollering at the official scorer, who was Ken Nigro of the *Sun*. Rick jumped all over him, threw a beer can at the wall, and poor Kenny didn't know what to do. I came out of my office and said, 'Hey, cool down. We won tonight, Rick. You're not mad that we won, are you?' He settled down. That kind of comment works with him sometimes."

Not long thereafter Weaver tried to get Dempsey out of his distemper. Earl quietly told Elrod Hendricks, the bullpen coach, to speak to Dempsey. He suggested that Elrod say, "Rick, why don't you apologize to the manager?" and Hendricks did.

"Apologize!" Dempsey said angrily. "I didn't do a goddamn thing wrong! I was right and I'm not apologizing to that guy!"

Weaver laughed and decided to just leave Dempsey alone until a means of breaking the communication block turned up. It always did, in time.

A week before he had been much more concerned about Doug DeCinces. He was then batting .193 with no home runs and his back, which had troubled him for years, was acting up again. DeCinces had taken himself out of a game in the sixth inning. Weaver subsequently said on his radio show that the Orioles might have to make a change at third base.

"I was definitely starting to look around for somebody else," Earl said. "Doug went and cried to Elrod about my comments, but they were the honest truth. He didn't come to me to hear the facts because he knew them. I'm just glad I stayed with him an extra week. Those four home runs in three days have bought Doug a *long* time unless his back really goes."

In the game that night Scott McGregor had control problems and gave up 11 hits and 4 runs in 4⅔ innings. But after the O's had gotten only 1 hit off Nelson in 3 innings, Crowley yanked a curveball into the right-field stands in the fourth. John Lowenstein singled and stole second ("He was out from the dugout," Weaver thought), then Graham fanned for the second out. But number 8 hitter DeCinces doubled in a run and Belanger tripled to score the Orioles' third run. They got 3 more the next inning to move ahead 6–4. Singleton's good eye earned him a walk, Murray doubled to right, and with a man on third, Crowley swung at the first pitch trying to hit a long fly that would bring in the run. The pitch was a high change-up, and Crowley got all of it and 3 runs as the ball sailed into the stands. Terry *was* the man tonight.

Sammy Stewart earned the win in relief, allowing only 1 hit and no runs in 4⅓ innings. The highlight of his appearance occurred with 2 out in the ninth. Stewart, a strapping right-hander, got 2 quick strikes on left-hand-hitting Dave Revering. Then Stewart—whom Rick Dempsey calls "a crazy country boy from Swannanoa, North Carolina"—suddenly slipped the glove off his left hand and onto his right. He started into a left-handed wind-up and was about to throw the ball southpaw, but Revering stepped out of the batter's box. Then Stewart reversed his glove and threw a right-handed pitch that Revering popped up to end the game.

"I can throw left-handed," Stewart said afterward. "Hard, too. The guys have seen me do it in the outfield before games. I was going for the element of surprise. Trouble was, Revering picked it up and backed out. Maybe next time."

But pitching coach Ray Miller and general manager Hank Peters were upset about Stewart's glove switch, as if they feared the Yankees might think he was trying to show them up. Weaver thought "it was one of the greatest things I've ever seen."

He was laughing about the incident in his office. "I would have been *delighted* if he'd thrown left-handed," Earl said. "If it had been a strike, I would have used Sammy 3 innings tomorrow night left-handed. Sammy says he's got a good curveball lefty and he was thinking of throwing one to Reggie Jackson, who was up before Revering. I love it! Hell, it's things like this that have kept me in the game so long! You can always come to the ball park and see something you've never seen before."

Earlier Stewart had been "pouting" because he hadn't been assigned to start in this series, Weaver confided. Steve Stone was still on the disabled list and Mike Flanagan had been experiencing stiffness in his arm ever since he had shut out the Blue Jays in the rain and cold in Toronto twelve days before. But Flanagan had done his between-starts throwing on Monday without stiffening and would start again tomorrow.

"Hell, Sammy saved Flanagan after five innings on Saturday and won for Scotty tonight," Earl said. "Sammy got us two wins in four days. I can't afford to start a guy like that now. He's too valuable in long relief. He's one of those rare guys who can warm up for three innings one night, then come in and give you four good innings the next night. Few pitchers can do that. But Sammy is a physical marvel and he's *invaluable* to the Baltimore Orioles. Now, if he could only perfect that left-handed delivery . . ." Earl laughed loudly.

Once the game discussions ended, the impending baseball strike was the topic of conversation among the few remaining writers and Weaver. A year before the owners and the Major League Players Association had reached an agreement on all issues except that of compensation for free agents. A player-management committee had negotiated that issue for months without reaching accord. In February 1981 the owners had unilaterally implemented a compensation plan that would require a team signing a "premier" free agent to give up a player from its twenty-five-man roster along with an amateur draft choice. Ray Grebey, the chief negotiator for the owners, was adamant on this issue. Marvin Miller, executive director of the Players Association, said the owners were trying to restrict the movement of free agents and reduce the number of big-buck contracts they had been passing out since free agency came into being after the 1976 season. Impartial observers suggested that if the owners used a little restraint in their bidding for free agents, they would solve the problem and avoid the strike scheduled to occur in three days. But the owners would not compromise on their compensation plan, and the players simply weren't buying it.

"Why should they?" Weaver said. "If the players give in to the kind of compensation the owners want, there goes free agency as we know it. And after winning something from an employer, who in his right mind would turn around and give it back? I sure as hell wouldn't. Ballplayers are the most competitive people, and they'll back Marvin Miller all the way because he's done so much for them. Hell, he's done a lot indirectly for my income, too."

One of the writers said that when Miller became head of the Players Association in 1966, the average major-league salary was $22,500 and the top salary was $150,000 per year. "Now the average salary is over $150,000 a year and the top salary is over $1 million a year."

"That's why, I'm sorry to say, there will be a strike unless the owners compromise," Weaver said. "The players have to stick with Miller, and he won't back off. In the 1972 strike, which took the first thirteen games of the season, Miller improved the pension plan tremendously. You used to need five years in the majors to qualify for it and now you're in after one year. In the current battle with the owners Miller is not trying to *gain* anything for the players, but simply to keep what they already have."

Earl Weaver is a management man whose sympathies were clearly with the players. Despite what fans thought, he knew all too well what salaries in baseball were like before free agency. Earl was himself a union man in long-ago off-seasons and he had worked twenty-one years in professional baseball before he earned as much as $15,000 in a year. Under baseball's former feudal system, Weaver had witnessed or heard about innumerable owner transgressions against ballplayers. For example, in 1941 Ted Williams was reportedly paid $100,000 by Tom Yawkey, the generous owner of the Red Sox. He was not being overly generous, for Williams batted .406 that season—an average no major-leaguer has matched in the forty years since. During that same season Joe DiMaggio achieved his famed fifty-six-game hitting streak, another record that will likely never be equaled. DiMaggio had been paid $43,000 in 1941, but Ed Barrow, GM of the prosperous Yankees, offered him a contract for the '42 season that called for a $5,000 pay cut. "Don't you know there's a war on?" Barrow told DiMaggio. "Take the $38,000 or sit in San Francisco all season." Joe D. did what ballplayers were forced to do before arbitration—he accepted management's terms.

"Then the player came to spring training mad at the club, and that never helped his concentration on playing the game, which is hard enough to do when your head's clear," Weaver said. "Or the player was a holdout and came in late; then we had to worry about injuries. Now salary disputes are decided by an impartial arbitrator. What can be better than that?"

As Weaver left the stadium and drove home, he said that until recently "the players had been chattels of the owners throughout the history of baseball. When players first started leaving their teams for better contracts elsewhere, it really annoyed me to hear all that talk from owners and fans about loyalty. 'Those guys have no loyalty to their ball clubs,' everyone said. 'The players should be loyal to the teams that invested all that money bringing them through their minor-league system.' What a joke! When did the owners show the players any loyalty? I remember growing up in St. Louis and following all those great Cardinal teams in the thirties. I loved Joe Medwick, Mickey Owen, Leo Durocher, and Dizzy Dean—but the owners traded all of these guys out from under me. I was very upset. Now, after wearing a uniform myself for thirty-four years and watching so many players get traded and knowing how it bothered them, I can certainly sympathize with players today making their own moves to better themselves. Remember, the team that stands to lose a free agent can also keep him by offering a satisfactory contract.

"The system's working fine from every aspect," Earl went on. "Baseball is drawing more fans every year—and the free agency has generated the interest that's resulted in attendance records— and also producing record profits. These will be astronomical when pay-TV comes in, which I guess is why ball clubs are selling for over $20 million now where only a few years ago Ed Williams bought the Orioles for just $12 million. And we've never had better competitive balance in the game. You'll never again see a team win nine pennants in ten years as the Yankees did."

Earl Weaver has been all for free agency from the beginning.

During the negotiations between the players and owners in the spring of 1980, he praised the system and criticized the owners' proposal that compensation for premier free agents come from among ten players on a team's major-league roster. The comments did not sit well with Ray Grebey and most owners, though Orioles owner Edward Bennett Williams, probably the most enlightened in the game, was not troubled.

But many people were surprised that Weaver liked free agency, because he had lost so many excellent ballplayers under the system: Reggie Jackson, Bobby Grich, Wayne Garland, Ross Grimsley, and Don Stanhouse. Jackson was the player he truly hated to lose. "Reggie wanted a million dollars for four years," Weaver said, "and Hank Peters said the figure 'boggled the mind.'" Weaver laughed. "This was after the '76 season, and it did seem like a lot of money then. Now $250,000 a year would have been a bargain for Reggie. And with him we would have won the pennant in '77 and probably in '78. Just think of Singleton, Jackson, and Murray as your three, four, five hitters."

Weaver had proposed that thirty-five players be protected and that five players from the forty-man roster be made available for compensation. He felt it would be a plus for everyone, helping to equalize rosters and also enabling "a kid who's stuck behind a star to get to an organization where he can have a chance to play." Weaver had managed a number of third basemen who might have earned a shot at a major-league job with an organization that didn't have a fixture named Brooks Robinson at that position . . . one he held for some twenty years.

"The Orioles won't need a first baseman for at least ten years," Weaver said, "not with Eddie Murray there. It'll be a shame to hold players back because of Eddie, but that's what'll happen unless they can become outfielders."

The owners, who had controlled a player in perpetuity until the reserve clause was ruled illegal by a federal court, still can retain control of a player for up to twelve years before he can become a free agent. Free agency is available only to players who have six years in the majors. What most fans don't realize is that when an organization signs a player it has three minor-league options on him and then three major-league options before it either has to bring him up to the majors, allow him to be drafted by another organization, or release him. So for up to six years in the minors and six more in the majors a player has no say in where he plays.

"Now how many ballplayers survive for twelve years?" Weaver said. "A very small percentage. And it seems to me that anyone who pays those kinda dues should have some say in his destiny. If you're extraordinarily talented like Eddie Murray and make the majors at twenty-one, you can capitalize. But there aren't many Eddie Murrays.

"Our brightest prospect now may make it at twenty-one, too, next year. He's Cal Ripken, Jr., the son of my third-base coach. Cal was highly regarded in high school and we were fortunate to be able to draft him in round two. We used the amateur pick that we got from the Red Sox after they had signed Dick Drago as a free agent off our roster. That is the current compensation, an amateur draft pick. Cal started in the Rookie League in '78, played A ball in '79 and AA ball in '80, hitting 25 home runs for Charlotte. He had a good winter season in Puerto Rico against some major-league pitchers, and he had a good spring with us. But Jim Palmer and Dave McNally are the only two players in all my years with the Baltimore organization who have skipped Triple-A ball. The Orioles would always rather a youngster put an extra year in the minors than be brought up a year too soon into major-league pressure. Cal's slugging percentage at Rochester is over .600 right now. My last words to him in the spring were, 'See you soon.'"

Weaver was asked what he would do if, as seemed inevitable, there was a strike. "Well, I've already told Mark Belanger [who was on the executive board of the Major League Players Association] that I would perform any appropriate duties for the organization, but that I would do nothing that would be detrimental to the players. I suspect what I'll be doing is tending my garden and hoping the front office doesn't come after me. I will get paid and have my first summer vacation in thirty-four years." He cackled. "Of course I'd get paid if I got fired, too, so I'm all right whatever happens. I'm sure baseball will be as well. It's bigger than the dunderheads who try to screw it up."

Weaver filled in his right-handed lineup—Roenicke in left,

Ayala as DH, and Dempsey catching—against Yankee left-hander Rudy May in the final game of the series. May had been having his problems lately, but Weaver knew that if the game were close in the late innings, the O's would have to face New York's awesome relief pitcher Rich Gossage. The Goose, as he's called, had struck out 27 batters in 19⅔ innings and achieved a miniscule .46 earned-run average. He already had 11 saves even though he had been out for 10 games with back spasms. But Gossage had been ready to return last night if needed.

"With Terry Crowley on the bench we got a chance if they bring in Gossage," Weaver said, chuckling and recalling when the Orioles had last faced Gossage in 1980. The man with the 95-mph fastball and the 92-mph slider had struck out 6 of 7 Oriole hitters that night. "Crowley was the only one of our guys to touch the ball. He ticked a couple." Weaver cackled.

"Our radar gun measures 4 mph less than the Jug gun that many teams use," he said, "but they're both equally accurate. We just set up our rating system accordingly. We rate an 85–86-mph fastball as average and a 95-mph fastball as virtually unhittable. When Gossage has that velocity, the batter simply can't get the bat around quick enough. There's not enough time from the moment the ball is released until it gets there; it's already by you. And if you do start your swing early enough and the pitch is a slider, you're dead. It looks like a fastball till the last instant and you break your back."

Weaver went over the Yankee hitters with pitcher Mike Flanagan and the catchers, then headed out to the dugout. "Dempsey still ain't talking to me," he said, smiling and shaking his head. He posted the lineup, then Rudy May waved to him from the field where the Yankees were taking BP. Weaver walked over by the batting cage and chatted with May, a former Oriole.

As Weaver turned toward the dugout, Lou Piniella—whom Earl had managed at Elmira, New York, in the early '60s—stepped into the batting cage. Weaver paused and his eyes twinkled. "I'm starting another left-hander for you tonight, Lou," Earl said. "I know you can't play no more against right-handers. That's what happens when you get old." He laughed and walked away.

"I ought to keep my mouth shut on Lou," Weaver said in the

dugout. "He still hits us pretty damn good." Piniella had gone 2-for-4 the previous night. "But I can't help riding him, he's got such a snap temper. You know, he still owns three water coolers in the Eastern League from that year he played for me. He also had to pay for four doors and at least fifteen batting helmets he smashed.

"I started riding Lou way back when he was with Kansas City and I just kept it going with New York. Whenever he'd pop out or ground out I'd give him a whistle." (It is shrill enough to cut through crowd noise.) "Then I'd wait for Lou to throw his batting helmet." Weaver laughed and lit a cigarette.

He said he finally got Piniella "to the cracking point" in New York a couple of years ago. Piniella had gone 0-for-3, each failure underscored by a piercing whistle and a flung helmet. The next time Piniella came up, Weaver whistled as he stepped into the box. Angered, Piniella stepped out and hollered, "You want to hit, Weaver?"

"Get back in the box," Weaver shouted from the dugout, where he was standing behind the bat rack.

Piniella took a step toward Weaver and threw his bat at him, the length of ash bounding and skidding all the way to the bat rack. He walked over and picked up the Louisville Slugger and said, "You better get off me or I'm gonna hit you in the head with this bat."

Weaver moved up on the first dugout step and said, "Get back over there where you belong before you cause trouble."

The umpire came over and told Piniella to return to the batter's box, but the Yankee outfielder waved his bat and said again, "If you don't stop it, Weaver, I'm gonna hit you in the head with this."

"It was a good thing I kept my cool," Earl said now, "because Lee May was coming over to us in a hurry. I sure didn't want him involved. Piniella had just snapped, which is his history. But the umpire escorted Piniella away. He cooled off, stepped into the box—and I whistled. On the next pitch the SOB hit a double!" Weaver cackled and stepped on his cigarette.

"I said to myself: I've been on this guy for years and years—and he's been wearing us out! So I got off him. And he *still* kept wearing us out. That's why I went back to riding him a bit tonight. But I don't know. Lou may be like that proverbial pile of dogshit. It never bothers you until you step on it. He has to be one of the best damn 'guess' hitters I've seen. And he's a patient hitter, too, which is why he's still up here after thirteen, fourteen years."

Weaver went through his nightly routine of responding to questions from more than a dozen reporters. Another attractive young female TV person, her hand shaking as she held the mike, won the evening's top query award, "Why do you always want to deck the umpires?"

"I don't think I can answer that kind of question," Weaver said. "I'm a Christian. But I have no problem with umpires. I love 'em all. I'm at peace with the world. Except on close plays."

The reporters drifted off and Jim Palmer sat down next to Weaver. "Jeez, Dempsey's really down, Earl," he said. "Why don't you have a talk with him."

"Dempsey pays as much attention when I talk to him as you do," Weaver said.

"What do you mean? You talked to me after I volunteered to go to the bullpen, and since then I've pitched three good games."

"But did you *pay any attention* to me?" Weaver asked.

"No," Palmer said, and they both laughed.

Palmer went into the clubhouse and Weaver said, "Jim is always worried about things that he shouldn't be worried about. He likes to help me manage, as almost everyone does. The only thing is that after fifteen years, Palmer comes up and makes his comments to me directly. That's a helluva lot better than two guys making their comments to themselves at a locker. That ain't no good because it does no good. At least Palmer's got a chance when he comes up and speaks to me. He's said many things over the years that have been valuable, helpful to the ball club. His concern about Dempsey is worthwhile. I still have to find a way to reach him."

In the game that night Dempsey, as he had on Monday, demonstrated patience and a good eye at the plate by orchestrating 2 bases on balls. He also exhibited the relentless fire with which he plays baseball when he tagged up at third and tried to break a 5–5 tie by scoring on a short fly to right. The relay beat him by five steps, but Dempsey crashed into Yankee catcher Rick

Cerone with the drive of a linebacker. However, the impact did not dislodge the ball, which did not improve Dempsey's mood.

Earlier he had hit another hard line drive to left, as he had on Monday, and was heard to groan when it found no hole. Ken Singleton subsequently came up and took a mighty swing at a ball that squibbed off his bat twenty feet in front of the plate. Cerone, who was just back from an injury, overran the ball and Singleton had a single. Weaver heard Dempsey moan and say, "Oh, shit!"

The manager walked over to Dempsey and said, "You got to learn to hit the ball like that, Rick." Weaver noted the slightest suggestion of a smile on Dempsey's face and hoped maybe the ice had been broken.

"He doesn't mean to do it and in his mind he's not—but Rick actually roots against his teammates," Weaver said later. "He's happy Kenny got a hit, but Kenny's hitting .370 and he got a 20-foot hit. Rick's hitting .218 and he hit a liner right at the fielder. So on Kenny's hit Rick couldn't help moaning. Rick always seems to be saying, 'Why me?'"

The game was the most exciting of the three. DeCinces was the early hitting star for Baltimore. He slammed a 2-run homer off May in the fourth and another off Ron Davis in the sixth to give the O's a 5–2 lead. Then Flanagan lost his control in the eighth and, with 2 out and the bases loaded, Weaver brought in Tim Stoddard. The club's top right-handed reliever in '80, Stoddard had been inconsistent in '81. But he had to have work because the Orioles would need him if they were going to win it all.

Left-handed-hitting Oscar Gamble pinch hit for Barry Foote, and Stoddard lost him, walking in a run. Weaver then brought in left-hander Tippy Martinez to face the left-handed-hitting Graig Nettles. Tippy had retired him 15 times in 17 meetings, and he pitched well. But Nettles, a veteran pro, fouled off 4 good pitches that he couldn't handle, battling to stay alive. Martinez threw a low fastball on the outside corner of the plate—and Nettles slapped it on a line into left field. With the score tied, Martinez got the final out.

But in the bottom of the eighth, the Yankees brought in The Goose. His velocity was off a bit; the Oriole radar gun clocked him at *only* 91 mph. Mark Belanger, who had a .181 batting average on the season and a career mark against Gossage of .390, stroked a single, but The Goose shut down the other O's. The Yankees got 3 singles but no runs off Martinez in the ninth, thanks to a nice spear of a liner by Belanger that started a double play and his moving pick up of a Dave Winfield grounder that resulted in out number 3.

With one out in the Orioles' ninth, Dauer collected his second single of the night. Weaver sent in Bob Bonner to run for Dauer ("We time him from home to first with a calendar," Earl says). Jim Dwyer, who had pinch run for Singleton in the seventh and stayed in defensively in left field, pulled the first pitch from Gossage to right for a single that moved Bonner to third. The Yankees then intentionally walked Eddie Murray to set up a force-out. John Lowenstein pinch hit for Gary Roenicke. Gossage tried to blow Lowenstein out of the box, but the left-handed hitter hung in and worked the count to 3–2. Then he topped a pitch to second baseman Willie Randolph, whose throw home forced Bonner.

Up stepped Terry Crowley, who had replaced Ayala at DH the previous inning, and grounded out against Gossage. He had exactly 1 hit in 9 at-bats lifetime against The Goose. Yet the veteran Crowley said later, "I felt really confident, totally relaxed." Crowley looked at 2 pitches, then ripped a fastball to right that drove in the winning run.

The Orioles flew out of the dugout en masse to greet Dwyer, who scored the game winner, and Crowley. It was as if the 3-game sweep had been in the play-offs, and the 42,869 fans stood and cheered and applauded for many minutes. The total attendance for the week-night series, 124,464, was an Orioles' record, and prompted a reporter headed for the clubhouse to say, "Can you believe that owners who are doing more business than they ever have are actually going to force the players to strike?"

The National Labor Relations Board had just announced that it would seek a temporary restraining order in U. S. District Court in New York that would postpone the players' strike deadline, which had been set for midnight. The MLPA had already filed a charge of unfair labor practices against the owners and the NLRB had it under review. But a postponement itself would not resolve the compensation issue.

"I had a meeting with the team and told everyone to watch his weight if the strike comes down," Weaver told the writers assembled in his office. "I guess we'll find out something tomorrow, which is an off day."

A couple of the Baltimore writers asked why he'd brought in Stoddard to pitch to Foote, knowing that Yankee manager Gene Michael would counter with a left-handed pinch hitter like Gamble. "I didn't *know* he'd send up Gamble," Weaver snapped. "Look, a relief pitcher has to face one man before you can replace him. Michael had the final option. I have to respect Foote, who has five homers. Stoddard was just wild tonight."

One of the writers asked what Piniella had shouted at Weaver when he'd gone out to speak to Flanagan with Lou at bat in the fourth.

"I don't know why that man don't mind his own business," Weaver said. "I just told him to shut up and get back in the box. Then he grounded out for the second time in a row and I look in the dugout and Piniella's staring at me pounding his fist in his palm. So I imitated him by pounding my fist in my palm. Then I forgot about him. But the SOB got two more hits later."

Al Mari, a New York writer who had just come from the Yankee clubhouse, said, "Piniella's pinky's all swollen. He told me he'd punched the dugout wall and said he wished it had been Earl Weaver."

"Hey, all I said to him during the game was, 'What the hell are you hollering about?'"

"Well," Mari said, "you're doing everything right."

"I ain't doing nothing," Weaver said. "The players are winning. All I'm doing is second-guessing myself after I bring in Stoddard and he walks in a run. But that's baseball."

The Orioles now had a 27–14 record (.659) and were 4½ games ahead of the Yankees (23–19). The Orioles then lost 2 out of 3 games to Detroit, while the Yankees were winning 3 of 4, and traveled to New York on June 2 for another 3-game series.

The Yankees won the first in 11 innings, 5–3, as Dave Revering hit a home run off Sammy Stewart and later said, "Payback's a bitch, ain't it?" The Orioles had loaded the bases with none out in the eleventh, but Gossage got DeCinces and Dempsey to pop out and retired Roenicke on a fly.

"When was your last sacrifice fly?" a Baltimore writer asked Weaver afterward. "You check?"

"No," Weaver said. "Did you?"

"Dauer had the last one in the first inning of the 10–1 win over the Yankees on May 25," another writer said.

"A week ago," Weaver said. "We must be due."

When the writers left, Weaver said Dempsey was talking to him again. "But the poor guy still ain't hitting. He's only had one hit in his last twenty-six times up. Ralph Rowe's been working with him and says there's nothing wrong with him mechanically. Rick's just always fighting himself up there."

Willie Randolph had stolen a base that night, only the second of the season with Dempsey catching. "He'd thrown out ten of the eleven guys who'd run on him," Weaver said. "He's the best throwing catcher I've ever had. He gets rid of the ball so quick, and he's accurate." Going into this season Dempsey had thrown out over 46 percent of the runners who had attempted to steal on him. The league average is about 35 percent. "Actually, nobody steals on Rick, but on the pitcher. We don't have a guy on our club with a real good move to first. Even Palmer sometimes relaxes so much on the mound he forgets about the runner on base.

"Dempsey's also amazing on pick-offs," Weaver said. "He's already picked off five base runners. He got them at first, second, and third. I've never seen anyone throw better than Dempsey, though I wouldn't put him above Jim Sundberg of Texas. I'd hate to judge those two."

A problem developed the next night involving DeCinces and Palmer. It stemmed from an incident during a game against Detroit the previous weekend. DeCinces had failed to field a groundball to his backhand. The ball glanced off DeCinces' glove and he was not charged with an error, but Palmer apparently regarded it as such and gestured in disgust. Palmer reportedly had made some disparaging remarks about DeCinces since then, and they got back to the third baseman.

"He [Palmer] was cussing me out and throwing his hands in the air after that play," DeCinces told Baltimore *Sun* writer Ken

Nigro. "I wanted to let things drop. Then I keep hearing these comments made to people who shouldn't hear them. I'm upset that he has to make comments about a play that was a hit all the way. I don't want him destroying what we have on this club. Everybody's going to make physical errors, and we don't throw our hands in the air every time someone hits a homer off Jim. I don't think it's fair that he continually shows up guys on the field, and then says he gets no support. This has been a twenty-four-man team and one prima donna."

"Jimmy's an emotional person, and he lets his emotions show no matter where he is," Weaver said, on hearing about De-Cinces' remarks. "The groundball wasn't fielded and Jim threw up his arms. Whether it should have been scored a hit or an error, I don't know. It was one of those in-betweeners. But Doug took exception to Jim's gesture. A hundred times I've walked out on the mound and Jim's been waving and flailing his arms. I'm old enough where I can accept it and turn the other cheek. That's Jim Palmer. But there were a lot of times where it just became too much to take. Everyone has a breaking point. And that's when we've had our arguments.

"Jim's shown his emotions many times when a high flyball has dropped in or a groundball has gone through that he thought should have been caught. Again, that's Jim Palmer. Most people don't change very much."

Weaver lit a cigarette. "It's just disappointment. Jim don't mean to show nobody up. Now I've gone out to the mound many other times where Palmer's waving his arms and people think we're in an argument. All he's doing is gesturing while he's saying something like, 'How can they be so lucky! I threw that ball right where I wanted to, and he got a hit!' The writers think we're having angry words."

Palmer had left that game against Detroit after two innings, saying the trapezoid muscle in his neck was sore. Weaver, who had him scheduled to start the next night's game in New York, now called Palmer into the office. "How does it feel?" the manager asked.

"There's no pain," Palmer said.

"Then I'll start you tomorrow."

"I'll go out there, Earl. But the muscle's still not right, and I know it'll affect my control."

Weaver scratched Palmer. He had Dennis Martinez going tonight, and an enormous hole to fill tomorrow. Flanagan and McGregor had started the previous two games. With Palmer unavailable and Steve Stone disabled, Weaver would have to start Dave Ford. A long reliever, Ford had started only one other game in '81, a no-decision outing. His overall stats were not impressive: 1–0 record, 5.18 ERA, 31 hits allowed in 24.1 innings. A pitcher who gives up an average of over a hit per inning pitched through a season usually has given up a lot of runs. Still, it was early and Ford certainly had the arm to excel if given a chance. And Weaver had no choice but to give him the start.

That night Dennis Martinez demonstrated why he had been the Orioles' most consistant starter in '81. He gave up only 3 hits to the powerful Yankees in 10 innings, two of them infield singles. The O's managed 8 hits off young left-hander Dave Righetti and his explosive fastball, but no runs in 8 innings. Ron Davis relieved and sustained the shutout through the top half of the eleventh. A tired Tippy Martinez, the O's most effective reliever so far, got the first out in the bottom of the inning, then Dave Winfield reached first on an infield single.

After Reggie Jackson struck out, Graig Nettles stepped in. Remembering how Nettles had battled Tippy last week and finally singled to left, Weaver moved up on the dugout step and waved left fielder Jim Dwyer closer to the line. Just then Palmer came up behind Weaver and said, "Why don't we walk him?"

Weaver turned his head and said, "Because Nettles is 2-for-bleeping-18 off Tippy."

Then Weaver heard the loud resonant crack of bat meeting ball. His head snapped around to see Tippy Martinez' first pitch arcing toward the second deck in Yankee Stadium and Weaver whirled on Palmer, "And now Nettles is 3-for-bleeping-19! Shut up, Palmer!"

But Weaver could not have brought himself to put the winning run on second base with the left-handed-hitting Revering up next. He had gone with his best and been beaten. That's baseball.

The following night, with a long reliever starting and only the last man on his staff, Steve Luebber, possessing a rested arm in the bullpen, Weaver said, "Off the record, we're considerable underdogs. But Sammy Stewart says he's got all we'll need tonight. Can you believe that?" Stewart had been a workhorse, having already pitched over 45 innings and faced 14 batters only two nights earlier. "But if it comes down to a 'game' situation, I'm gonna use him. We're up by two after six, I'll try to get three innings out of Sammy."

"Left-handed?" I asked.

Weaver smiled. He was not dispirited at having lost four games in succession. "You'll run into this shit 8–10 times in a season," Weaver said in the visiting manager's office, "where you've got one pitcher disabled [Stone], another injured [Palmer], another who can't seem to find his rhythm [Stoddard], and your entire bullpen tired. You need a couple of complete games once in a while."

The Baltimore writers, a hard-working crew who were always questioning Weaver and his players in search of quotes and insights for their columns and game reports, were scattered around the room. One of them said to Ken Nigro, who was wearing a trench coat despite the 90 percent humidity, "What's that, your Colombo coat?"

"Take it off, for chrissake!" Weaver hollered. "Ken tells me it's a lucky coat—but every damn time he wears it we lose! He wore it in Rochester [for an exhibition game] and we couldn't even beat minor-league pitching."

A writer asked Weaver why he hadn't used the sacrifice bunt in the last game when he'd had two on and only one out in both the third and fifth innings. Weaver does not believe in giving away outs; hates the sacrifice bunt and seldom uses it.

"I put it on once and it was unsuccessful," he said. "The Yankees tried it three bleeping times and it was unsuccessful. We kept getting the out and leaving the runner on first. So please stick the sacrifice bunt up somebody's ass and leave it there.

"The Yankees didn't bunt when they won nine pennants in ten years. The '69, '70, and '71 Orioles didn't bunt while winning pennants. The '72 Orioles didn't bunt, either, and then Chan Keith wrote a four-part series on why we finished five games out of first and said, in essence, we lost because we didn't bunt."

Weaver shook his head. "There are more games won on two-run and three-run homers than on sacrifice bunts," he said. "And it don't take no philosopher or genius to make that comment."

Weaver grabbed his lineups and stats and headed for the dugout. En route he recalled a humorous incident on the bus to the park in Toronto a few weeks earlier.

"I heard the strangest damn noise coming from about a half dozen players in the back of the bus," he related. "I sat there thinking and thinking: What the hell are those guys doing? The noise they were making sounded like something between a cranky starter motor and someone clearing his sinuses. It made me laugh out loud. And when I heard my laugh—*it was the same sound!* The players were back there trying to imitate my laugh—and doing a good job of it!"

That night Bumbry led off the game with a single and stole second, but the Orioles didn't get another hit off the rookie they'd beaten in Baltimore, Gene Nelson, until the ninth. Dauer and Murray homered and Ayala singled in Crowley for 3 runs. By then the Yankees had collected 19 hits off Ford, Luebber, and Stoddard while scoring 12 runs. The first 4 were unearned as Doug DeCinces misplayed Bucky Dent's 2-out grounder. Dave Ford did not throw his arms in the air.

Weaver was anything but upset by the drubbing. No one despises losing more, but when his team is a decided underdog and loses, it is not unexpected. The only thing to do is forget it and march on, accentuating the positive.

Earl was actually smiling as the Baltimore writers trooped into his office. "We're still in first place!" he cried, though the lead was not prepossessing: .004 percentage points. "And I was happy to see three guys wearing gray uniforms finally touch home plate tonight. A good sign! Now we're going to California where there's more sun. Baseball—you can't beat it!"

He took a large bite from the hero sandwich on his desk, answered a question about Bumbry's muscle pull, then saw GM Hank Peters, who had come in for this game to make the West Coast trip, stick his head through the doorway. "We lost the other two as well, Hank!" Weaver shouted. "We just lost bigger with you here." Peters smiled and left. "If we'd held 'em in the ninth two nights ago and gotten a sacrifice fly last night, we'd be sitting on top of the world."

Weaver took another bite as a couple of writers peeled off. "Well bleep those guys who went to the other clubhouse," Weaver said. "I ain't giving them any of the good stuff. And they won't get to see me eat." He was biting and chewing as fast as he could now, relishing the sandwich.

"Wasn't the play DeCinces was given an error on very similar to that play against Detroit?" a writer asked, referring to the one that had led Palmer to demonstrate his charades' techniques.

"Not at all," Weaver said. "The play in Detroit was to his right and two-hopped him; the one tonight was to his left and one-hopped him. See, you get in fielding slumps, too. Even Belanger made three bad throws early in the season, none since. Now Doug's getting himself in a position where he *has* to play the short hops. He's got to make a decision to go back or come in and smother the ball on the first hop. The other thing, on that backhanded ball—and he's done this before—Doug planted his feet and reached instead of being fluid and moving back for the ball. Tonight he planted himself again.

"He played the balls wrong, that's about as much as you can say. Doug's not trying to, but you're gonna make mistakes in baseball. He's making tough hops for himself." You could almost see Weaver making a mental note to speak to DeCinces about the bad habit he appeared to be acquiring.

A writer asked about Gene Nelson's performance, and Weaver said, "I don't know why he was so effective, but that was why I was so happy we finally scored. For eight innings we couldn't have gotten a run off Nelson's sister. And I mean the younger sister, not the older one with the hard curve."

Peter Pascarelli of the Baltimore *News American* came in and said, "Reggie [Jackson] says this game don't mean nothing."

"It does," Weaver said. "The same thing it means every night —one goes in the win column, one goes in the loss column."

"You're late, Henry," Weaver said as New York *Post* writer Henry Hecht scurried in.

"Hey, I go to *my team* first unless someone hits a home run," Hecht said.

"We hit two bleeping homers."

"Big bleeping deal. What was the final score?"

"What *was* the final score?"

"Twelve–three."

"They got a lotta bleeping runs."

"What was the difference to you in Nelson between last week and tonight?"

"Crowley."

"Ooohhhhh."

"Well that's exactly what it was—two homers, four RBIs."

"Nelson pitched differently to me," Hecht said.

"Well, all right." Weaver shrugged. "Quote yourself."

"I want to know what *you* have to say."

"What I have to say is I'm feeling pretty good. We're leaving New York in bleeping first place. We got McGregor, Flanagan, Palmer, and Martinez lined up, and Tippy got a day of rest. They really helped us out, these bleeping guys."

"Earl."

"What?"

"I love ya."

Weaver laughed.

"I guess I won't see you again until the All-Star game," Hecht said. "You'll be one of Jim Frey's coaches, won't you?"

"Shit, Henry! I'm taking one of my suspensions."

"Come on, Earl—three glorious days in Cleveland."

"I'd rather be mixing cowshit and feeding my garden," Weaver said, turning to me. "I had to retie my tomatoes three times in a week since the first feeding."

He showered and dressed, looking weary when he emerged. "Monday and today are primary reasons why I'm looking forward to retirement," Weaver said. "Monday I awoke in Perry Hall, drove to the ball park, and took a bus to the Washington airport, an hour away. We flew to Rochester, New York, for an exhibition game that night, flew here after the game, then bussed to the hotel. Tonight we take a bus to the airport and fly all night to L.A., arriving at 7 A.M. EST, then get on another bus for an hour trip to Anaheim. This is a *young* man's game.

"Of course, in the minor leagues I thought I'd have to go through that exhausting travel all my life. There was no pension, no way to retire. That didn't bother me at all then. And if I still had to do it, I'd be doing it and not bitching about it."

A friend offered to drive Weaver to the airport, but he said he'd better take the team bus. "I have to be sure I make the plane. I miss it and the team wins ten in a row—and they won't need me!" He cackled.

A week later they didn't need him as the players went on strike. By then the Oriole record was 31–23, two games behind the Yankees' 34–22. When play resumed in August, Earl Weaver's cow-magic garden was producing elephantine vegetables, which made him happy. The fact that the owners (not Baltimore's) had voted to split the season and guarantee the Yankees a place in the All East mini-play-offs didn't even upset him.

His ball club was healthy again and also stronger. The O's had brought up from Rochester left-handed relief pitcher Jeff Schneider, who had 13 saves and a 2.35 ERA, and also "See you soon" Cal Ripken, Jr., who was batting .290 with 25 home runs for the Red Wings. A strong arm and an Intern Longball.

Just what the O's seemed to need, particularly for the final ten games of the season. Seven of those games would be against the Yankees, the last three at home. After those "play-offs" the Orioles would face the Yankees in the additional play-offs if they had the best record in the "second season."

Weaver expected the Baltimore Orioles to have the best record. Earl Weaver always expects, over the long haul, to win.

chapter ONE

According to the media, I am famous for three things: arguing with umpires, battling with players, and winning ball games. Well, you can't have the latter without the first two, I'm sorry to say. So the opening chapters in this book will deal with confrontations, beginning with those involving umpires.

I feel obliged to point out that an umpiring crew makes approximately 300 calls per nine-inning game. As I had managed over 2,000 major-league games, I have witnessed more than 600,000 calls. The fact that in this section I find fault with only a minuscule percentage of those calls testifies to the splendid job that umpires do overall. It is amazing.

Nevertheless, the names of some of the umpires have been changed or withheld to protect the guilty.

No owner of a rival American League team has ever praised me more than George Steinbrenner of the New York Yankees. Several times Steinbrenner has said, "Weaver's worth at least eight to ten wins for Baltimore a year." I'm just pleased as punch that my ballplayers, on their very own, manage to win a helluva lot more games than that every season.

But my old friend George was once again heaping praise on me in late May of 1981. We had just beaten the Yankees, 6–4, for the second successive night in Baltimore, and George told the press, "Give Earl Weaver credit. Every close call went against New York. He's a great manager and a master intimidator of umpires."

When the writers passed along George's words, I told them, "I'm happy to hear the nice things he has to say about me, as usual. And I invite George, as I did last year, to come to Miami on December 25 and share the Christmas goose I cook annually."

Then I had to laugh, because I regularly get mail from fans who write, "Please leave the umpires alone, otherwise their decisions will go against us." My father used to say as much right up until he passed away in 1980. He felt my relationship with umpires should be more akin to that followed by the subdued former Cardinal manager Billy Southworth, whom we observed for years when I was growing up in St. Louis. My dad seemed to regard my style as neo-Leo Durocher, who as a player was among my childhood heroes. Both of my parents were (my mother continues to be) embarrassed every time I've been thrown out of a game, particularly in the '69 World Series—from which I was the first manager to be ejected in thirty-five years. I could never convince them that if I had done what they wanted me to —not argue, not protect my players—I would not have lasted in the major leagues.

Even Jimmy Russo, who has been called the Orioles "superscout," but whose official title is Special Assistant to the General Manager, has publicly criticized my relationships with umpires. In 1975, after we had finished 4½ games behind the Red Sox, my friend Jimmy said, "We lost a bunch of games on plays that instant reply showed weren't even close. I've talked to Earl about the way he antagonizes umpires. I don't understand his brand of psychology."

Well, as I tried to explain to Jimmy—my colleague for more than two decades—I don't have a brand of psychology. All I have is an obligation to do my job to the best of my ability, as I have always attempted to do. When I accepted the job as manager of the Orioles after eleven seasons as a successful manager in the minors, I was told by everyone in the organization—from my associates in the minor-league department to the general manager and owner of the major-league club—"Earl, don't change, don't change anything." And I haven't, though experience has provided me with a tad more wisdom. I finally learned how to make certain points to umpires with appropriate forcefulness while perhaps avoiding an ejection or two or three.

During the 1980 season, for example, I was ejected from only four games, five below my '79 total. Overall, entering the '81 season, I had been ejected from 79 games in 13½ seasons as a major-league manager (and good old George says *I* control umpires?). In 2½ fewer seasons as a minor-league manager I probably accumulated more ejections. I have been thrown out of spring training games in Florida and exhibition games in California. I have been chased from the dugout at the Orioles' old minor-league training camp in Thomasville, Georgia, where fans did not even have to pay for their seats. Once I was even banished from a postseason ball game halfway around the world . . . and the Japanese fans who seemingly had never witnessed such an event before sat there in bewildered silence.

Historically, once I have been formally notified of my ejection I have been known to reveal my displeasure by putting on a show which even umpires have applauded. Fans regularly write and say, "*Please* get thrown out of tonight's game, Earl." On that last trip to Japan the sponsors met with us and asked that we put on a show. "I can't do that," I told them. "My actions are all spontaneous." It has been written that I have premeditated explosions to somehow reduce the tension on my ball club, deflect the pressure, spur the motivation (surely the most meaningless word in sports), and for a half dozen other reasons. What bullspit.

Each and every one of my ejections resulted from the simple fact that I was doing my job—and that has nothing to do with "motivating" professional athletes or any other amateur analyst theories. My confrontations with umpires have usually resulted from my attempts to:

• Save a player from ejection by stepping into an argument and saying what the player wanted to say, for it's far better for me to go than a man who might hit a game-winning home run.

• Wake up an umpire and get him to start concentrating and stop missing calls.

• Get a decision changed that was contrary to the rules of baseball, which the umpires don't always know.

And since the umpire has the authority to eject managers, players, and coaches from games for *any* reason, a manager is in danger every time he opens his mouth. For example, I have been ejected from games some ten times while standing on the dugout steps and hollering when the umpire could not have heard what I said over the crowd noise. I know that because I couldn't hear what the umpire had hollered at me amidst that roar from the stands. At least four times I have been ejected for trying to ask one of my players a question.

Yet Lee MacPhail, the American League president, accepts the word of the umpire that I was yelling at him. Every time MacPhail *has* agreed to hear an appeal, he has ruled for the umpire. He is far more consistent than some of his umpires. But until an appeal can be made to an impartial arbitrator, only one side of an argument will be heard and the status quo will remain the same: unfair. That's baseball.

Most umpires in the minors gave managers a little more time to express themselves than they do in the big leagues. I ran in from the third-base coaching box in the minors countless times when I felt the umpire was not in the game and said, "Are you gonna get any better, or is *this* it?" without being ejected. My first ejection in the majors occurred not long after I took over as Orioles manager in 1968. I protested what appeared to be a very bad call by grand old ump Larry Knapp . . . and he wouldn't give me a second.

"Old man, the game's passing you by," I said, and grand old Larry stepped on my toes and called me a dirty name. "You can say what you want and do whatever you want," I went on, "but you are not with it anymore." And he stepped on my toes again and called me another dirty name—which is one thing I never do to an umpire, though I have been known to use foul language in describing a call. Knapp gave me one final stomp and curse and ejected me.

After the game I was asked by the press what had transpired in the argument. "Well, he was cursing me and stepping on my feet," I said.

"Funny," I was told, "that's what Knapp said you were doing."

When I handed in my lineup card the next day, I said, "Larry, only three of us know the truth—you, me, and God."

Larry Knapp laughed—but not until twelve years later when I reiterated the scene to him while we were making a television commercial together. I'm sorry to say that I haven't come across a lot of umpires with a sense of humor. For example, although smoking is not allowed in dugouts, I would never get through most games without having a cigarette. So I move into the runway to light up, as do most uniformed personnel who smoke.

But there was a game in 1969 when umpire Frank Umont was bound and determined to catch me smoking. He was working third base and looking over at me so often I was afraid he might get hit with a line drive. But at one point I lit up without stepping far enough into the runway, and Umont came running over and said, "Okay, Weaver, I got you smoking. That's a fine."

I said, "My mother lets me smoke, Frank."

The next day when I took my lineup card to the umpires I was sucking on a candy cigarette. I politely offered the umpires a bite—and Umont threw me out of the game before it even started!

That was plain silly. But no sillier than many of my ejections, such as the time I was thrown out for tossing my cap in the dugout. Now hat throwing is not cause for automatic banishment, but an umpire can eject someone for throwing a cap if he feels it was done to protest a call. Several years ago Angels pitcher Paul Hartzell threw his hat in disgust when he missed a close double play. Hartzell was allowed to stay in the game by umpire Rich G. The next night I called to that same umpire, and threw my hat on the dugout floor. He ejected me and told me that was the reason. Ernie Tyler, the Orioles ball man who serves the umpires, heard Rich G. say the ejection was for hat tossing. The umpire later changed his story and said I was ejected for questioning balls and strikes—which wasn't true. Once I was booted, though, I tossed a batch of gloves, helmets, and bats on the field, deciding I might as well give Rich G. a legitimate reason for making me leave.

Naturally I've had to eject a few umpires from games myself for incompetence. The first time was in 1973 when home plate umpire John Flaherty called Paul Blair out on a third-strike swing. I argued that Blair had ticked the ball and, since the catcher had dropped the foul, Blair was still up. When I seemed to be getting nowhere with Flaherty, I ran out to first-base umpire Bill Kunkle and then to second-base ump Marty Springstead to see if they had noted the foul tip. Kunkle got angry and ejected me—by which time Flaherty had changed his call on Blair! So I turned to Kunkle and Springstead and hollered, "You and you. You're *out of here!*" and gave them the big thumb they deserved for not being in the game.

One of the umpires' favorite tricks in an argument is to get so close to you they hit the bill of your hat. When it falls off they claim you bumped them and throw you out. I have been ejected and even suspended for allegedly pecking at the faces of umpires with the bill of my hat. That is a physical impossibility—unless the umpire leans down to cause the bill of my hat to strike him in the face. I am five feet, six and one-half inches short, and the bill of my hat is a couple of inches closer to the ground—well below the face of any umpire. Even if I actually left the ground trying to hit most umpires, I could reach no higher than a neck because they are all much taller than I am. Umpire Larry Barnett has admitted: "Earl's cap only reaches my chest."

Yet Rich G. claimed I hit him in the eye with the bill of my hat during a game in 1980, and MacPhail suspended me for three games. That was a case of compound malfeasance by the umpiring crew of Rich G., Dale Ford, Steve Palermo, and Al Clark. The problem started in the seventh inning of a game against the Yankees. We had two men on base and two out when Pat Kelly checked his swing on a possible third strike. Palermo refused to call it a strike, but when he consulted with Ford, the third-base umpire signaled that Kelly had swung. I blew my cool a bit there, tossing a mitt out of the dugout. But then I decided not to make a big thing of it when we had two more times at bat coming and were down by only two runs. So I stepped into the runway for a smoke to cool down and sent Belanger in to play shortstop because Kelly had hit for shortstop Kiko Garcia. The next thing I knew, on the very first pitch of the eighth inning, Yankee DH Eric Soderholm hit a home run. That did it!

I *flew* out of the dugout—and Rich G. came running at me from second base. I chewed on him only briefly because Ford was the guy who'd blown the call on Kelly. And when Palermo joined us, I suggested that competent home-plate umpires could tell whether a batter had swung or not. I seldom see myself in these confrontations, but one writer reported, "Weaver stood in the midst of the three umpires, moving from one face to another in rapid Charlie Chaplin movements. He was a windup toy possessed." Well, I was wound up, all right, and I had to get the frustration and anger out of me. There was no point in keeping the argument going, so I ran out to second base, jumped on it, and stood there, refusing to budge. Rich G. came over and said I had one minute to leave the field or he would forfeit the game to the Yankees.

I headed toward the dugout counting the seconds to make sure he didn't job me out of a full sixty of them. But as I approached home Palermo was bent over, his back toward the mound and his legs straddling the plate that he was brushing off. The opportunity was too much to pass up. I swung my leg as if I were going to boot Palermo in the seat. Instead I swung my foot down and kicked dirt between his legs—all over his clean plate.

After the game, when the writers asked me about a possible suspension, I said, "No, those umpires shouldn't be suspended. The poor guys are doing the best they can."

As usual, though, MacPhail suspended me and announced, "It is clear that your ejection was unreasonably forceful and . . . unfortunately you hit Garcia in the eye with your cap." Yet when I met with MacPhail he conceded that the video-tape replay of my confrontation with Rich G. did not show my cap bill hitting the umpire, and I certainly didn't think it did. Again, though, if the bill of my hat did hit Rich G. it was the result of *his* leaning down and into me.

The umpires'-hat tricks on me had started years before this incident. And I had countered them until I left the dugout to argue with umpire Jerry Neudecker in 1978. As he came to meet me I reached up and turned my hat around so that the bill was in the back—as I had been doing with other umpires to keep them from bumping my hat off. Neudecker said, "You are not going to turn your hat around on me, Weaver!" And before I could even turn it back around if I wanted to, he threw me out of the game.

The next night when I had to have a discussion with Neudecker, I stepped out of the dugout and stuck my hat in a back pocket. "What are you going to do now?" I asked, and Jerry just listened.

Actually, Jerry Neudecker is one of the better umpires and I guess he felt I was trying to show him up by turning my hat, which I wasn't. But I wish every umpire—and the vast majority of them do—would adopt a key aspect of Neudecker's principles. "Each day is a new day and I forgive and forget," he says, and does.

I firmly believe in that, and as I have said many times, "There will be a reckoning for all of us someday. And if I die and get to heaven before any of the umpires who have been untruthful, I will be forgiving. In fact, I will stand at the gate and try to get them all in, as any good Christian would."

But I have felt that in the heat of pennant races I have seen an umpire or two slip, if you will, as far as "every day's a new day" goes. We had a series in New York late in the '79 season and in one game, while trying to keep Eddie Murray from being ejected, I got into an argument with both the home-plate umpire and the first-base umpire. Well, in the midst of this argument, second-base umpire Steve Palermo suddenly ran to our dugout and threw out coach Frank Robinson. Palermo said Frank had called him a dirty name. Now if Palermo had been able to hear anyone from the dugout over the noise of 50,000 fans in Yankee Stadium he must have a hearing capability that ranks with Ted Williams' eyesight. Later Frank told me he'd had a number of skirmishes with Palermo in the Puerto Rican League.

Two weeks later in Kansas City, Frank White attempted a second-inning steal of home, and plate umpire Bill Haller called him out. Then Palermo, who was umping at third, overruled his own crew chief and called a balk on Dennis Martinez, thus allowing the run to score. Martinez did not balk, and if he had more than one umpire would have called it, as usually happens. I couldn't see how Palermo, who had been in the major leagues about three years at this time, could call a balk when plate umpire Bill Haller—who was in his eighteenth year in the league—detected nothing.

I called Palermo "a young punk" and said "there's no place in baseball for a person like you. I question your integrity. You've got a chip on your shoulder going back to when you threw Frank Robinson out of that game in New York."

I said these things as loudly as I could because it's almost always a 100 percent shouting match out there. I also emphasized my points by shaking my finger in Palermo's face, which is my habit and which the umpires counter by gesturing in kind. But Palermo slapped my hand, then grabbed it. Now if I had slapped *his* hand in retaliation or grabbed *him*, I would have been subject to the same kind of large fine, seven-game suspension, and lawsuit that Billy Martin was hit with in 1981.

Palermo told the press at game's end, "Earl kept waving his finger in my face and his hand brushed the bridge of my nose . . . that's why I grabbed his arm."

"I never touched the guy," I told the writers, angry that Palermo would make up such a thing. "I have respect for the umpires' uniform and wouldn't touch Palermo as long as he wears it. If I ran into him in street clothes and he laid a hand on me, his parents would have to visit him in the hospital."

I was hot, for sure. There are certain young umpires who could get anyone upset because they came into the league thinking they knew it all. They were wet behind the ears, as most youngsters are, and they did not like to be told that. Worse, they had trouble controlling games, and as a result they tended to eject players even before I could get out there and intervene, either to take up the argument for my player or to tell him he was out of line and to forget about the umpire and concentrate on the game. Either way I'd keep an invaluable ballplayer in the game. It's a shame that certain younger umps didn't learn some lessons in control from Nestor Chylak, the former crew chief, who was probably the best umpire in the American League.

One of his greatest assets—and it was possessed in abundance by a number of the older umpires—was patience. Chylak knew fans came to see the players, and he was happy to see a manager come out to save a player. He allowed a manager to do his job by never acting precipitously, even when some other umpires might blow up and worsen a testy situation.

I remember a doubleheader against the Royals early in 1977 that was plumb full of arguments from both teams. We lost the opener and I was ejected in the first inning of the second game by Joe Brinkman, who cursed me. Well the background on Brinkman was this:

In our final series of the '76 season Tony Muser of the Orioles got into an argument with Brinkman, who told him, "I'm going to get you every chance I get." Now I've heard those words from an umpire or two over the years, but they were usually just angry words, which we all issue in the heat of confrontations and then forget. I never saw umpires follow through on such threats . . . or almost never.

But in the first Baltimore series of '77 that Brinkman worked, in Seattle, I repeated those words to him—and the man confirmed that he had said them. That didn't give me a whole lot of confidence in his objectivity. Two days before the Kansas City doubleheader, in a game against Milwaukee, Brinkman had made a couple of questionable calls against us . . . and naturally his words came back to me. I went to Nestor Chylak. Nestor said he would speak to Brinkman, and you can bet your life he did so. But as far as I was concerned, the counsel of the crew chief didn't do much good—Brinkman threw me out of the K.C. game for a picayune reason.

I sat in my office seething and watched the game on television. In the third inning Palermo ejected my shortstop, Kiko Garcia. I said the hell with it, ejected or not—I wasn't going to let my players be intimidated by umpires. I ran into our dugout and told everyone to wait before taking the field again. "We may have a couple of umpires out there who are against us," I said, "but don't quit. Keep fighting out there. We're in first place, we're going good, and we ain't gonna lose this second game if you guys keep battling. And if any of you want to do some yelling about questionable calls—go right ahead. Because this goddamn ball club is gonna stand behind you!"

Royals manager Whitey Herzog was out protesting the fact that I was delaying the start of the fourth inning with my pep talk. Nestor Chylak headed toward us, but by then I had finished and the Orioles ran out like it was a play-off game. Dennis Martinez, who was a rookie, pitched his first complete game after a wild start and we won, 7–2.

At game's end Nestor Chylak said he had been prepared to act during our brief delay "if the Orioles made a travesty of the game." An inordinate delay of a ball game is valid grounds for action. Nestor was asked what kind of time limit he was thinking of imposing, and he said, "I hadn't made up my mind yet. At that point I was very cool. I was adjusting my mind."

God bless Nestor Chylak's "cool." And bless any umpire who "adjusts his mind" and weighs situations and circumstances before acting. Isn't that what arbiters—whether they sit on a bench in a court of law or work on a baseball diamond—are supposed to do?

A lot of the umpires used to. Another thing that umpires like Nestor and John Stevens, John Flaherty, Arthur Franz, and John Rice, among others, used to do—and Jerry Neudecker and few other veterans still do—was establish a presence that often kept you from arguing once you got out there. They'd say something like, "What are you *doing*, Earl?" in a way that made you feel embarrassed for coming out to question a call they were so positive about. You'd feel ridiculous and say to yourself: "How can I argue with a guy who's so sure of himself?"

I don't know why this posture has disappeared among the umpires who've reached the majors in recent years. Maybe they no longer teach this in the umpiring schools.

I also have to wonder if the schools are putting any emphasis on teaching the rules of baseball. There are a number of umpires who have made it clear that they don't know the rules. They even make up their own rules as they go along. Consider:

There was a game in Toronto in September 1977 in which rain was falling steadily, but not hard enough in the umpires' judgment to call the game. The Toronto playing field is artificial turf, except for the pitcher's mound, home-plate area, and the bullpen mounds. The latter are situated in foul territory off the outfield foul lines. The Blue Jay bullpen mound adjacent to the left-field line was covered by a tarpaulin. I asked crew chief Marty Springstead to have it removed because the tarp constituted a hazard to any of my players who might have to pursue a ball hit in that area. Springstead said he didn't have the power to order the tarp's removal. Didn't have the power? I thought for a moment I was speaking to an alien creature. Umpires have fans remove coats hanging over railings because they could interfere with play.

I strode back to our dugout and explained the situation to my players. I said I could not see proceeding with a game in which one of them might be hurt as a result of a safety hazard. I told them that if we refused to take the field because of the danger, Springstead would forfeit the game to Toronto. But we would file a protest with the league president, and we might get a suspended-game ruling from MacPhail, though I wouldn't wager my salary on it considering his record. Still, we were losing 4–0 and had only two hits in five innings . . . and if we got lucky and could resume later when it wasn't raining we might pull out a win. I left the decision up to the players.

When the forfeit was announced, the Baltimore writers seemed to think I should exchange my baseball shirt for a strait-jacket. We were still very much in the pennant race with 16 games left to play, only 2½ behind the Yankees (which is where we would finish, as it turned out).

"I would rather play the last sixteen games with everybody healthy than risk having somebody possibly ruin a career running over that tarpaulin," I said. "I also want to say that in all my years in baseball I've never seen a forfeit until tonight. But then I've never seen part of the playing field covered during a ball game until tonight. All the umpire had to do was have that tarp removed and we would have finished the game."

Lee MacPhail ruled that the forfeit stood, saying judgment as to whether or not hazardous conditions existed "must rest with the umpires." He said nothing about the fact that Springstead had made a mistake in maintaining that he was not empowered to have a tarp removed.

The Orioles were also forced to forfeit a 1981 preseason game because an umpire didn't know the rules. We were playing the Royals in Ft. Myers and in the seventh inning manager Jimmy Frey sent in five new players. Now there are so many players you don't know in spring training that you need the names in writing. First you want to get a line on them for the future. I don't want to look like a dummy if my GM asks me what I think of so-and-so player. But that's what I would be if I said I didn't know the guy and the GM said, "That's strange, you played three games against him in the spring." I also need to know where everyone's hitting in the lineup, because I wouldn't want anyone to hit out of order, and it's my job to see that they don't. I'm getting in shape in spring training myself, getting used to keeping track of all the details I have to be aware of during the season.

So when Frey sent in those five players I asked umpire Vic Voltaggio to give me the names in writing and where they appeared in the lineup.

"We don't do that here," Voltaggio said.

"What do you mean you don't do it? How can you run a ball game without an official lineup? Do you know where these players are hitting?"

"They're all straight up and down." (They'll bat in the position of the man they replaced on the field.)

"How do we know if they're straight up and down," I asked, "if we don't know their names?"

"Earl, we don't do that here," he said. "This is spring training."

I got angry and hollered, "If I don't know the names of the players and in what order they hit—this game can't continue."

"Well I'm not going to give them to you," Voltaggio said.

Jimmy Frey offered the lineup changes to Voltaggio, but he said that wasn't necessary. Frey knew the rule, the essence of which I quoted to the umpire: "The minute there is a multiple substitution, the manager should inform the umpire, who should immediately write on his card the names of the players, the positions they will play, and their places in the batting order. If the manager fails to do so, the umpire has the authority to place these players wherever he sees fit in the lineup."

So even if I didn't want to tell Voltaggio about my changes, he was *obliged* to list the new players on his card. Yet Voltaggio adamantly refused to, so I told my players to pack their gear and we left. Voltaggio called the game a forfeit—I called it a travesty.

But it got worse. Another umpire came over and told me, "We were told we didn't have to write down the changes here, Earl. We were told to come down here and relax, wear our sun glasses, and have a good time." Now I have this on tape, because the man who introduces my radio show, Tom Marr, was standing there with his recorder on. Yet when I reported to Lee MacPhail what the umpire had said, the president of the American League denied that the umpires had been told any such thing.

I then asked MacPhail why Vic Voltaggio was not following the rule book. Not surprisingly, Lee had no satisfactory answer. As far as I know Lee MacPhail either didn't know the rule or chose to ignore it, even though he is the man who makes final decisions on rule violations. Figure that one out.

Later MacPhail issued a directive ordering umpires to keep written lineup cards.

The most ridiculous result of the entire episode with Voltaggio was that MacPhail *suspended* me from three exhibition games! Can you imagine any rational person penalizing someone by sentencing him to take three days off from work during the spring in Florida? Billy Martin said, "Weaver's smarter than the rest of us." I just wish I was as smart as the umpires who get away with making mistakes concerning the fundamentals of the game. Yet it seems like every time an umpire makes a mistake, a manager gets fined or suspended or both.

And because some umpires don't know the rules and make up their own, we run into inconsistency. For example, in 1979 I had an argument in Oakland with umpire Jim Evans—who has a hair-trigger boiling point. I mean, a few words can send steam hissing out of all his orifices, so I try to keep that in mind when I have to discuss anything with him. But as I started talking to him this day, he suddenly ordered my pitcher, Sammy Stewart, to stop throwing warm-up pitches until I left the field. Well that ignited *my* boiling point. I told him there wasn't a damn thing in the rule book that prevented a pitcher from warming up when an argument was in progress. I told Sammy to keep throwing, and Evans threw me out of the game. The umpires all applauded as I walked toward the dugout.

I didn't leave, though. If the umpire could break the rules, I could too. I slipped into the toilet off the dugout and continued to manage from there—until A's manager Jim Marshall spotted my cigarette smoke. Evans came over and chased me. After the game Jim Evans said, "Earl Weaver is the Son of Sam of baseball." Now I don't know what the hell Jim was trying to say, but I'm sure he didn't mean I had killed a lot of people. I guess Jim's metaphors are as mixed up as some of his rulings.

I protested that Oakland game over Evans's misruling on warming up. Then we returned to Baltimore, and Angels manager Jim Fregosi went out to argue a point with the plate umpire. The Angels pitcher threw warm-up pitches during the discussion. I strolled out to another umpire and asked him to have the young man cease and desist. The umpire said, "There's no rule in the book . . ." I thanked him, and at game's end we filed another protest with that ultimate arbiter of justice, Leland S. MacPhail. The umpires couldn't have it both ways, right, Lee? Wrong. The umpires can do anything they wish to as long as the American League is presided over by a president who not only doesn't know the rules but won't correct *opposite* rulings on the exact same activity.

I made my strongest statement on the rules situation on June 18, 1979, in Cleveland. The trouble started in the fifth inning when Eddie Murray was ejected for the first time in his major-league career. On a pick-off throw to first base, Eddie appeared to tag out Cliff Johnson, but umpire Fred Spenn called him safe. Eddie argued and was gone before I could get there. After that home-plate umpire Ted Hendry started squeezing our pitcher on the ball-strike calls, and things got ridiculous.

In the bottom of the eighth, the Orioles leading 7–6, Mike Hargrove of Cleveland led off with a single. Dave Rosello then tried a sacrifice, bunting right in front of the plate. Catcher Rick Dempsey, who is cat quick, pounced on the ball and came up to throw as Rosello brushed him going by. I hollered, "Interference!" Rick was certain we had the out because he'd pushed Rosello with the ball, but just in case that wasn't called he threw to second thinking he would get the automatic interference.

The plate umpire said, "No." I ran out screaming, "The rule book states the runner is out when he fails to avoid the fielder in the act of fielding the ball. Rosello did not avoid Dempsey!"

Crew chief Larry Barnett came in from second and I said, "You should know the rule, of all people."

"I know the rule, and that was not interference," Barnett said.

"Are you really gonna blow the call *again?*" I said. "You blew it in the '75 World Series when Ed Armbrister [Cincinnati] bunted, collided with Carlton Fisk [Boston], and you didn't call interference. I almost kicked in my television set when you screwed it up then."

"No interference."

I ran into the dugout and grabbed our rule book. I found the rule while running back out and waved it as I approached the umpires. "Just look at this."

"You're out of here, Weaver," Barnett said. "You can't bring a rule book out on the field."

"Whaaaat? There ain't no rule that says you can't bring a rule book on the field! Now look at the interference rule—it's right here in black and white." I jabbed my finger at it.

Barnett and Hendry turned away, refusing to even look at the rule. I held my head in disbelief. I ran to the first-base umpire waving the book, then to the third-base umpire . . . hoping to find one arbiter who had some respect for the rule book. It was like trying to find another Frank Robinson.

I raised the rule book overhead in two hands—and tore it in half. I tore it in quarters. I tore it in sixteenths. I tore it in thirty-seconds. Then I threw into the air the pieces of the baseball scriptures that these umpires would not even deign to consult . . . and some of the confetti symbolically descended on the heathens.

The 31,506 fans in Cleveland's Municipal Stadium gave me a thunderous round of applause. It continued as I picked up some scraps from the book and handed them to Hendry as I strode toward the dugout. The applause grew even louder and I tipped my cap, then stepped down into our dugout where the Oriole players were doubled over laughing. I glanced at the Indian dugout and saw the players there doing the same.

With the score tied, I wasn't about to go into the clubhouse. I hid in the runway behind a few players and watched another obscene call go against us. The Indians missed a bunt attempt and Rick Dempsey threw behind Hargrove at second. The relay to Doug DeCinces at third beat Hargrove by at least five feet. It wasn't far enough for Jim Evans. Doug said, "If Evans said I'd missed the tag, that might have been a little reasonable. But he said Hargrove beat the ball—which was absurd." Thankfully, we won the game in the ninth.

But I was fearful, as I said afterward, "Oh are we gonna get a

royal screwing the next two nights." Actually that very seldom happens, and as it turned out the Barnett crew gave us a
very professional job in the subsequent two games.

Even when I'm concerned about an umpire, it never keeps me
from arguing like a crazy man again the next night. You've got to
go and tell a guy when he's wrong, just as you've got to tell a
guy when you feel he may be harboring some kind of grudge.
But that feeling will dispel itself; it'll pass in time. There will be
something said or done that will convince you that umpire's
going to do the best he can from that point on.

There are exceptions, of course, to just about everything. Ron
Luciano, for example, was an umpire I preferred not to associate
with right up until he retired a few years ago to work for NBC-
TV. I say that not merely because Luciano ejected me more
times (seven) in fewer games than any other umpire.

I've known Luciano from my days in the minors when he was
definitely one of the better umpires in the league. I remember
offering him counsel, though, based on my fifteen years in professional baseball. We had a big argument in York, Pennsyl-
vania, and I'll never forget standing there looking up at Ron's
chin and hollering about all the dedication it takes for a ballplayer to go to the big leagues. And I suggested that anyone who
wants to advance has to bear down all the time. I don't know
whether Ron heeded that advice, but he did move up to the majors rather quickly.

And he introduced a new style of umpiring, one that had more
entertainment value in it than anyone I'd seen since Emmet
Ashford. Luciano wouldn't just call a man "safe." He'd make the
call a dozen times, dramatically slicing his arms through the air
like a non-swimmer trying to stay afloat. And his "out" signals
looked like a spastic trying to hitch a ride on an L.A. freeway.
But it was fun and gave fans something else to cheer about.

Luciano, who is a massive man, about six-foot-six and 300
pounds, was indeed a showman. I think his antics were definitely good for the game . . . until he began putting more effort
into them than he did into his work. It suffered along with those
of us who were engaged in our profession that particular day.
Luciano just got caught with his thumb up his butt too many
times. I remember a game in which he was working the bases.

During the fifth-inning break when they drag the infield, Ron grabbed a Coke and began talking to fans in the stands. He was still standing there chatting when the first pitch of the next inning was thrown. He looked like a fool and so did his crew chief, Bill Haller, who is supposed to be sure all the umpires are in position before an inning begins.

And I don't know how many times Luciano gave one of his multiple "out" signals, then suddenly realized he had yelled "Safe" and had to switch signs. *That* was entertaining, too, but more than a little confusing. We'd be jumping around in the dugout saying, "What the fungo did that big boob call? Can't he make up his goddamn mind?" Then someone would say, "He ain't got one."

Still, I didn't have any more problems with Luciano than I did with other umpires until he started saying publicly that he hated Earl Weaver. The quote appeared in a California newspaper in 1975 and was picked up all over. Now I did not feel that a man who admits that he hates you should be umpiring your games. After I questioned Luciano's attitude and protested his performance in a game against us, he proceeded to eject me from both games of a subsequent doubleheader, and I wasn't even fined. That suggested that MacPhail saw some merit in my charges.

It didn't do me much good, though, because in the first Oriole game Luciano worked behind the plate in 1976 he got me for nothing. He'd missed some calls on Jim Palmer in the first two innings, and when the initial pitch of the third was "Ball one" I called to catcher Dave Duncan:

"Was that a strike, Dave?" He motioned that it had been.

"Where did Luciano say the pitch was?" Duncan motioned high.

Then Luciano, who had been staring at me, gave a little jerk with his thumb. I went out to him incredulously. "Are you throwing me out?"

"You're out, Earl. You know you can't question balls and strikes."

"I wasn't! I was asking my catcher about the pitch! I have every right to question my catcher!"

Luciano turned his back on me. I charged him, cupped my hands by my mouth, and hollered as loud as I could into Luciano's face that he was a disgrace to his profession and several other unprintable things. Then I kicked dirt all over home plate and went into the runway. I saw Palmer start to pitch with the plate still covered. Luciano didn't clean it off until Jim walked in as if to clean it himself.

After the game, which we lost 3–1, I was still enraged and I told the writers, "I wish Luciano hadn't uncovered the plate. If he'd let Palmer do it, Lee MacPhail would have had to fire Luciano, which he should have done long ago."

Just a few weeks later Ron Luciano gave MacPhail incontestable reasons for relieving him of his duties. In an interview with a Chicago *Sun-Times* writer that was syndicated nationally, Luciano said, "I don't care who wins the pennant as long as it isn't Baltimore." He also said he didn't like Earl Weaver and "I hope he doesn't win another game."

Now, how can a man who openly admits that he roots against a ball club and its manager, how can that man possibly be objective in umpiring any of that ball club's games? The Orioles front office called for Luciano's immediate termination.

In July, before we played the Angels in Anaheim, Luciano called a press conference and apologized to me for his anti-Weaver, anti-Oriole comments. "To start with," Luciano began, "I've got a big mouth and I've said a lot of dumb things. Everybody makes mistakes, and I'm at the top of the ladder when it comes to saying dumb things."

I certainly agreed with that, but I was still unconvinced that I could rely on Luciano to be impartial. I said, "I'll try to forgive and forget. But the first time a close play goes against us, I'm gonna feel it was a chance to get the knife in deeper."

In all truth, by making that statement after Luciano's public apology to me I thought he would not dare give us any quick thumbs. And in the game against the Angels that night Luciano was exemplary. But his crew chief, Bill Haller, ejected me in the fifth inning. The next night he got me two innings earlier.

Both were blatant instances of Haller standing up for the Umpire's Association in what amounted to a slap in the face of the president of the American League and the supervisor of umpires . . . with me paying the price. In other words, *no* authority was going to chastise an umpire without the umpires retaliating. As I said after the second successive ejection, "We got no chance with this crew. Evidently Luciano will stand back and let the other members of the crew get me."

Luciano didn't work any of our other games that season and very few in subsequent seasons. The next time we saw the Haller crew in 1976, Dale Ford had replaced Luciano, and again we received no bargain. During a Sunday afternoon game in Baltimore, Lee May contested a called third strike, and once again it was a case of an umpire ejecting a player before I even had a chance to try and protect him. I don't think anything infuriates me more than the gratuitous loss of a player. By the time I reached the plate umpire, May was already gone and I really tore into Dale Ford. Unfortunately, in waving my hands in Ford's face my fingers accidentally cut his lips. When MacPhail asked me if there had been contact with Ford, I said yes.

But I also told him that the entire incident could have been avoided if the league had used a little foresight and not assigned the Haller crew to Baltimore. Taking Luciano off of the crew just alienated the others, in my opinion. That crew had already thrown me out of five games, fined me once, and I now received a three-game suspension—and the season was only half over!

But we had very few inordinate problems with the Haller crew thereafter, and I don't know as we even saw Luciano again until the 1979 season. Of course, I heard from him occasionally, or rather I heard from what he has characterized as his "big, dumb mouth," particularly after he had appeared at off-season banquets.

Luciano made a speech in Rochester in the spring of '79 and said, "I hate Earl Weaver with a passion. I met Weaver in my second year in baseball. I threw him out that first night and three nights after that. Our relationship has gone downhill ever since. He's about three-foot-one and I have to tell him to get his nose off my kneecap."

When the writers sprang these quotes on me I got annoyed and said, "I'm sorry Luciano's mentally ill and won't umpire any of our games again this season. He's a sick man."

The only time Luciano worked one of our '79 games, on August 26 in Chicago, he grabbed the first opportunity that presented itself to eject me—and I ended up with another three-day suspension. There were no problems whatsoever through the first four innings. But Doug DeCinces led off the fifth and worked the count to 3-2. The next pitch was so far off the plate that Doug flipped his bat and was 25 feet down the base path when Luciano called strike three . . . another of Ron's cute mannerisms. Doug turned and charged Luciano, and I jumped out of the dugout to get between them—when Doug suddenly stopped and headed for the dugout. So I was left standing there, bare and exposed five feet from the dugout. I threw my hands in the air helplessly. Someone thought I was raising my arms to the heavens imploring a higher power to grant us patience . . . if He couldn't provide us with another home-plate umpire.

It seemed to me Luciano had just been waiting to get me out of the dugout to throw me out. He made only the slightest pointing motion at me, then quickly brought three fingers to his lips and gave me the kiss-off.

"Are you throwing me out?" I asked.

"Yes."

I went right to crew chief Russ Goetz. "I am protesting this game," I told him, "on the grounds of the umpire's integrity." Then I went to the White Sox P.A. man, Bob Finnigan, and had him make the announcement to the 25,000 people in the stands. Lee MacPhail happened to be one of them, and I felt it was about time he took Luciano off our case permanently.

MacPhail was of a different mind. "I exploded when I heard that announcement," he said. "I sure as hell can't let him publicly question the integrity of an umpire. What does that mean? He's dishonest? We had Luciano apologize when he said what he said." Thanks, Lee, I thought, that did me a world of good. "We've tried to keep Luciano away [from Oriole games]," MacPhail went on, "but you can't carry these things on forever. Earl Weaver is suspended for three games. That strike call was the first decision even debated today."

The fact that the call led to my ejection raised legitimate questions in my mind about the umpire's integrity—particularly since my part in the "debate" consisted of stretching my arms to the skies. Is that just cause for ejection? I could have been airing my pits, for all anyone knew.

Oriole GM Hank Peters was angry, too. "I don't like the grounds of the suspension," Hank said. "They don't suspend an umpire when he calls Earl 'baseball's Son of Sam.' Luciano has said all those things about how he doesn't want the Orioles to win. We asked Lee to fire him and he refused. I haven't seen why Luciano hasn't been suspended."

I didn't waste my time protesting the suspension. But then suspending managers is really a waste of time, because every manager has a means of communicating with his ball club following an ejection or suspension from games. It certainly would not be difficult to communicate if I so desired. I have closed-circuit TV and a phone to the dugout in my office, as well as messengers available if needed. I can sit back in comfort and see when the count goes to 3–0 with a man on second and put on the hit sign just as I would if I were in the dugout. But I cannot confirm the reports that I have continued to manage after being thrown out of a game. There is no way I would want to give Lee MacPhail any groundless grounds to suspend me.

It has also been reported that I have continued to manage while under suspension. After that '79 suspension in Chicago we traveled to Minnesota and before each game I made out the lineup, then sat in the stands next to scout Jimmy Russo throughout the series. Newspaper stories stated that I made all the calls during those three games, with Russo relaying them via signals to coach Frank Robinson in the dugout. I can't comment on this kind of pure speculation, of course. But I will say that a manager can find ways to manage his team from anywhere if he wishes to. In truth, a manager can do just about anything he wants to, even sit in the dugout during games if he is resourceful enough. I heard about a minor-league manager who managed a 1981 game while wearing the tiger suit of his team's mascot. I'm thinking of donning the Oriole mascot's Bird suit during my next suspension. Maybe I could "debate" balls and strikes through a beak. Would umpires dare eject the beloved Bird?

Lee MacPhail has even placed me on "probation" a time or two. Probation is a word Lee uses that nobody pays any attention to because nobody really knows what he means by it. It sounds something like being in purgatory . . . but the next step from there is heaven, so it's not exactly the same.

What blather. I would like to inform baseball's powers that be that whenever Lee MacPhail puts somebody on probation or places somebody on suspension or levies a fine against somebody —he is accomplishing absolutely nothing. These measures are all archaic and asinine; strictly for show. If such measures were effective, would they have to be used over and over again?

For as long as a manager is going to serve his ball club properly—by trying to see that his players stay in the game and that the umpires do the right thing on the field—eventually the manager is going to be suspended again. It is inevitable. And who gives a fungo?

Like myself, the umpires do exactly as they please. They are not effectively supervised, and they take advantage of it. Dick Butler is the supervisor of AL umpires and Nestor Chylak and John Stevens are his assistants, but they don't really have any authority to hire and fire. That is where all authority starts and finishes. But umpire Joe Brinkman has told me flat out, "We're not going to pay any attention to what Nestor and those guys say. We don't care what they say because those guys are living in the past." Vic Voltaggio has said the same thing to me.

I questioned Dick Butler about the umpires' stated positions, and he said, "We can't do anything."

I said, "Well that's ridiculous. If a ballplayer tells his bosses to go stuff themselves, he gets fired. Anybody in this country can be fired. The President of the United States would have been fired if he hadn't resigned. You mean umpires are bigger than the President?"

Dick Butler just shook his head. Lee MacPhail took the same posture when I talked to him about the situation, which has been reported in the press. Off the record, the umpires have said their union is too strong for them to be dismissed. The Association of Major League Umpires should not be more powerful than a league president, but that appears to be the case. That is why a number of umpires are not performing to the best of their ability; they go uncorrected and fully employed because their superiors are failing. As I said on my radio show early in '81, things rot from the top as well as from the bottom. And until umpires are made to do what they are told to do by their supervisors, American League baseball will continue to be subjected to some rotten officiating. It is far from widespread, but there is a grave danger that it could become so in years ahead.

The solution to the problem may lie with a new president of the American League. Lee MacPhail does a portion of his job excellently. As far as his control of umpires, though, he simply does not have enough knowledge of on-field procedures. Lee Mac-Phail has never gotten his teeth dirty on a ball field. Neither, for that matter, has Dick Butler. But the game would benefit, I feel, from having a man atop the league who has spent some years on the ball field. It's for certain that somebody has to get in there and make some changes.

If I were the president of the American League, the first thing I would do is visit each club in spring training and talk to the players for a couple of hours. I'd put on their uniform and say, "I used to wear one of these. Nobody got thrown out of more ball games than me. So I know there will be times when you're gonna aggravate an umpire because you think you've been wronged. And you have a right to talk to that umpire. But the umpires working for me demand respect, and they will get respect. You don't have the right to call an umpire a dirty name. You don't have the right to unduly delay a game." And I would proceed to lay out boundaries beyond which players could not go. Once those boundaries were breached, the offender would be ejected from the game. I wouldn't take a penny of their money, as I know fines don't work. "It's penalty enough when your ball club loses your services for a number of innings. And if there are repeated violations, your ball club is going to lose your services for a number of games—three, five, seven, whatever—depending on the circumstances. If that happens, you are penalizing your club by your absence as a result of taking advantage of my umpires. Losing a manager is unimportant because he can still perform his duties. But losing a player is destructive to every team's goal of trying to get to the World Series.

"Any time I receive a protest of an ejection, there will be a due-process proceeding. All sides will be heard from in writing and in person if necessary, for I will fly out and meet personally with the principals and weigh all the evidence before any final ruling is made. Most rulings, however, should be cut-and-dried hereafter, as we will now begin utilizing the technology available to us. Every umpire will now be equipped with a highly sensitive tape recorder that will produce a record of the words that pass between umpire and player. We will have voice prints on file of every umpire, player, manager, and coach in the league so that each individual can be readily identified."

Once the above was known, there would no longer be many harsh words between umpires and uniformed personnel. For I would see that the truth was known. The Major League Umpires Association might not be happy about this innovation. But I would ask, "What are you afraid of? If an umpire is right, you should not be afraid of a machine that will confirm he is right." Why not use the technology available to end the hassels with umpires that often diminish the quality of the game by resulting in the ejection of players who should be out performing. I'd get the umpire situation straightened out very soon by finding out who was wrong and making sure the offender was not habitual.

It is apparent to anyone who is regularly on the ball field that there are some AL umpires who have not demonstrated the ability to perform their job consistently. They should be given cram courses to get their work up to major-league level or be replaced. I don't know of an umpire who has ever been dismissed for other than off-the-field behavior, cashing bad checks, or some such. I read a story in which Nick Bremigan was still annoyed with the non-union umpires who worked during the MLPA strike of a few years ago, four of whom are still employed. Bremigan said, "There are better umpires in the minor leagues who can't get called up because they wouldn't work during the strike." He seems to be suggesting the league is behind this, assuming it's true. Many people feel that the only reason the less-than-proficient umpires aren't fired is fear of the union. I would put an end to this nonsense as league president and hire umpires strictly on their ability.

I would also upgrade the umpire's standard of living. Umpiring is no easy occupation. Ballplayers complain about fifteen-day road trips, for example, yet umpires will hit the road for sixty days or more at a stretch. If baseball expects to attract and keep top men, the salary structure and expense allowance must increase. The umpire's starting salary in the low $20,000 range should be moved up closer to the player's major-league minimum of $32,500. Senior umpires now earn about $50,000 per year; $75,000 would be a more equitable figure in our economy. And a daily expense allowance of $77 is chintzy when hotel rates in some cities run $50 while umpires also must pay for meals, cleaning bills, clubhouse fees, and local transportation. So umpires should be paid more, but not hired for life as if they were members of the Supreme Court.

I don't know how often umpires read the rule book, but I would see to it that regular refresher courses were given on the rules. I can read the entire book in ninety minutes, and I'm a slow reader. It would not take a lot of time for supervisors to meet with crews periodically each season to review the rules in depth.

Knowing the rules helped win us a ball game in 1977. We had lost the opener of a doubleheader in Cleveland and appeared to have the second game won when, with two outs in the ninth and the bases loaded, the Indians hitter grounded to Rich Dauer at second. Dauer, who made only seven errors all season, threw the ball into the dugout. We had a two-run lead, but plate umpire Vic Voltaggio waved the three runners around the bases and everyone left the field. I turned to coach Jimmy Frey and said, "That ain't right, is it? Let's reconstruct the play."

"The bases were loaded and they let the guy score from first," Jimmy said. "He should've gotten only two bases."

I ran out and told crew chief Marty Springstead, who said, "There was an intervening play."

If there had been, the runner could keep going. But I pointed out that the throw would have had the runner by six feet, that the ball was out of play *before* the batter even reached first. The runner at first could not advance beyond third, so the game was tied.

Marty thought for a moment and said, "You're 150 percent right."

We came back, scored two runs in the top of the tenth to take the lead again and held it. Meanwhile, the Baltimore television and radio stations had given the "final" score with Cleveland winning and had gone to a commercial as the players left the field. Many fans in Baltimore turned off their sets thinking we had lost, only to be surprised in the morning.

I was also surprised in 1975 when I actually had a Ron Luciano decision changed by his colleagues. It was a May game in Baltimore against the Angels, who had two men on when Tommy Harper hit a drive down the left-field line that everyone in our dugout could see was foul. Luciano, umpiring at third, signaled home run. I went running out to protest as the umpiring crew convened and told Ron he had missed the call. When it was changed to a foul ball, Angels manager Dick Williams protested in a rage and was thrown out—another instance of an umpire's mistake resulting in a manager's ejection.

Luciano admitted after the game that he hadn't seen the ball enter the stands, but felt he had to make a call. "I had a fifty-fifty chance of being right," he said.

When Luciano was hired by NBC-TV before the 1980 season, I said, "I just hope he takes this job more seriously than he did his last one." I meant that sincerely.

And I mean it when I say I don't care what an umpire says about me—unless his words taint his impartiality, as Luciano's did more than once. Luciano has also said, "Weaver gives me the impression that he wants everything—that he wants you to cheat for him. He wants an unfair advantage."

Here are a variety of other umpire comments on Earl Weaver.

Dave Phillips: "Weaver's main objective is to intimidate. He doesn't use any curse words. He just fights for everything he can get."

Rich Garcia: "He's a disgrace to the game."

Larry Barnett: "He goes goofy. He can't control himself, screaming, ranting, and raving. Every time he comes out, he's shot out of a cannon."

Marty Springstead (who was tied with Luciano in the Weaver-ejection race going into the '81 season with a total of seven): "Weaver never shuts up. The way to test a Timex watch would be to strap it to Earl's tongue."

Nestor Chylak: "He always used to have me thinking, what's he gonna do next? It made me a better umpire."

Jerry Neudecker: "I'd just as soon have Weaver out there as anybody else. He's been fair to me. He won't take up for a ball-player when he knows the player is wrong. I remember when Earl came out to complain about calls on the bases twice in one game, and later he said he had seen television replays and we were right on both plays and he was wrong."

I apologize every time I find I'm wrong. I try to say I'm sorry as quickly as I possibly can, too, no matter who I've wronged—umpire, ballplayer, newsman.

That's one reason why I feel that, overall, I get along with umpires just about as well as any manager. As I've said many times, the umpires are going to be right 98 percent of the time. But that's not going to deter me from trying to help them achieve 100 percent. I get upset when they make a mistake, just as I get upset when my players do. With a player you can wait until after the game and speak to him privately. With an umpire you have to jump right out immediately and make your point in front of thousands of spectators, which doesn't build warm and loving relationships.

Still, for all the battles I have had with umpires over all the years, there is only one man in the league with whom an animosity has built up. Generally I have to say I've been satisfied with the way Bill Haller has umpired our games. But he's not crazy about my personality and I'm not crazy about his. I respect the fact that he can go out and give a good ball game any time he so desires. And I would just as soon see him give it to California-Oakland as Baltimore-New York.

I don't recall a single run-in with Bill Haller until the 1972 season when the Orioles fought Detroit all season for the pennant. Haller was behind the plate in the first game of a doubleheader against the Tigers that year, and we seemed to get the short end on every pitch. We weren't getting any of the close calls, while the Tigers seemed to be getting everything that was around the plate. We lost the game and afterward the writers asked me why we had seemed so perturbed by the calls. I told them I felt Haller had favored the Tigers and I couldn't understand why, as I'd never had a problem with him going all the way back to the minors.

Just then Jim Palmer came up behind me and whispered, "Wouldn't you call 'em like that if your brother was catching for the other team?"

It hadn't even occurred to me that Tom Haller, Bill's brother, had caught that game. He was a seldom-used reserve, and I'd paid no attention to that until Palmer whispered. Then I heard myself say, "Well the league can't let Bill Haller umpire an important series in which his brother's catching. An umpire should not be leaning over his brother. There is no reason why a league president should let this kind of situation come up. If MacPhail has any sense he'll keep Bill Haller away from the contenders so there can't possibly be any questions."

That was what happened: Bill Haller was taken off the contending teams, and to this day I doubt that he rejoices over that decision. I don't believe that Haller would intentionally retaliate on a ball field for a personal offense, though I do feel he represented the umpire's association when he ejected me twice after Luciano's command apology.

But Haller didn't act like a professional a couple of years ago when he secretly agreed to be wired for sound by a Washington television station during one of our ball games. The fact that he told no one on the Orioles or Tigers that they were being recorded for public broadcast not only showed bad judgment on Haller's part but could have made him a defendant in an invasion-of-privacy lawsuit. As it turned out, what transpired suggested to some who viewed the telecast that Haller ejected me to spice up the taping, though I wouldn't go that far.

The confrontation started after Haller, working first base, called a balk on Mike Flanagan of the Orioles and Eddie Murray told Haller he was wrong.

"That's not a balk," Eddie said.

"Behind the rubber," Haller said.

"He did not go behind the rubber," Eddie said.

"For me he did," Haller said.

That was when I got out there and said, "Ahh, bleep."

"Bleep yourself," Haller said.

"You're here and this crew is here just to screw us."

"Boom!" Haller said, and jerked his thumb.

"You couldn't wait to get me out."

"Oh, Earl, you run yourself," Haller said, jabbing his finger in my face.

When he brushed me I slapped his hand away and said, "Get your finger off me."

"You hit me?" Haller said.

"Yeah, because you put your finger on me. You do it again and I'll knock you right on your nose."

"I didn't touch you. You're lying."

"You ain't no good."

"Nah, you aren't either."

It is this kind of scene that has led folks to say that the umpires are out to get me. But if that were true, we would not have won forty one-run games in two seasons. The fact is that in my major-league career I have won more ball games than any other manager in that time, and if the umpires truly had been after me that record would not have been possible.

That is why I honestly would like to thank the umpires for all of their generous help.

A few years ago *Time* magazine reported, "Earl Weaver and his players yell at each other so much that the dugout sounds like a session of primal-scream therapy, but the anger quickly passes." Well as far as I'm concerned, yelling's just a way of communicating loudly, and a manager has to tell a player when he's out of line or he may stay there. And my players are welcome to yell back at me. I don't take it personally, and I make sure they don't either.

Mark Belanger, who played for me in the minors and every year since I've been in Baltimore, has said, "If Earl has to tell a guy to go to hell, he'll do it. But he does not have a shithouse like some managers. You can argue with Earl for six hours and call him every name in the book. But if he thinks you're going to help him win, you'll play the next day."

Winning is the only meaningful final score, and my desire to do so has been the underpinning of every confrontation. I've had them ever since I started managing, and I will have them until I retire. One of the first in Baltimore occurred late in the 1970 season. We loaded the bases in the ninth inning of a game with Bobby Grich due up. Grich was a rookie who had batted .383 in half a season at Rochester and was hitting about .210 for us. I sent up a pinch hitter for Grich.

Bobby exploded. "How the hell am I ever going to build any confidence in myself," he hollered, "if you keep hitting for me?"

And I exploded, angry that he had broken my concentration

on the ball game. "I don't give a shit about your confidence—I want to win this game!" I hollered.

"This is bullshit!" he yelled.

"Get the hell out of here!" I shouted and stepped toward him, just as I do in arguments with umpires. But Bobby also lunged forward and bumped me down the runway steps. Ellie Hendricks grabbed Bobby and I sent him into the clubhouse and told him I'd see him in my office after the game. Then I sat him down and explained to him that the goal of the Baltimore Orioles was to win games and that any time I could make a substitution that I thought would give us the best chance of accomplishing that goal—I was going to do it. When Bobby Grich convinced me that he was the best hitter in a similar situation, he would go to bat. Eventually Bobby did convince me, and then he called me "a great manager, a brilliant composer of lineups and tactics."

But it takes time for some players to understand the manager's job. Doug DeCinces thought I was picking on him for years every time I corrected him. Early in the '78 season I played DeCinces at second base in the first game of a doubleheader and Eddie Murray at third. Rich Dauer was in a slump and I had to try something to score some runs. I'd used DeCinces at second in a number of games in previous seasons and to say he was accomplished at that position is stretching the truth. But I was desperate.

In this game against Cleveland a ball was hit in the hole behind second with a man on second. Mark Belanger fielded it and shoveled the ball to DeCinces, who came across the bag with his back to the infield. He apparently never thought the runner from second might keep going home. We hollered from the bench: "Home! Home!" But DeCinces stood there holding the ball while the run scored.

We got out of the inning and when the infield came into the dugout I said, "Damn it, we got to stay on our toes out there! We've got to be alert! Somebody's got to holler, for chrissake!"

DeCinces thought I was singling him out, even though I was speaking to the entire infield because everyone was at fault.

"You mean me?" he said angrily.

"Yes," I said, "you're part of the infield. Everyone's supposed to be alert."

"You little shit!" DeCinces yelled. "I've had it with your stupid mouth!"

He grabbed for my shirtfront and I went for him. Pat Kelly jumped in between us and wrapped his arms around Doug. "Let him go, Pat!" I said. "If he wants a piece of me, he's got it!" I don't back down from anyone in the heat of anger, but I was damn glad Kelly didn't let go of the six-foot-two DeCinces.

Kelly and one of the coaches took Doug into the clubhouse. He was out of the game. Then he worried that because he'd hollered something that hurt my feelings I wouldn't play him in the second game. That was silly. As every player who's ever had a screaming match with me knows, I would never sit down a player who could help me.

The next day Doug asked for an audience with me. He asked for more audiences than any other player I've ever had, which is all right because that's what I'm there for. And I was not unaware of Doug's situation. It was no easy task for him to replace a legend in Baltimore named Brooks Robinson. Doug would misplay a ball at third and fans would holler, "Brooks woulda ate that up!"

When Doug came into my office and closed the door, I said, "Just relax, Doug. No apologies or nothing. Just go out and play ball." Most ballplayers respond positively to those kind of words, but Doug was still worried.

"You know, you're in charge of my whole future, Earl," said Doug, who hadn't been signed to a new contract and who had been having back problems that concerned all of us.

"You're probably right that I'm in charge of your future here," I said. "But you got nothing to worry about if you can play, 'cause you'll make a lot of money. If you can't play, you won't. It's all on your shoulders. You got a decent glove—use it. You're good for 20–25 home runs a year and some big RBIs."

When Hank Peters consulted me about whether to sign Doug or not, I said, "We don't want a ballplayer of DeCinces' ability to get away from us." And Doug DeCinces went out and tore up the league the rest of that '78 season, leading the club in slugging percentage. That screaming incident may even have been the spark that ignited him, you never know.

But DeCinces is a worrier. Even after six years with me he still thought I kept him out of a game because he'd said something that offended me. This was in Kansas City during the '80 season. The Royals had men on first and second with two outs in a tie game and George Brett coming up. Brett already had a double and triple off Scotty McGregor, whom he hits at about a .570 clip. I had Scotty walk Brett intentionally and brought in Timmy Stoddard to pitch to Amos Otis. Otis can't get the bat around on Stoddard's heater.

But Stoddard ran the count to 3–2 and then threw a fastball so far out of the strike zone nobody could hit it. Otis fouled it off. That gave Stoddard another chance if he could get the ball over the plate because Otis had made up his mind to take. He took ball four and the winning run scored.

The next day I read what had to be the dumbest criticism of me from two intelligent players, DeCinces and Belanger. De-Cinces said we shouldn't have walked Brett because then we were taking a chance on somebody making an error that would let in the runner from third.

Belanger said the intentional walk put all the pressure on the pitcher and the infielders: "What if we made an error?" Well Mark must've been thinking of somebody other than himself. He'd only been the best defensive shortstop in the major leagues for fifteen years, and if he makes an error it's a freak. I had been *praying* Otis would hit the ball to Belanger. You can't worry about all the possible ways a runner can score from third on *your* misplays. You have people in the game who don't often make misplays, period.

In the next game, Kansas City started a right-hander that De-Cinces didn't hit, and I played left-hand-hitting Dave Graham at third. Doug's back had been troubling him and Graham's bat had been troubling opposing pitchers. But DeCinces saw the lineup posted and came running in to me. "Why aren't I playing?" he demanded.

"Because you're a horseshit hitter off this guy," I said, "and you're 2-for-22 in the past week."

He knew damn well why he wasn't playing, and his .212 average should have been a clue. But DeCinces wanted to know if I wasn't playing him because he'd second-guessed me in the papers.

Rick Dempsey is another guy who always thinks I'm picking on him. "If Weaver picks on anyone else," Rick has said in the papers, "I sure haven't noticed it." He's been saying that ever since 1976 when he joined us, and he's too stubborn to ever change his views.

In our system, for example, the pitchers call their own games. But Dempsey kept trying to call the pitches. He'd put down the same sign no matter how many times the pitchers shook him off. I'd say, "Rick, Jim Palmer's only won three Cy Young Awards."

"You think that SOB's smarter than me?" he'd say.

"Smarter don't count," I'd tell him. "He knows what he wants to do with the hitter, so let him do it."

Oh, was he stubborn! I tried to point out to Rick some fundamental truths. A manager manages. A pitcher pitches. And a catcher *receives*. We had a big fight on this subject. "Rick, a catcher catches the ball," I said. "When you're given more responsibility, then we'll change the title. We'll call you an executive receiving engineer or something."

Our most celebrated battle occurred in the first week of the '79 season in Milwaukee. Rick is a good guy, an excellent catcher, and a very aggressive ballplayer. But aggressiveness on the basepaths isn't worth a damn if you get a hit and stretch it into an out. Rick had made several baserunning mistakes in spring training as a result of being overaggressive. I'd spoken to him after he'd doubled, taken a big turn around second, and stopped, then been thrown out trying to get back. I'd told him to make up his mind and either go or stay—but not to stop halfway between bases.

So in Milwaukee Rick singled in the second inning, rounded first, and stopped. The outfielder threw in behind him and Rick didn't slide back into first. He was out.

"You forgot how to slide?" I said when he came in. Rick mumbled something I couldn't hear, and I didn't say anything. It's always better to keep your composure in the dugout and speak to the player who's errored in private after the game. But you can't always do that. When a guy makes a boo-boo, his teammates *expect* the manager to holler at the guy.

Well, in the fourth inning of that Milwaukee game Rick dropped a pop foul, and when he came in my composure dissolved and I hollered at him.

"Why am I the only guy you ever holler at?" Rick said.

"Because you're the only guy who's making the same mistakes all the time!" I shouted.

"I'm not the only one!"

"You're sure as hell the one today!"

"That's bullshit!"

"Shut up!" I hollered.

"I'll shut up when you get off my back!"

"Well that's it—I don't need this shit! Call in Dave Skaggs from the bullpen," I told coach Frank Robinson.

Dempsey threw his mask on the dugout floor.

I picked it up and flung it down, too.

Rick grabbed a batting helmet off the rack and slammed it on the floor. I yanked another helmet off the rack and smashed it on the floor. He grabbed another helmet and smashed it on the floor. So did I.

"That's my helmet!" someone yelled. "What am I gonna bat in?"

Rick picked up a shin guard and flung it on the floor. I went scrambling around looking for the other shin guard when someone yelled, "What's wrong with those two nuts?"

Frank Robinson bear-hugged Dempsey from behind and later said, "It was a case of two guys getting things off their chest. But there comes a time when someone has to back off. And the manager should have the last word."

That's one thing I insist upon. Jim Palmer came over and told Rick, "Pick up your gear and put it on," thinking I was going to keep Dempsey in the game.

"He don't need that gear," I said. "Skaggs is catching." I turned to Dempsey and said, "If you're not gonna play baseball my way, then I can't play you. The only reason I'm hollering at you is because you're making mistakes and I think you can correct them. If I didn't think you could correct them, I wouldn't bother to tell you. That would be pointless, and I'd trade you.

But you've gotta start listening. Now go out and warm up the pitcher until Skaggs gets his gear on."

That was the crowning blow—having to warm up the pitcher after being yanked from the game. But Rick did what he was told.

Dempsey thought the dugout incident was going to be old news once we went on the road. But when we arrived in Anaheim the writers there asked me about it, "I hear you and Dempsey had a battle." "It wasn't much," I said, trying to keep things low key.

Rick came storming into my office all upset. "Why the hell are you starting all this crap again?" he said.

"Look, Rick," I said, "this is something that happened. It's something you don't like to think about, and I don't either. But writers in every city are gonna ask about it and we have to live with it. If we don't tell them the facts as you see them and as I see them, the incident's gonna get more and more distorted. So when someone asks you what happened, just relate the facts."

Dempsey gritted his teeth and left. But Rick's always gritting his teeth. When a foul tip hits him in the finger, Rick's the kind of guy who says, "Damn, that feels good."

You're always going to have problems with intense players who can't see the manager's point of view. Even individuals who have the interest of the team at heart can foul up because they can't really see the overall picture. In 1969 Donny Buford wanted to steal on his own, and I called him in and told him we had too many good hitters coming up behind him. If he stole, it opened up first base for an intentional walk and I didn't want a Frank Robinson or a Brooks Robinson to get a free pass when they might hit the ball out of the park. Donny nodded.

A few days later he took off and stole second on his own. When the inning ended I sent another player out to his spot in left field. Buford was upset and I hollered at him in the runway and then saw him again in the office later. I had to have it out with him if we were going to have a good ball club. I don't think Donny ever understood or agreed with what I was saying. But he stopped running on his own when he saw he'd be yanked from the game for doing so.

Now Eddie Murray did that once as a rookie—about the only

thing that Eddie's done wrong since he's been with us. Murray's no speedster like Al Bumbry, but Eddie is like Frank Robinson in that he can get you the big stolen base when you need it in a late inning. But in Eddie's first year he tried to steal third base with two out in the ninth inning. He was thrown out and that was the ball game. He came trotting in with his chin on his chest, and I'm sure everyone was waiting to see what I'd do. I called him into the office and I didn't have to say much. I knew he felt bad enough. I also read Murray as a ballplayer who wasn't going to make a foolish mistake twice.

Before the '79 season, pitcher Steve Stone became the first "expensive" free agent signed by Baltimore. I liked Stone with the White Sox in '77 and '78, as did my pitching coaches, first George Bamberger and then Ray Miller. I feel I'm an astute judge of pitchers, and with the assistance of my coaches, I know how to help them get the most out of their ability. As testimony I cite the fact that we had twenty-two twenty-game winners in my first thirteen years as the Orioles' manager.

We acquired Stone as a fifth starter. You're invariably going to have some arm problems among your first four starters, and Stone appeared to be the kind of guy who could sit out for a week or more and still be sharp enough to give us six or seven good innings in a spot start.

But he did not have a good spring. Every other time out I said to myself, "Jesus, he's getting whacked pretty good!" When the season opened and Scotty McGregor came down with tendinitis, Stone filled in as the spot man between Jim Palmer, Mike Flanagan, and Dennis Martinez. Early rainouts limited Stone's starts to once every seven or eight days. He went 2–3 in his first five starts and came to me complaining.

"How the hell am I going to do a good job pitching sporadically?" he said.

"Steve, that's your job here," I said.

"I can't pitch well going eight or nine days between starts."

"That's why we signed you, because we think you can," I said. "We think you can go eight days between starts and give us a good game, then come back in four days if necessary and give us six or seven good innings. If you can do that, it's gonna be beneficial to the club."

"Earl, I've never done that. I just can't pitch that way."

"Well, Steve, that's how you're gonna pitch here. That's why we signed you as a free agent."

"Money's not the most important thing to me," Stone said. "I may be overpaid now for the work I'm doing. I want to pitch in rotation."

"I'm sorry, but you haven't beaten out the guys ahead of you," I said, realizing Stone's pride demanded that Baltimore get its money's worth out of him. "Just take your money and do what we tell you. You'll be successful and the ball club will too."

Stone also maintained that I had pulled him from games too quickly, and I told him I relieved him only when I felt it was necessary. His performance alone controlled how long he stayed in a game.

Shortly after this meeting we were in Oakland for a series. I left the hotel for the ball park at 3 P.M. and who did I see outside with a woman at his side but Steve Stone. I didn't think anything of it until I reached the ball park and started writing out the lineup card. Steve Stone was scheduled to pitch that night! I'll be damned! I thought. Stone is a single guy who is a restaurateur and a wine connoisseur. But he is also a ballplayer who knows how to take care of himself, so I wasn't *that* upset. His bad form didn't trouble me as much as his pitching that night. I relieved him early.

The next afternoon he came into my office furious, and we really lit into one another. "You didn't give me a chance to pitch out of trouble!" he yelled. "I hadn't started in nine days—and you relieved me instantly! That's an asshole thing to do!"

"Hold on there!" I hollered. "You didn't give me a lot of confidence in you."

"You've relieved me too soon before!"

"I've relieved you every time you haven't been pitching good!" I said. "You came to us as an under-.500 pitcher, and if you ever start doing what you're told—you'll be a winning pitcher! I know what I'm talking about because I've done it before."

"You keep telling me to throw my curveball over the plate— and I'm giving up too many home runs!" Stone said.

"I don't tell you to *hang* the bleeping curve!" I said. "You keep throwing it high and over the middle of the plate—you're gonna see the ball flying out of the park!"

"You think you're always right!"

"I know you got a good curveball if you'll concentrate and use it right!"

"You're not only an egomaniac—you're a stupid egomaniac!" he shouted.

"And you're a loser!" I hollered. "You'll always be a loser until you're willing to do things the right way!"

I never doubted that Stone could win for us and I kept starting him after Palmer came down with tendinitis. By the All-Star break Steve had started 19 games and had improved, though his record was only 6–7. I kept preaching the powers of positive thinking—which I steadfastly believe in—and Steve started applying it and concentrating on the mound. In his first start after the All-Star break, Stone struck out 10 batters and won 12–1. In his last 13 starts he was 5–0 with a 2.94 ERA. The following season he was 25–7 and won the Cy Young Award as the league's best pitcher.

Steve Stone may have been right in saying he wouldn't have been successful had he remained a spot starter, but that would have been his role if we hadn't had injuries among the starters. Yet I was right in assigning him the role he had qualified for, and for elevating him as he came on.

I think we both learned something in our confrontations. I learned to leave Stone in longer to work out of trouble once he convinced me he could do so regularly. When valid points are made on both sides of an issue, people have got to learn something if they have any sense at all.

I've certainly learned more than a few things from Jim Palmer, as would any manager who has watched a man pitch his way into a Hall of Fame reservation. But we are both emotional, intractible, and fiercely competitive. And because I've almost never been right as far as Palmer's concerned in our fourteen years together, we've battled every other step of the way. We've had so many high-decibel arguments that the players once referred to us as Oscar and Felix of *The Odd Couple*. Still, life with the greatest pitcher to ever gain even more fame selling underwear has indeed been an education.

Jimmy is the guy who introduced me to the ulna nerve, for example, which I thought he'd invented. He's had so many physical problems—back, shoulder, elbow, forearm—that I thought he'd just run out of ailments and had made one up when he told me his ulna nerve was bothering him. Then I had to see a doctor about swelling in my right hand and he said, "You've got an ulna nerve problem."

"I must've caught it from Jim Palmer," I told him.

But I finally learned to take Palmer out of a game when he complains that he needs relief. Some years ago in Baltimore I talked him into going back out to pitch the ninth after he'd gone eight tough innings against the Red Sox. He said his forearm was hurting, but with his fluid motion you sure couldn't tell it. "You won the Cy Young Award pitching complete games," I told him. He went out and gave up three homers in the ninth. He came in boiling. "Damn it, Earl, if just once you'd ever listen to me!"

"From now on, I will!" I hollered back.

And I do whenever he says he wants to come out of a game because he's hurting. The trouble with Palmer is that he's as high-strung as I am, and he has tried to leave games simply because I've hollered at him. I remember an incident in Texas when he laid in a fastball to Juan Beniquez that became a double. Now Beniquez can't hit a hard breaking ball with a tennis racket, so I ran out and asked Palmer what the hell he was doing. He took off his glove and extended it to me saying, "Here, you pitch if you can do better."

That wasn't the first time he's made *that* cute move. At game's end I reamed him for embarrassing me and he yelled back. Then he said, "I'm sick of this shit! I want to go to a ball club where I can just pitch."

I called a team meeting and said, "Is there anybody here who wants to be traded?" No one answered. "Well *that* guy does!" I said, pointing at Palmer.

"Really bush, Earl," Palmer said and ran into the trainer's room, which he likes to do when he thinks he's gotten the last word. But I chased him down in there with a few more choice words of my own. I was so angry I was jumping up and down, and Palmer said, "Earl, I've never seen you so tall."

Only once have I ever gotten my point across to Palmer without saying a word. That was in 1976, one of the years in which Jimmy kept complaining about the defensive ability of our outfielders. It was bad enough that he was knocking his teammates to the press, but he went too far during a game in Oakland. A flyball was dropped and another that might have been caught fell in. Palmer was furious when he strode in off the mound. He reached the edge of the dugout and fired his glove against the wall—about two inches from my ear. I told him off loudly, and after the game I said, "You've got to apologize to the ball club. You're lucky you're standing up, the way you've put down your teammates. It's a wonder somebody hasn't knocked you on your butt."

Palmer refused to apologize. So the next day I called a meeting and told the players to get together on their own and decide why we were playing poorly. "The coaches and I are getting out of here. I want you guys to discuss among yourselves what's wrong with this ball club and what can be done to improve it. Then let me know."

I knew that in a closed-door meeting Palmer would be forced to apologize for cutting up the outfielders, and he did say he was sorry. But Jim wants to win so badly he can't help reacting to situations when he thinks he can improve them. Though my coaches and I have positioned the outfielders behind him, Palmer has moved them from the mound many times. I even did an underwear commercial with him where he tried to move the cameraman "to improve the angles." I laughed when the director vetoed the move.

To be successful it is imperative that a manager have the last word with his players, otherwise you have anarchy on a ball club. The Anarchists have never won anything anywhere, even in the Mexican League. With no one in charge, nothing gets done right. Although the players might not always like all the words, they have to like the Baltimore ball club's overall record. That speaks for itself.

It would have been better if I had been able to get things done without all the public confrontations with players. I have avoided a helluva lot of them by counting ten and waiting until the end of the game when I could see the player in private. But there were certain situations where I just couldn't control my temper. The mistake had to be corrected right *then* if the message was to be effective. At least that is my belief. But I've had enough screaming matches with players to know they are not the ideal.

The ideal manager and the greatest manager would avoid *all* confrontations, public and private, and still win consistently. He would get his points across without any screaming and hollering and smashing batting helmets and hurting people's feelings. I've just never learned how to do that 100 percent of the time while winning ball games. I guess eventually some sonofagun will come along who can do that, maybe the next manager of the Baltimore Orioles. I'll certainly applaud his ability.

I've never enjoyed walking into the clubhouse after pinch-hitting for a guy, pinch-running for another, and sending in a defensive replacement for a third . . . and seeing those cold glares and angry darts headed my way. Managing a ball club ain't always fun.

Still, I have to say that virtually every player who's left the Orioles has found that our way of doing things is as good as or better than anybody else's. They would agree with what Bobby Grich and Don Baylor have said to me: "Earl, I appreciate what you tried to tell me." It might have been a little loud at times, but in the long run it was beneficial.

chapter three

Growing up in St. Louis, Missouri, where I was born August 14, 1930, my whole world was built around baseball. When I was five my parents gave me a uniform that displayed Dizzy Dean's phrase, "Me 'n' Paul," on the back. I wore that uniform and played ball every day I could from then on . . . until it had to be replaced. And every day my father or grandfather would pitch to me in the yard behind our house, and they never got upset about the panes of glass I broke in our garage. From the beginning I never had a single doubt that one day I would be a major-league baseball player.

Once I started playing games, St. Louis summers were so hot that within a few innings my uniform would be soaked through and the heat radiating off the field made all of us do a little dance to cool our feet. I never gave that a thought until in the minors we went into Ft. Smith, Arkansas, for a series with the temperature stuck at 110 degrees and the hard-packed infield was such an inferno that we had to stand back on the grass. Between innings we dipped our shoes into buckets of ammonia water, then dipped in our caps and dumped the water over our heads. That was when I remembered the St. Louis summers and told myself: Hell, I'm used to this; it's simply something you gotta do when you're becoming a major-league ballplayer.

I was exposed to major-league players from the age of six. My father handled the dry cleaning for both the Cardinals and Browns, and he often took me with him to pick up and deliver the uniforms. It was a thrill going into the dressing room and seeing all my heroes from the Gashouse Gang and the Browns. With this access I got quite a few autographs over the years, but I lost them . . . which I'm certain has been the fate of most of the scraps of paper I've signed for fans. I remember getting Ducky Medwick, one of my favorite players, to sign a scorecard for me after a game. On the way home, though, I rolled the scorecard into a bat and started hitting a paper ball with it (I was always trying to improve my swing). The scorecard ended up too tattered to keep.

I got to see over a hundred ball games every year at Sportsman's Park, where both the St. Louis teams played. My Uncle Bud Bochert saw to that. Uncle Bud was the well-to-do member of the family, a shrewd and good-natured man who numbered bookmaking among his professions and stashed his cash in the large, hollow hassock in our living room (I once saw him count out $70,000 from that repository). Uncle Bud annually bought a block of tickets to all the weekend, holiday, and night games at Sportsman's Park, and he always took me along. Afternoon games I attended as a member of The Knothole Gang. Even when I was playing ball I could get to the park after my games by the fifth or sixth inning. So throughout my childhood I sat in the stands and studied baseball day after day, second-guessing one of the game's greatest managers, Billy Southworth of the Cardinals and wondering why in the hell a smooth-swinging switch-hitter like Roy Cullenbine of the Browns could never hit to the opposite field.

In 1944 we had an all-St. Louis World Series. The Cards had won their third successive pennant and the Browns had won their first ever, and I was able to buy a bleacher ticket to see all six games. It seems amazing now that I could just stroll over to the park from high school and purchase a Series ticket. But baseball had attendance problems during World War Two, and neither of these teams had drawn over 500,000 spectators that year. It was wonderful seeing all those players I had followed so closely competing for the world championship. And it was a good Series as the Browns surprised everyone by winning two of the first three games; then the Cardinals' pitching took control and won the final three.

I was only thirteen when I began my freshman year at Beaumont High School in January 1944 and I was small. But I was determined to become the regular second baseman on the baseball team, which had to be one of the best high school squads anywhere. Bobby Hofman, who went on to play for the World Champion '51 Giants, was a senior on that team. Roy Sievers, the American League rookie of the year in 1949, was a junior. Two other teammates, Bobby Weisler and Jimmy Goodwin, became major-league pitchers. I was damn proud to make that ball club, as well as the Stockton Post American Legion team that many of us played on in the summers. We won the state championship twice.

Missouri was a prime area for baseball scouts in those days. There were more than fifty minor leagues and the practice was to sign players in quantity out of which quality would eventually emerge. Today, with minor-league baseball being little more than a license to lose money and no major-league team having more than four or five affiliations, every player signed is a solid prospect. But during the war the rule against signing players before their high school class had graduated was suspended, which was how Joe Nuxhall pitched for the Cincinnati Reds at age fifteen.

I must have really impressed one scout, George Sisler, Sr., of the Dodgers, my freshman season. As soon as it ended he phoned my father and asked, "Would your son Earl be interested in playing professional baseball, Mr. Weaver?"

My father, Earl Milton, who had named me Earl Sidney, was momentarily taken aback. Then he said, "Yes he would, Mr. Sisler, but Earl won't be fourteen years old until August."

"Oh, I didn't realize he was so young," Sisler said. "Obviously it's too soon to talk about signing him, but I'll be keeping an eye on that young man."

That didn't damage my dream any, nor did the fact that during the next three years both the Cardinals and Browns invited me to all of their tryouts. My father was particularly friendly with Browns coach Freddie Hofmann, who was proud to have lasted nine years as a major-league player and also survived rooming with Babe Ruth. Freddie was awfully nice to me at the workouts, hitting me 50 groundballs each time and making sure I got all my swings.

But the man who scouted me and encouraged me the most was Walter Shannon, who was in charge of the lower minor-league teams for the Cardinals. He saw most of my high school games and any time I got an important hit or made a big play in the field he'd slap me on the back and say, "You're gonna be hitting like that for the Cardinals in a few years."

My father leaned more toward the Browns, though, because of Freddie and because he'd known the team's owner, Bill DeWitt, ever since they had sold newspapers on a corner in North St. Louis as kids. So just before my graduation from high school my father phoned his friend Freddie Hofmann and said, "Freddie, I want you to tell me something. The kid's gonna graduate here in a few days and I want to know honestly, what do you think of his chances in pro ball?"

"You really want to know, Earl?"

"Yes, I want to know what you honestly think of his potential in pro ball."

"He's a Class-A player, tops."

My father didn't speak to his friend for over a year after that. Earl Milton knew, just as Earl Sidney did, that I was going all the way to the majors.

Yet my father still favored the Browns, so we went to their offices in Sportsman's Park and saw DeWitt and Jim McLaughlin, who was running the farm system (McLaughlin would move with the team to Baltimore in 1954 and give me my first job as manager a few years later; Jim would also break in Harry Dalton with the organization, the man who would give me my first major-league manager's job). Bill DeWitt was frank, to put it much more mildly than I would have when I heard his words, "Earl, as far as we're concerned you don't run very well. Your arm is average; it's a second baseman's arm, period, which means you can't play the other side of the infield. Now you hit over .400 in high school, but we don't know if you can hit on the professional level. The competition is that much tougher."

Then he offered me a contract, $175 a month for five months and a $2,000 bonus if I was still with the team on June 15. My father gave me the slightest nod indicating he thought I should sign. But I knew about those contingency contracts. Dick West-ling, who had played with my Legion club, signed a contin-gency contract with the Yankees and was released before the deadline. A contingency contract puts a lot of pressure on a player to do well immediately, and for teenagers away from home for the first time it can be overwhelming. Teams were al-ways looking to save the bonus money. But if they gave you the bonus money up front, they usually let you play out the year to try to get their investment back.

So I looked at my father and shook my head, then said, "Mr. DeWitt, we'd like to think over your offer."

I led my dad down the corridor to the Cardinal offices, where Walter Shannon greeted me as if I were the next Frankie Frisch, "We want to sign you, Earl, and there won't be any contingency contract. I'll show you why." He slung his arm around my shoul-ders and walked me over to the big window that looked down on the manicured playing field of Sportsman's Park. "You'll be playing right down there in a few years, Earl."

I signed a Class-B contract for $175 a month and a $1,500 bonus, which seemed like a pretty good buck to me in 1948 when you could buy a new car for that figure. Two of my high school teammates who graduated that June would sign for $4,000 bonuses, yet Roy Sievers had been so intent on signing with the hometown Browns that he had agreed to do so for a pair of spiked shoes.

Until free agency and arbitration came to pass in 1976, the owners of major-league baseball teams had done a very nifty job of controlling players and their salaries. When I signed they had a rule that anyone who received a bonus of $4,000 or above had to be counted on the major-league roster of forty. They put in this rule so they wouldn't be inclined to bid against each other for players and inflate all salaries. The owners protected them-selves at the players' expense for seventy-six years, which was a pretty fair run. Now that the owners can't pass a law to hold down bids on free agents, Philadelphia Phillies' owner Ruly Car-penter abruptly announced in 1981 that he was selling the team. He said, "I don't think it's wrong to pay big money to quality players. I just can't accept the direction my peers seem to be tak-ing." Well no one said Ruly Carpenter had to follow that direction. But why he wanted to sell a world championship team that had a lucrative television contract and that drew 2.6 million people into his ball park in 1980 is beyond me.

At age seventeen I had never been out of St. Louis when I boarded the train for Albany, Georgia, site of the Cardinals' central spring training camp for its fifteen Class-A-and-below minorleague clubs. I had with me the shaving kit and the suitcase that relatives had given me at my going-away party. Also with me was the center fielder from my Beaumont team, Harley Beavers, who had been signed to a C contract, which meant he'd gotten a little less money than I had. I was nervous and it was good to have a guy I knew along. I was more nervous the next day, after arriving in Albany late at night and being bussed to a rooming house, when we reported as instructed at the YMCA. There were literally *hundreds* of young men standing around. "My God, Harley," I said, "where the hell are all these guys going?"

We were assigned to the Class-B Lynchburg club, and I found out where everyone was going when I was given a number to pin on my uniform—521. We were bussed to the Lynchburg diamond, and I was in for another shock. There were six guys on the field at every position. I stood there staring at the dirty half dozen by second base, thinking, *Maybe I should get right back on the train and go home*. Then I said to myself: Shit, I had made the high school team and I had made the Legion team. It's up to me to make the Lynchburg club.

There was pressure every morning, because numbers were called and guys were sent packing daily. But I kept getting pretty good wood on the ball and handling everything in the field. The other second basemen were all cut and I thought I had the Lynchburg job. Then another guy showed up from an A club, and I was optioned to the D club in West Frankfort, Illinois. I was decimated, so I sought out Walter Shannon, who told me the initial decision had me going to the Duluth club in C ball. But he thought I'd be much better off starting in D ball: "It's easier, Earl, and you won't be eighteen until the season's almost over. So burn up that league and you'll be moving up right on schedule."

I was still disappointed. En route to the West Frankfort diamond I passed the Duluth players and decided at a glance that I was as good as them and should be with them. I may have been lucky that I wasn't. Two months later the Duluth team bus crashed and ten of those kids were killed. Harley Beavers was lucky, too. He didn't do well at the plate in B ball, but after the accident he was sent up to play center for the C team and somehow he found his stroke in the higher classification.

I loved West Frankfort, even though I had to live in a rooming house and eat at the Little Egypt Cafe. But the food was reasonable and plentiful, which was important when you were trying to stretch $1.25-a-day meal money. At the Little Egypt we got two eggs, bacon, toast, grits, and coffee for 29¢. We played 120 games that season, many of them on fields that featured knee-high weeds in the outfield or surfaces on which no plant would grow. But I was seventeen years old and making a living doing the only thing I ever wanted to do: play baseball.

Although there was no way at 5′ 6½″ and 155 pounds that I could be a power hitter, in my first at bat I drove a ball over the left-field fence. Fans took up a collection and presented me with $40. They liked my style of play because I was always in the game, a Pete Rose type who went all out and chattered constantly. We won the pennant, and fans voted me the team's "MVP," which was really the most popular player. Although my batting average was only .268, I averaged a hit a game and scored 96 runs.

That summer a girl I'd known casually in St. Louis, Jane Johnston, visited her grandparents in West Frankfort for a few weeks and we started dating. I liked the way Jane looked and the way her grandmother cooked. At season's end I went home and dated Jane exclusively, and I began thinking about the married players who always had someone to go home to, someone to do their laundry and cook for them . . . someone to dissolve their loneliness. I took a job as a warehouseman with the Inland Steel Company for $60 a week, bought a new Chevrolet for $1,400 with my bonus money, and in February Jane and I announced our engagement. We planned to marry at the end of the 1949 season.

In spring training, though, loneliness gripped me like a fever you can't seem to shake. Jane and I spoke on the phone or wrote every day and we decided to marry as soon as possible. I was assigned to St. Joseph, Missouri, a step up to Class C at $275 a month, and within a week after I arrived there I arranged for a church, a place for the reception, and found us a dingy little apartment.

On May 7 my entire family and Jane's father, mother, and stepfather assembled for the church ceremony at 3 P.M. We then had dinner at the reception and received about $400 in gifts, and by 5:30 I was at the ball park. I was much happier being married, even though it was a lot of responsibility for an eighteen-year-old. In those days you were supposed to be married and have a family, and I was thrilled when my son Michael was born eighteen months later.

St. Joe was in the Western Association, which took us—via eight- and ten-hour trips in battered old buses that could seldom accelerate beyond 40 mph—to towns like Muskogee, Oklahoma; Ft. Smith, Arkansas; Salina, Kansas; and Joplin, Missouri. They all had two things in common: temperatures of 100 degrees and dilapidated hotels that forced us to develop our own crude air conditioning nightly. We would fill a wastebasket with the luke-warm water from the cold tap and soak our sheets and mattresses. Then those antique ceiling fans that are so fashion-able today would evaporate the moisture we slept in and cool us . . . ever so slightly.

I had a great year with St. Joe, making the All-Star team and again being voted the team's "MVP" by the fans. I batted .282 with 141 hits in 138 games, and I also had over 100 bases on balls.

Yet my personal statistics weren't important to me. It sounds like a lot of crap, but any time I went 3-for-4 and we lost, I was angry. If I went hitless and we won, I was happy. I always con-centrated all of my efforts on doing whatever I could do for the ball club because as far as I was concerned that was the little guy's job. I couldn't hit the ball out of the park; I never had over six home runs in any of my thirteen seasons. But I sure as hell could take a lot of pitches to create a base on balls. If I was lead-ing off an inning with us behind by two runs, I would take two strikes without giving it a thought. I never struck out more than 30–35 times a season . . . until the last years of my career when the slider came in big and ate my bat. I just never learned to go to the opposite field with the slider, which is the way you handle that pitch. I could go to the opposite field with the fastball and curve, though, and I always tried to when the game situation called for hitting behind the runner. I figured if I did everything I could to help the team win and it did, I was doing a job that would eventually carry me to the big leagues. Of course, if I was starting as a player now I would definitely concentrate on building good stats. As I tell my players—you get nine guys on a ball club building good stats and you're going to win.

In 1950 I moved up another notch to Winston-Salem in the Class-B Carolina League. Then I began to see some real baseball talent, including quite a few major-league veterans who were on their way down. As it turned out, not one of my teammates at West Frankfort or St. Joe ever made the big leagues. But it quickly became apparent that one kid at Winston-Salem was destined for the majors. He was called "Vinegar Bend" Mizell, and he was the main reason why we won the pennant by 19 games. Several times he went into the fourth inning without anyone having hit a fair ball off him.

He entered the ninth inning of one game with a 1–0 shutout as the result of his own home run, and the hats that were passed through the stands for Mizell were getting full until he abruptly gave up 2 home runs. In the bottom of the inning we rallied and, with 2 out, I doubled home 2 runs. Fans brought $400 into the dressing room and Mizell thanked them, but he was told that $150 of the collection had been designated for me. Vinegar wasn't too happy about that. He got rid of most of the change on me, though I sure as hell didn't mind.

For the third successive year my team finished first, I again made the All-Star team, and led the league's second basemen in fielding percentage. I batted .276.

That winter the Cardinals signed me to a Class-AA contract with their Houston team in the Texas League, and I won the starting job in spring training. I was feeling good, because this was far and away the toughest competition I'd played against. The Houston team was loaded with veterans, eight of whom were over 30, including the second baseman I'd beaten out, Ben Steiner. I had negotiated a good contract, $600 a month, but Steiner was earning more and it was no secret that the team's management wanted him to play. I got off to a slow start at the plate, hitting .233 in 13 games. I wasn't worried, though, being confident that I could handle the pitching if they stayed with me. They didn't. And since my three minor-league options had been used up, I was sold outright to Omaha of the Class-A Western League. That depressed me enough. When Omaha tried to cut me to $400 a month, I said no way, jumped in my car, and drove home to St. Louis. The next day the Omaha management called and said they really wanted me, that the $600 a month would be no problem.

Great. I had suffered a bit of a setback, but what the hell . . . I was only twenty, I had had three solid years of experience, and if I had a good year in A ball, I had to move up next year closer to the majors. I did have another fine season, rapping out 35 doubles among my 141 hits and compiling a .279 average. Again I made the All-Star team and again we won the pennant, although we lost the play-offs.

The Omaha manager in 1951 was one of the sharpest men I ever played for, George Kissell, who later earned his pension coaching for the Cardinals. (There was no pension for career minor leaguers; only those men who were employed in the majors for five years qualified for retirement income.) I learned a helluva lot from George, including some strategies we still use—with certain modifications—in Baltimore, such as his cutoff-and-relay system. His double steal while the pitcher has the ball is one of my favorites. It's one play that we practice only in secret during spring training, and it's been very effective for us.

In the pressure of a close ball game, a pitcher has so much to think about with runners on first and third that it's impossible for him to do everything right at every moment. In 1979, with two out in the twelfth inning and a rookie left-hander named Guy Hoffman on the mound for the White Sox, I put the play on. As Hoffman came off his stretch, Doug DeCinces broke from first. And as the pitcher stepped off the rubber and froze—Eddie Murray raced in from third base. By the time Hoffman threw home, Murray had scored standing up.

But the pitcher doesn't have to be a rookie and he doesn't have to be left-handed. We have a play for right-handers, too. It's just easier against a pitcher who is staring at first base. Still, we worked this play against Vida Blue when he was with Oakland, and in the last two years we've used it successfully against

Cleveland and against the Red Sox twice. Veteran Boston reliever Tom Burgmeier was the victim early in 1981. You get a feeling when a pitcher's concentrating so hard on the batter and the man on first that the runner on third is the last thing on his mind. It's the element of surprise in the extreme, so you pick your spot and try it. When it works, I've been known to do a little dance. When it doesn't, I look like a jerk. But when it's successful, the play usually wins us a ball game.

So I felt like I went to school with George Kissell. He was a great fundamentalist, but he was also a grating perfectionist, a manager who had rules for everything imaginable, and who assessed fines for the least infraction.

He hated cigarette smoking and strictly forbade it in the dugout. That merely frustrated those of us who needed an occasional puff to relieve the tensions of ball games. But like most minor-league managers Kissell coached third base. So we'd sneak a few puffs when we were up, then clip our butts and hide them behind the bench. We had to be careful because the manager was always shooting looks into the dugout trying to catch us.

One day George walked into the clubhouse before a game holding a carton of Tareytons and said, "Somebody gave me these nasty things. Does anybody smoke them?"

I smoked Raleighs because I liked the taste and the gifts I could get with the coupons, but I wasn't going to turn down a free carton of cigarettes. Right away I said, "I smoke 'em."

George had been looking at outfielder Wally Moon, who I later found out did smoke Tareytons. George turned to me and said, "I wondered who was smoking these damn things in the dugout; I found these butts pinched all over the place. You're fined ten dollars, Weaver."

He handed me the Tareyton carton. It was empty.

Kissell was a stickler on curfews. He not only ran bedchecks on the single guys—he would actually call the married men at their homes and ask to speak to them. He wouldn't even accept your wife's word that you were home. Now I've always felt that almost any time a manager wants to catch a player out after curfew he can. I've also felt that if a guy is performing well on the ball field, leave him alone. Playing baseball successfully is difficult enough for even the most talented individuals, and there is no point in harassing them when they are trying to unwind in the off hours.

At season's end the Cardinals either had to buy my contract—my minor-league options having been used up—or chance losing me in the draft. When I was informed that I had been placed on the major-league roster, I was ecstatic. I would get a shot at making the Cardinals in the spring of 1952. Eddie Stanky had been named manager of the team, and I didn't see how he could have any prejudice against a little guy who demonstrated a lot of desire and hustle, because that was Stanky's game as a player.

The spring started well. I checked into the Bainbridge Hotel in St. Petersburg, where the Cards trained, and I had never stayed in a place so fine. We just signed chits for all expenses at the hotel and were also give twenty-five dollars a week "Murphy money," which was for incidental expenses such as tips and laundry. I thought I'd arrived in heaven, and that feeling carried right into the clubhouse where I dressed with people like Stan Musial and Harry "The Cat" Brecheen and Enos Slaughter.

In one of our early spring games I went running out for a high pop-up in short right. I turned and backpedaled under the ball, when suddenly I heard footsteps pounding behind me and a distinctive Carolina voice crying, "I got it! I got it!" I could hardly believe it was actually me out there as I hollered, "Enos! Enos!" and moved out of the way. I remembered those countless times that I had leaped to my feet in the stands at Sportsman's Park and shouted, "You got it, Enos! All yours!" as he ran down a line drive and speared it.

All of the veterans were pleasant, most of them openly friendly. But none of them was happy about Eddie Stanky's manner or demeanor. He was downright atagonistic toward *everyone*. This was his first managing job and, in truth, he wasn't ready for it. Brecheen was a ten-year veteran who always played by the rules. Yet before a game later in the season Harry was in the clubhouse changing his shirt after pitching batting practice, and Stanky fined him fifty dollars for not being out when the national anthem was played. Stanky simply could not accept incapabilities from any of his players, even though he had a lot of them as a player. In fact, he still had himself on the active roster when his own skills had diminished dramatically. But every manager has to remember that he made mistakes as a player, that there were certain things he simply could not do on a ball field. No manager can expect any player to perform beyond his physical limitations. Eddie Stanky frankly scared the hell out of me.

He set up a pitching machine and a net for a bunting drill that he personally supervised. Now if there was one thing that I did well at the plate, it was bunt. But I stepped in with him standing there and I must've gone after thirty pitches without ever laying down an effective bunt. Not one. Then Stanky took the bat and demonstrated how to bunt. I watched him carefully, observing his technique, and he was good. Then I stepped back into the cage . . . and I still couldn't bunt. I was just too nervous.

When the games started I had no trouble at all. I regained my confidence and was pleased with my performance, getting into 19 games and hitting close to .270 against some pretty damn good pitchers. I knew I wasn't about to win a starting job in St. Louis because the incumbant second baseman was Red Schoendienst, then a youthful veteran who was holding out in a contract dispute. When he reported he was not in shape, but that didn't take long under Stanky—who ran the most exhausting camp I've ever experienced.

Stanky included in his conditioning program a couple of very strange drills. In one we practiced diving back into first base, which I thought was a dumb thing for a major-league club to work on. But the other drill was even more dangerous. I kept thinking, What the hell's Stanky gonna do if a guy like Stan Musial gets hurt in this exercise? The drill was designed for a man-on-third, one-out situation when the runner is given the sign to run on any groundball. If the runner can't make it home safely, every team expects the runner to retreat and force a rundown so that the batter can make it to second. Stanky introduced a little football into this play. The runner was to stop and get the catcher moving toward him. Then, just as the runner was about to be tagged, he was to throw his body at the catcher's ankles. The catcher would then fall over you. Except in our drills the Cardinal catchers—all of whom weighed over two hundred pounds with their equipment on—tended to fall right on us. Stanky lined up the whole team and had us go through this.

Musial did it once, then kept slipping back to the end of the line. The manager having told me to do something, I executed the drill with such enthusiasm that Stanky said, "Hey, you're good at this." He had me demonstrate until I was black and blue. Some of the veterans gave me a hand to keep me out there diving so they didn't have to. But I'm sure that if any manager tried that drill today, he'd be run out of baseball.

I was still with the Cardinals on April Fool's Day when I received the shocking word that I had been optioned to Double-A Houston. I was so disappointed. I'd talked myself into thinking I was going to stick as a utility infielder, which was ludicrous given my barely adequate arm. But when you're a twenty-one-year-old kid and you think you've come *this close* to realizing your unremitting dream, only to suddenly see it hook foul and out of play . . . it can do grave damage to your head and heart. For the first time, I had doubts about my ability, serious doubts that occasioned the worst period in my life to that point.

I reported to Houston with bitterness camped in my throat and indecisiveness swirling in my head, and I played miserable baseball. I couldn't even pick up a groundball. I don't think I got one hit with a man on base. I went to bat twenty-four successive times without getting a hit, a slump that I had never approached before. Manager Al Hollingsworth, who had optioned me the previous year, stuck with me, giving me every chance to get straightened out. I couldn't, batting only .219 in 57 games. Back to Omaha again.

When I got there I thought things over and had to acknowledge one thing to myself. In my depression I had begun drinking far too much beer. To this day, as player or manager, I have never had an alcoholic drink of any persuasion before a ball game. But I had periodically stopped for a beer or two with teammates after games through the years. I don't think I ever had more than three no matter how gala our celebration may have been. When I first arrived in Winston-Salem I saw two of our veterans—guys in their late twenties who were on their way down—come to the ball park with so much booze in them that they were only marginally ambulatory. One player fell down and the other threw up. I knew those guys weren't going to the big leagues. I now realized I wasn't either if I kept beering up.

I got myself together in Omaha, deciding that if I could produce in Double-A there was a possibility that a major-league club would draft me over the winter. I concentrated, regained my consistency in the field, and got my batting average up to .278. I was hopeful.

Sure enough that December the Cardinals left me unprotected in the draft . . . but no team took me. The Cardinals had put me on their Triple-A Columbus roster, so I said to myself: I'll show them all. I'll have a good spring and make the Columbus team. Johnny Keane, who went on to manage the Cards and Yankees, had Columbus . . . and I didn't impress him. It was back to Class-A Omaha once more. My average dropped to .243. I had reached the level Freddie Hofmann had predicted I would: "He's a Class-A player, tops."

At the close of the 1953 season I was traded to another Class-A team in the Western Association. Denver was an independent club that had a partial working agreement with Pittsburgh. And in Denver I got to play for a very good manager named Andy Cohen, who liked my pepperpot brand of ball and encouraged me. He also taught me a lesson I've never forgotten.

I had always been the kind of player who, when an umpire missed a call, let the man in blue know about it in the bluest language imaginable. My theory was—that if you gave the umpire enough hell when he blew one he would be less likely to blow two on you. I was particularly vehement in this 1954 season because I knew that if I didn't excel and move up to Double-A, I was very likely on my way out of baseball. Although I was having a good season both in the field and at the plate, my inner tension got to me on a tag I made at second in which the runner was so clearly out that he was about to run off when the umpire called him safe. I threw every curse word I knew at that umpire, and he threw me out of the game. I didn't leave. I continued to call the umpire every profanity I could think of until Andy Cohen came running out and angrily said, "Weaver! Get your ass in the clubhouse right now or it's gonna cost you a hundred dollars!"

Cohen was furious as he followed me into the clubhouse. "You know what would have happened if you'd called that man those names off the field?"

"We'd have fought," I said.

"You're damn right," Cohen said. "And you know he can't punch you without losing his job. How do you think he feels? You think that's fair?"

"No, I guess it's not," I said, and I knew it wasn't. Since then I have never called an umpire a profane name. I have cursed in describing an umpire's call, but I have never cursed the man. And if I hadn't learned that then, I would not have lasted long enough to allow my career ejection record to reach its present proportions.

I batted .283 for Andy Cohen in '54, and he took me with him to Double-A New Orleans the following year. That was when I was introduced to the incalculable benefits of using a corked bat. One of my teammates met a fan who happened to be a bat mechanic. He drilled a hole six inches deep into the barrel of my teammate's bat and packed it with five inches of ground-up cork. The man then topped off the hole with plastic wood and sanded it smooth. You couldn't tell the bat had been doctored even if you viewed it through a magnifying glass. When you swung the bat it whipped around so much quicker than normal that balls literally leaped off it. We had the man cork bats for everyone on the team and instantly went on a homer binge.

I had never hit more than six home runs in an entire season, but I hit six in one month with that splendid bat in '55. Then outfielder Bobby Honor cracked his bat in Mobile. But he insisted on continuing to use it. Finally the bat broke open at the top and the cork flew out. A couple of days later we received a tip that the league president would be coming to inspect our bats, so we got rid of them.

Norm Cash admitted after he retired that he used a corked bat throughout his major-league career. And in 1974, Graig Nettles of the Yankees hit a single against Detroit and the end of his bat fell off. During the '79 season Milwaukee manager George Bamberger, who had been my pitching coach in Baltimore for ten years, accused Kenny Singleton and Rick Dempsey of using corked bats. If Rick had been, he sure as hell would have hit a lot more than six home runs that season. But I thought Bamberger's charge was funny. First of all, George was always trying to get us to cork some bats when we worked together. Secondly,

I have to believe that Cecil Cooper of the Brewers uses a trick bat ever since I saw him hit a homer against us with one hand.

I cried when our corked bats were discovered in '55. I didn't hit another homer that season. Actually, I didn't hit much of anything after I was hit in the head with a smoking fastball in early August. The ball crushed the bones beneath my left eye and put me in the hospital for eleven days. That beaning crouched in my mind till the end of the season.

Even so, my final stats weren't bad: a .278 batting average and 69 RBIs, a substantial total for a lead-off man. I thought there was a chance I might be drafted by a Triple-A club that winter. In the meantime, I was invited to play ball in the Dominican Republic that fall. The money was pretty good and the winter ball would keep me sharp for, hopefully, spring training with an AAA ball club.

My wife and I flew to Santiago and our first trip overseas was enjoyable. But my performance on the field was not exceptional. I guess I was still a little gun-shy at the plate. Under league rules in the Dominican Republic, when teams were eliminated from the play-offs their players could be signed by the contenders. My team made the play-offs, but I didn't. Another second baseman was brought in to replace me. I got paid, but my spirits fell.

They plummeted when every Triple-A club passed me by. I wrote to the Pirates asking for a chance with them in spring training. I received no answer, and now I had to deal with the reality that had finally and irreversibly devoured my dream. I was never going to make it to the major leagues. No way, I thought, as scenes from sandlot ball and high school ball and Legion ball and games at West Frankfort and St. Joseph and Winston-Salem ("Mr. Mizell, a hundred and fifty dollars of that is for Earl Weaver") and Houston and Omaha and Denver swept through my head like ghosts of wonderful moments past. I was heartbroken.

I headed for the New Orleans camp in the spring of 1956, thinking, I'll be twenty-six in August, I have a wife and two children to care for (my daughter, Rhonda Lee, having arrived fourteen months after my son, Michael) and mortgage payments to make on the house. I'll take my $800 a month this season, then look for a new profession in the fall. I had my shot and I gave it my best. How many men in a lifetime of working manage to spend nine years doing exactly what they want to? I wouldn't want to have missed any of it.

chapter FouR

I would have happily skipped the first two months of the 1956 season. The Double-A pitching that I had handled the year before was suddenly beyond me. It seemed that every right-handed pitcher I faced at New Orleans not only had a crackling slider, but one that he could consistently get over the plate. I had long known that the secret of hitting was, conceptually, very simple: Lay off the pitch you can't hit because eventually most pitchers will have to come in with a pitch you *can* hit. This bit of common sense has been confirmed so many times over the years by the statistics we keep at Baltimore that I wonder why more batters don't make use of it. Willie Randolph of the Yankees, for example, obviously does against us. I noted some years ago that Randolph had 19 hits in 22 at-bats against us one season—and 19 of them had come off fastballs above the belt. Randolph simply laid off everything else and waited for the pitch that he could nail.

Anyway, after 26 games at New Orleans my batting average was .228 and I was sold to the Class-A Montgomery club in the Sally League. I reported, rented a house, and had my wife drive the kids down from St. Louis. Three weeks later the team was sold to Knoxville, Tennessee. Shit, I said to myself, this is foolish. I thought about quitting right then and heading on home with Jane and the kids. But after consulting our bank account I made a decision. There was no job that I could start in St. Louis that would pay me the $800 a month I was earning playing baseball.

I sent the family back to our house in St. Louis and trudged to Knoxville alone, wondering what other business I should go into at season's end. My background had not prepared me for any of the lucrative professions like aerospace engineer or brain surgeon. In fact, my non-baseball background could be described in one word: varied.

For the first couple of winters of my baseball career I had been a warehouseman in Teamsters local 688, loading and unloading galvanized steel. It was hard work for good money, which was fine with me except I kept banging up my hands. An infielder's hands are his prime asset, so I asked my favorite uncle, Bud Bochert, if he could help me find another job. Uncle Bud, whose bookmaking business was booming, had lines into most of the labor unions as well as good political connections. The city of St. Louis was going to install parking meters the winter of 1950, and Uncle Bud knew the engineer who was laying them out. The engineer hired me and another fellow as his helpers.

The job called for considerable precision. The engineer would measure off a block and divide it into parking spaces as my associate and I held the ends of a tape measure. The engineer would chalk an X where the meter was to be installed and I would then slap yellow paint over his X. We had not quite finished laying out the entire city when I had to leave for spring training. To this day I don't know how they ever found a man capable of replacing me.

The next winter I became a member of the maintenance crew that checked and serviced the meters, doubtless because of my ground-floor experience in '50. The meters had a Magic Washer in the handles that I could replace on the spot. I seldom had more than three broken meters a day among the 500 I checked. It took me all of two hours to walk by 250 meters in the morning. I then had four hours off before I made my afternoon pass, finishing just in time to sign out at 4:30.

In 1953 I was hired by the city tax collection department, a boring office job. Real estate taxes were bad enough, but St. Louis also had a personal property tax on things like furnishings, jewelry, and automobiles. New license plates could not be obtained for a car if the personal property tax was unpaid. That did not result in a lot of smiling people coming into my office.

But I was empathetic to everyone except those who showed up with a $1200 assessment and handed me that amount in single dollar bills or all coins—which I had to count.

Wanting to get out of an office and earn a little more money, I asked Uncle Bud to get me a union card as a common laborer the next winter. As an apprentice I could make over $420 a month. My first day the foreman took me into a room with sand piled to the ceiling in one corner. He said, "This was dumped in the wrong place, right where the plumbers have to work. Move the sand into the opposite corner." I grabbed a wheelbarrow and shovel and went to work, wanting to make a good impression. In three hours I finished, wiped the sweat off my face, and reported to the foreman.

"You moved that whole pile of sand *already?*" he said.

"Yeah. You said the plumbers had to work there."

"Not until Wednesday, for chrissake. I thought that would take you two days, and I won't have anything else for you to do till then."

He sent me home. I had cost myself a day and a half's pay by hustling.

On Wednesday I was assigned to carry mortar in a hod up ladders to the bricklayers. I saw this guy in his fifties, who was built better than any ballplayer I'd seen, fill his hod to the brim—about 150 pounds' worth—and zip right up the ladder. I filled mine to the standard point, about 130 pounds' worth, and struggled up with it. I hadn't learned the technique of dumping the mortar properly, and I let the hod get away from me. The mortar spilled all over and plopped onto the bricklayer's foot. He was bent over a row of setting bricks, and he didn't even unbend. He glanced up at me as his trowel went down and neatly scooped a mound of mortar off his shoe—then he flicked it right into my face. I wanted to kill the SOB, but I needed the job.

The following winter, 1954, started even more disastrously in my new gig as a stone mason's helper. I was a definite menace until I learned how to operate a jimmy pull to raise and lower into place huge blocks of cut stone, granite, and polished marble. I lost a slab of polished marble that would've killed somebody on the floor below if anyone had been standing where it landed. I did become a competent stone mason's helper, but I knew it would never be my life's work. I had no idea what that might be.

So there I was in Knoxville buying time at $800 a month. The team was one of the few totally independent clubs in all of baseball, with some of the players belonging to major-league organizations and the rest of us being owned outright by the group of businessmen who operated the club. Knoxville had a nice ball park and we managed to draw over 4,000 people to each game even though we got off to a slow start—and got slower. We were in last place in late July when the owners fired our manager.

They asked me to become manager for the final weeks of the season, offering me a $200 salary increase. The first thing I did was bench our second baseman. Although I was hustling as usual, I wasn't hitting. The kid I put in was no terror with a bat, either. But he *might* have a future on the playing field. I sure as heck didn't.

I also put an end to the poker games that I had found enjoyable and profitable, as well as a good way to unwind after road games in which we didn't get to our hotel until midnight. But the poker often ran until 3 or 4 A.M. That was okay for a player on his way out, but not for the guys who would now be playing for me. I wanted to see how I could do as a manager, even for a few weeks. I guess somewhere in the back of my mind it had occurred to me that managing a ball club was something I could do pretty well.

By chance, the day after I became manager Orioles farm director Jim McLaughlin sent his assistant, Harry Dalton, to Knoxville to see about adding the club to the Baltimore system. I coached third base and apparently made a good impression on Dalton, even though we never got out of last place. He gave McLaughlin a good report on me, he later confided, because he dug into back issues of the local newspaper and read that I was a hustler, a guy who was always in the game, and something of a character who excited fans.

I went back to St. Louis in search of a new career. I registered with an employment agency that sent me to the Liberty Loan Company. There was an opening in their management-trainee program and I was given an aptitude test. I was surprised when I was informed that my score was the highest recorded to that point. I started at $350 a month and was told that I could work my way up to supervisor within three years and be earning over $7,000 a year. I enthusiastically applied myself to the job. I interviewed and screened small-loan applicants, handled collections on the phone, and tracked down delinquents.

In December Jim McLaughlin, who was in St. Louis to visit his family, phoned me. He asked if I would like to manage one of the Orioles Class-D clubs. The salary would be $3,500 for six months' work. That was $500 less than I had made as a player for the same period of time, I said to myself, but this is a chance to stay in baseball! I accepted, asking that I be paid $500 a month over seven months. My boss at Liberty said he liked my work and that I could come back every winter if I wanted to. I thanked him kindly and in early March set off for Baltimore's central spring training camp in Thomasville, Georgia. I was excited. I had crossed the paths of a lot of former players who had made a decent living by staying in this game they loved and had learned so much about. Many of the most successful managers had been mediocre ballplayers like myself because those of us with limited abilities had to think more and play smart baseball to sustain a professional playing career on any level.

The Orioles had eight teams of Double-A classification or below at Thomasville. I was to get one of the three D clubs. Harry Dalton told me to get a good line on the players as we would have to cut about a hundred kids in making up the teams. Initially, we just had workouts on various aspects of the game: hitting, pitching, running, throwing. We graded players on these skills plus power on a scale of one (excellent) to four (poor). All the managers and scouts sat around a long table that was headed by McLaughlin and Dalton. Harry would say, "Let's have today's nominations for cuts." I would say, "I'd like to bring up number 242. He's a four in every category." Then Dalton would ask around the table about 242 and if somebody wanted to keep 242, he would get another look. The first cuts were all fours, and the only way they ever lasted another day or two was when the scout who had signed the youngster protested. The scouts *had* to defend their signees because they had to go back to the same area for other youngsters and face their coaches.

But I quickly became known as "The Hatchet" that first year.

I was the only manager who didn't have a team after the veterans picked theirs, and I was anxious as hell to get my guys together and start working on fundamentals. The grading was even easier once we started playing games and I could observe the youngsters in competition. The names of those cut were posted every day in the mess hall: "After eating, will the following please report to Mr. Weaver" or one of the other lower-classification managers. I didn't mind cutting numbers in meetings, but I dreaded having to face the youngsters in person. Before I did so, I consulted with the two veteran Class-D managers, Barney Lutz and George Staller. They both said you had to be honest with the kids about their weaknesses. Lutz told a funny story about a tough kid from Detroit who, seeing his name posted, walked into Barney's office and before the manager could say a word announced: "I know what you got in mind, man. But I want you to know that if you cut me"—he pulled out a switchblade—"I'm gonna cut *you!*"

I never had a kid threaten me, but some would get snotty. "Why the hell are you cutting *me?*" the youngster would say. "I can outplay half the guys in this goddamn camp!"

"Well, it's the consensus of the baseball people here," I'd say, "that we probably would be wasting your time sending you out to play Class-C baseball. We're not saying you might not be successful in Class-D ball again, but we're trying to judge your ability to make the major leagues. And we don't think you're gonna hit enough to do that."

Some kids simply refused to leave camp, swearing they were going to stay on until we gave them another shot so they could prove what they could do. But they didn't stay long without mess-hall privileges.

Most of the scenes were poignant. The kids would choke up and use the very words that I would have used had I been released two or three weeks after reporting to my first camp as a professional. "Oh no, Mr. Weaver, you can't do that . . . you can't send me home already," they'd say, "not without giving me a chance. What am I gonna tell my mom and dad? What can I say to my high school coach? He said I had the ability, that I'd go all the way to the majors. . . ."

When the tears started coming, I quickly learned, you had to stop talking instantly or they would totally break down. I had kids sit there and cry uncontrollably for twenty minutes, the tears coursing down their cheeks as they sobbed, "Play baseball, that's all I ever wanted to do. My mom and dad, they expect me to. . . ."

Those kids all tugged my heart, though I couldn't show it. The decision had been made and it was my job to be honest and ease the kids out in the most painless fashion possible. The problem was that there was no painless fashion. And I had to be the truthful rotten little bastard.

The cut player's bottom line was that I wasn't as smart as his high school coach. That was understandable, the view that has encouraged you being much more acceptable than the one that says you can't do it. But I realized from the very beginning that I could not let my heart intrude on my judgment of a ballplayer's skills. And as I listened and learned from the veterans like Lutz and Staller, I think my ability to recognize baseball talent showed itself immediately. I said to myself: If I can do this job right—and I'm damn sure I will—I've got it for life!

We had some horrendous arguments in meetings revolving around baseball judgments. One of the managers would say, "Get rid of that SOB, he can't play," and several others would concur. Then the scout who had signed the player would cry, "Wait a minute! The kid's only eighteen and he's had trouble at home. But he hit .480 with power in high school, and you guys are gonna run him outta here in three bleeping weeks?"

"Yeah, but he ain't touched the ball with his bat here in two weeks!"

Although cutting ballplayers was never easy, The Hatchet never faltered. And it's been a helluva lot harder in the majors when I've had to tell a guy who for years has done everything he could to help you that, suddenly, he was no longer wanted. I had to tell two veterans that at the end of the 1980 season. Pat Kelly had been a great pinch hitter for us, and Lee May had averaged 90 RBIs for 5 seasons in Baltimore. He had one off year and, at age 38, that was it.

But I'm sure Lee suspected it was coming. For the first time in his fourteen years in the majors, a pinch hitter batted for him in '80. His reaction showed what kind of a man Lee May is. Eventually just about every ballplayer sees a pinch hitter step up for him, even Ted Williams did. It's almost inevitable if a veteran plays for a guy like me who is not going to let *anything* interfere with winning a ball game.

That's what we were trying to do. I had just pinch hit for Rick Dempsey, who was playing on a bad leg. Everyone on the bench knew, with Lee due up, I would be going for a left-hander, and everyone looked away. I hated to look him in the eye, too, but I had to, saying, "Lee, I'm gonna hit for you." Lee nodded and calmly put his helmet back in the rack as Dempsey picked up his mitt to go out to the bullpen on his bad leg. Dan Graham was on his way in to replace Dempsey at catcher. When Dempsey limped up the dugout steps Lee May grabbed him and said, "Gimme that glove, Rick. I'll warm 'em up in the 'pen."

After the game, the writers asked Lee how he felt about being hit for, and he said, "The man did what he had to do, what he thought was right." And at season's end when I had to tell Lee May we wouldn't be offering him another contract, he said, "Well, I'd like to stay in baseball, and if I get a job, fine. If I don't, I know I've given baseball all I could . . . and it sure has been good to me."

I was so happy when the Royals signed Lee May, who's one of the greatest people I've ever met in this game and who should always have a job in baseball if he wants it. Pat Kelly, another very unusual man, sent me a note after I told him the sad news. Kelly wrote, "Whatever happens, Earl, I love you." Then Cleveland signed him, praise be.

Out of all the players we cut in that first camp only one went on to make the majors, Fred Whitfield. But the most astounding comment on the Oriole organization and the judgment of its personnel over the years is that from 1954, when the team started in Baltimore, through 1967, my last year as a minor-league manager—only Whitfield and Chuck Cottier, were cut players who made the big leagues. I actually had the final say on Whitfield, Dalton asking me if I wanted him. By then I had selected my team and had what I thought was a better first baseman. Whitfield had such a bad arm he could barely throw the ball across the infield. But "Wingy" hit well enough to last nine years in the majors. My first baseman, Dave Bednar, never got there, nor did any of the other guys from the '57 Fitzgerald team because I didn't listen to Barney Lutz.

He told me to take more than the minimum number of rookies if I felt they had potential, even if they seemed raw in the spring. I was determined to win the pennant in my first year on the job, and I decided the way to do that was go with players who had pro experience. I didn't take a wild-armed kid pitcher named Steve Barber because he couldn't locate the plate. Lutz took him and won a pennant, and in a few years Barber became Baltimore's first 20-game winner.

We got off to a good start, then were passed by several clubs as I had a revelation: players in their second season of D ball don't improve. Rookies may have to make adjustments through the first half of a season, but those with ability improve and pass the vets. It was an insight I wouldn't forget. From then on I tried to select a majority of youngsters who were on their way up. That was the way to win in the minors, and the way to develop ballplayers for the Baltimore Orioles, which was what my job was all about.

I did a lot of learning that year. I saw early on that I could outhit a number of my players and in my desire to win I played second base enough to bat over 350 times. I batted .288 and had 6 home runs with Fitzgerald.

And, of course, I hustled 120 percent to set an example, and expected everyone to emulate me. I got angry when anyone missed a sign or a cutoff or failed in any way to play heads-up ball. Then I realized a number of guys who played for me were just like a certain number on every team I had played on. No matter how much they tried, there were aspects of the game they would never learn and there were plays they could never make. I worked trying to correct these weaknesses, but in many cases I discovered I simply had to manage around them. The key was never to ask them to do what they could not do—only what they *could* do.

Some of my players, mostly the nineteen- and twenty-year-olds, tried to do considerable foul-mouthed bench jockeying initially. I put a stop to that by saying that crap would not help them move up baseball's ladder. In fact, it could hold them back, so they had better change their attitude. There were a lot of smart-aleck kids in D ball, particularly on the Waycross, Georgia, team that was in last place all year but often beat us badly and continually hollered scurrilously at me. Having struck out the first two times up in a game just before season's end, I was pretty frustrated the next time I went to the plate. One guy had yelled something unprintable about my forbears, and I swore that if he said one more thing I was going into the dugout after him. Sure enough, I grounded out and he hollered as I turned right at first base and trotted head down until I was parallel with the Waycross dugout. Then I cut left and sprinted into the dugout swinging at my tormentor. I don't know as I ever landed on him, because seven guys started pummeling me. My guys charged to my aid, but by then I'd been shoved backward and fallen on the edge of the dugout steps. I emerged with a separated right shoulder and several large knots on my head.

I finished the season with my arm in a sling and decided that unless there was absolutely no way that I could avoid it, that would be my last fight. And while I may have come close a time or two in subsequent years, I have kept my vow.

I stayed in the Georgia-Florida League the next year as we affiliated with Dublin, a larger town that drew better. This time I picked Steve Barber, who still couldn't find the plate, and another young pitcher named Steve Dalkowski, who many people feel may have had the best arm in the history of baseball. Fast? Dalkowski once threw three wild pitches that went right through the *screen* behind home plate. He once hit a batter in the head and the ball ricocheted so hard it sailed over Steve's head and carried almost to second base. In his rookie year of pro ball at Kingsport, Dalkowski struck out 10 of the first 12 batters he faced (the 2 he walked were picked off), and not one hitter even *ticked* the ball. The first man to do so in the fifth inning managed a long foul to left, then Dalkowski struck out the side. When he returned to the dugout, Steve told his manager, "You'd better get somebody ready. I'm losing my stuff."

Even with the two hard-throwing, wild Steves we finished third. But I got a promotion to Aberdeen in '59, my salary was raised from $4,200 to $5,000 and we finished second. Dalkowski was our star whenever he managed to locate home plate. But he let the booze destroy what could have been an unbelievable career. I had to get him out of jail four times in three years, and no matter what I told him about the damage he was doing to his talent and his health, I couldn't reach him. If he'd only had the head to go with that astounding arm of his! One night he threw 280 pitches in a game—the equivalent of 2-plus games—and he lost no velocity on his fastball. He struck out 16 and walked 17, winning 4–3. I think my first gray hairs appeared that night, as I watched Dalkowski go through the sequence of loading the bases on walks, wild-pitching a run in, then striking out the side . . . three times.

In the minor leagues the umpires, like the players, were not all candidates for the major leagues. The umpires were also trying to develop their skills, and some tried a helluva lot harder than others. It was obvious that no matter how hard certain umpires tried, they just didn't have it. But I still attempted to help them improve their performance, just as I did with the players. Sometimes my efforts to educate umpires called for drastic measures.

The arbiters in Class-D ball were particularly remiss. I was coaching third in a ball game when one of my players hit a hard groundball that hopped right over the bag but was knocked down by the third baseman in foul territory. The umpire called it a foul ball and my arguments could not change his decision. Later in the game my cleanup hitter lined a shot over third that hooked foul down the left-field line. "Foul ball!" the umpire cried. Incensed, I charged him and wondered aloud if there was an eye chart anywhere bearing a letter large enough for him to identify correctly.

"You're out of here!" he yelled, flailing his thumb. I raced back to third and tore the base out of the ground and headed into the clubhouse with the bag under my arm.

"You're not using this anyway!" I hollered.

Another time the plate umpire was calling so many balls on pitches that were well inside the black of home plate that I just couldn't take it anymore. I went out and got down on my knees in the batter's box and completely covered home plate with dirt. "What the hell are you doing?" the umpire demanded. I stood up and said, "You're not paying any attention to this thing. I might as well cover it up."

During the 1962 season at Elmira we were trying to catch Williamsport in the Eastern League pennant race and we scored a run on a questionable play. Williamsport manager Frank Lucchesi ran out and convinced the three-man umpiring crew to reverse the decision. Since umpires almost never change a call, I hurried out to the men in blue gathered at the mound and protested. When the umpires explained their ruling, which was correct, I clutched my heart, threw my head back, and cried, "Oh, that's more than I can bear!" as I collapsed to the ground. I lay there with my eyes clamped shut, the obvious victim of a heart attack.

That was not obvious to crew chief Fred Blandford. He wasn't even impressed when my next batter, Charley Johnson, knelt and fanned my face with his cap saying, "Hang on, Skip!"

"Weaver," Blandford said, "that's a good act. But the instant you open your eyes—you're out of here."

"Got it, this is page one!" I heard Frank Lucchesi say, laughing. I opened my eyes to see him bending down snapping away with an old box camera he must've gotten from the stands.

"Get going, Weaver," Blandford said. "Delay of game."

"What about him?" I shouted, jumping to my feet and pointing at Lucchesi.

"You started it," said Blandford, who was now grinning.

"Good show, Earl," Lucchesi said.

And I can't remember whether it was Lucchesi or another manager named Grover Reisinger who came up with a unique way to challenge a delay-of-game threat in the minors. The umpire pulled out his pocket watch and announced that the manager had one minute to return to his dugout or he'd be banished. The manager asked to see the watch. When the umpire handed it over, Frank or Grover threw it into the stands.

In 1960 I moved up again, getting a $1,000 raise to manage our B club in the Three-I League, which was so named because its franchises were originally from the states of Illinois, Indiana, and Iowa. My team was situated in Appleton, Wisconsin, and was called Fox Cities. As another St. Louis product named Joe Garagiola once said, "Baseball is a funny game."

In the Baltimore system, as I noted, the managers get to select the players in the spring that they will win or lose with during the season. So each spring you put your ability to judge talent on the line, and as the season progresses you adjust, adding and subtracting players as they falter or are called up to a higher classification. The manager is always under pressure from the local owners and general manager to win, as they must attract fans to the ball park and sell hotdogs and such in order to survive. I was under considerable pressure from the Fox Cities GM to make some personnel changes at the start of 1960. But I told GM Bob Willis, a great guy, that I was determined to stay with my players. After all, this was the best team I ever had.

Four of the players were bonus babies whose professional experience consisted of a couple of months in the rookie league. Two were pitchers: Dean Chance, who had some 20 no-hitters in Ohio, and Arnie Thorslin from New Jersey, who had an even livelier arm than Chance. I had a massive power-hitting first baseman from Florida named Boog Powell and a switch-hitting shortstop from Connecticut named Bobby Saverine whose speed and arm were both rated one. I also had a young third baseman named Pete Ward who'd torn up the California League in '59, as well as three other pitchers who were destined to make the majors—Pat Gillick, Johnny Papa, and Buster Narum. A helluva ball club.

Thorslin and Chance were still training with the Orioles when we opened the season on the road in Sioux City, Iowa, which was managed by my old friend and high school teammate Bobby Hofman. I could hardly wait for Bobby to see my team in action.

Sioux City won the first game 23–2. The only good thing to come out of it was the intensity my guys showed. Throughout the debacle they kept battling. With the score 21–2, Pete Ward argued a call on the bases so vehemently that he was ejected. I liked my team's spirit.

We lost the next day 14–4.

We lost the third game 18–14.

Afterward I went over to see Bobby Hofman, who was standing with a newspaperman laughing. "Earl, you've got some bunch of garbage there," Bobby said through a smile.

The writer said, "I guess you'll have a lot of new faces the next time we see you in Sioux City." He chuckled.

"New faces, hell!" I said. "I don't need no new faces, my friend. The next time we come in here we'll be ahead of this ball club—and you can write that down!"

Bobby Hofman bet me a dinner his club would be ahead of us on our next visit. Done.

We bused to Cedar Rapids and had to sit around chewing on

those horrendous losses during two days of rain. We finally got to play and my guys hung tough for 12 innings. In the thirteenth my center fielder dropped a flyball and Pat Gillick, who had gone all the way, lost 2–1.

When we got home our GM, Bob Willis, was waiting for me. "Earl, let's get on the horn to Baltimore and get us some players."

"Bob, let's just relax and see what we do the first few weeks," I said. "It may take these kids some time to get going, but when they do I know we're gonna win."

I went to the house I'd rented and Jim McLaughlin phoned. "You need some help, Earl?" he asked. "It looks like we may have these kids in over their heads."

"No, Jim, I don't think so. Let's stay with them."

That afternoon I met Thorslin and Chance, who had just joined us. Dean strode up to me and said, "Weaver, I want to tell you something. You start Arnie and me every four days—and we'll win the pennant." He was probably the only nineteen-year-old who ever called me "Weaver."

I didn't mind Chance's outspokenness if he could pitch. But there was no way I could start him every four days. I had five pitchers to groom. Furious, Chance got right on the phone to Orioles' GM Lee MacPhail. Chance was not about to let some stumpy little Class-B manager impede his march to the majors.

"Mr. MacPhail, this manager you got down here is out of his mind," Chance said. "He refuses to pitch me every four days. Now what are you gonna do about it?"

"Dean, keep your mouth shut and do what you're told," MacPhail said, which was required behavior in the Baltimore system.

I never held Chance's temper and brashness against him, those having been paramount ingredients in me as a player. A manager can never let a man's temperament warp his judgment of the player's abilities on the field. And Dean Chance could pitch. His stubbornness and independence were overshadowed by his determination.

Chance was a godawful fielder, a guy who never learned how to pick up groundballs, and with a bat in his hand he was about as dangerous as a Sister of Mercy. When I met Dean Chance I kept thinking about what Freddie Hofmann had once told me,

"You separate pitchers from the rest of the players, because 99 percent of the time pitchers are freaks. They don't have to field, they don't have to hit, they don't have to run fast. They got one tool, their arm, and they don't have to do nothing but pitch. They are the freaks of baseball." Freddie had a lot of insights.

We were playing in Green Bay late in the season with Chance on the mound and runners on first and second, none out. I called time and went out to Dean as Pete Ward came over from third. "I think they have to bunt," I said. "I want you to get off the mound and field the ball, Dean, and see if you can get the front runner; if not, go to first."

Ward nodded and I turned back to the dugout. As I walked I heard Chance say, "Pete, lookit. You come in and field the bunt and throw the batter out at first. Then I'll strike out the next two guys."

I kept right on walking. I had learned you were going to have to accept this kind of thing from players with true grit, or whatever you want to call it. Chance had pitched well against Green Bay earlier, so I figured he must have something in mind for those hitters. And since my philosophy insists on getting the sure out, *always get one*, it was fine when Ward charged the bunt and got the out at first.

Dean Chance then struck out the next two hitters, and went on to win the game.

It took us a little time to get rolling, and one reason was that Boog Powell *was* over his head for half the season. He didn't hit one ball to the right side of the infield in that time, and his batting average was under .200. He never let it bother him, just kept working and working, and gradually he taught himself how to get the bat around and pull the ball. Then, of course, the balls started sailing over the fences. Two years later Boog was hitting balls out of major-league parks for the Orioles.

Bobby Saverine also made the Orioles in '62, as a utility player. His problem was that while his rifle arm and quickness allowed him to make spectacular plays at short, all too often he bobbled routine grounders or watched them go through his legs. Yet he wouldn't listen to instructions on how to field groundballs, how to position himself, and concentrate. Saverine preceded Roberto Duran as the original "Hands of Stone" by more than a decade, which is why he ended his career in the outfield (with Washington). But Bobby was a tremendous B ballplayer and he led us offensively all season.

Needless to say Chance was not pleased by the defense behind him. Though he couldn't catch a common cold, he expected his teammates to snare every ball he served up that was hit anywhere near them. His record at the midway point of the season should have been better than 8–9, but he seemed to think it should have been closer to 17–0. He came up to me and said, "Weaver, there's no doubt in my mind that I shouldn't be playing in this chickenshit league. I should at least be in Triple-A."

"How can you say that, Dean?" I asked. "You're not even a winning pitcher in Class-B ball."

"That's not my fault," he said. "It's the fault of that big dumb first baseman and that guy with no hands at shortstop."

Pat Gillick had no problem with our defense after his opening loss. He won his next twelve decisions and was moved up to Triple-A Vancouver. We were still in very good shape, and the next time we traveled to Sioux City I won my bet with Bobby Hofman. We had moved ahead of them in the standings and we soon lunged into first place and stayed there. But I was never overconfident. I wanted desperately to win my first pennant.

We had a 6-game lead with only 12 left to play when Harry Dalton phoned with an order. Brooks Robinson had been up and down with the Orioles since 1955 trying to learn to hit major-league pitching. There had been no question about his glove from the beginning, and Harry said Robinson had been stinging the ball all season, hitting close to .300 with power. Harry was now certain the Orioles would be set at third base for years.

"Everyone agrees with you about Pete Ward's potential," Dalton said, "but there's no sense wasting him at third base when he can't win a job with us there. So play him in the outfield for the rest of the season."

"You want me to blow the pennant?" I protested. "If I move Pete to the outfield I'll have to bring an outfielder in to play third."

"Whether you like it or not," Dalton said sharply, "play Ward in the outfield. You can't get hurt that much in a dozen games."

"All right, Harry, but if the situation gets sticky, can I bring Ward back to third?"

"Well, I suppose so. But as soon as the situation is resolved, put him back into left field."

I had my out. Box scores list a player's starting position first without noting how many innings he performed there. If I played Ward one inning in left and then shifted him to third, the box score would read, "Ward, lf, 3b." Who would know? I had to file a box score along with daily game reports of about two hundred words noting who played well, who messed up, and so forth, but I could fudge those a bit.

I played Ward in left for an inning, then brought him in to third for the rest of the game. What had not occurred to me in my raging desire to sew up the pennant, though it should have, was that the Orioles would send in a scout to check Ward's outfield play. In two games the scout saw Ward make exactly one outfield play. Then Dalton called and screamed at me.

Ward dropped a couple of flies in left field, but we still won the pennant by ten games. And two years later Pete was up with the Orioles. It was amazing how swiftly so many kids from that B ball club shot up to the big leagues. And winning that pennant was the most exciting moment of my first three decades on earth.

I was still a player-manager in 1960, but I filled in only in a dire emergency, say when someone twisted an ankle or came down with the flu. The sliders were getting more and more wicked, and I couldn't see any future in standing in against them and chancing getting hit in the face again. I just couldn't compete in B ball anymore. I guess what convinced me to quit for good, though, was embarrassment. In my last at-bat I came up with men on first and second and none out. Figuring the opposition would be looking for a bunt, I swung away and hit a hard grounder to third. The third baseman scooped it up, stepped on the bag, fired the ball to second for two—and I just beat the relay to first by a half step. *The hell with this*, I said to myself. *It's ridiculous when you run as hard as you can just to barely beat hitting into an around-the-horn triple play! Hang it up, Earl.*

I did make one more appearance in the field five years later while managing at Elmira. My second baseman banged up his leg in the ninth inning and I filled in for three outs. The first was

a strikeout, after which we threw the ball around the infield—
and I dropped it. At least I left 'em laughing.

That fall we had an unusually long and intensive organizational meeting as the Oriole management, all the scouts, and
minor-league managers assembled to decide which 25 players on
our 40-man major-league roster should be protected. The American League was adding two new teams, in Los Angeles and
Washington, D.C. (the original Senators were moving to Minnesota), and we would have to make 15 players available for the
expansion draft, 8 of whom could be taken. Among the pitchers
it came down to a decision on whether to keep Thorslin or
Chance, as one would have to be made available. Both were exceptional prospects, though Thorslin's record was 13–5 and
Chance was 13–13. Thorslin threw much harder than Chance,
but both had averaged a strikeout per inning. An important consideration for any pitcher, however, is his ratio of hits given up
per innings pitched. Thorslin had 40 fewer hits allowed than innings pitched. Chance had given up 208 hits in 204 innings.

As I had observed both pitchers all season, Oriole manager
Paul Richards asked me right off, "Earl, which one would you
protect?"

"Chance," I said.

"Chance allowed more hits than he had innings pitched."

"Yeah, Paul, he did, and I'll tell you why," I said. "Dean
started twenty-six games and in every one of them he gave up
two hits simply because he couldn't field his position. He falls off
the mound after his delivery and is in no shape to field anything
hit back to him or any ball that's bunted toward the mound. I
think his fielding can be corrected, and if you subtract those
fifty-two hits that any other pitcher would have handled, you
can see he had a helluva year. In addition, I think Chance has
better baseball instincts, a youngster who already knows how to
set up hitters and come in with a pitch they're not expecting."

Someone said, "I've seen major-league pitchers who never
learned how to field their position."

Still, I added one more thought. Freddie Hofmann had told
me in the spring as he watched Thorslin work, "That boy can't
last. He's throwing across his body. In three years he'll have a
sore arm." During the season I had seen that Hofmann was right.

Thorslin, instead of getting his hips, back, shoulder, and legs into his pitches, was throwing entirely with his arm. I related this observation.

When the vote went around the table, though, the decision was made to protect Thorslin, the harder thrower with the better record. Dean Chance was drafted by the Angels and in two years was their best starter. He pitched 11 years in the majors and had a career ERA of 2.92—and he never did learn how to field his position. In fact, he started the last game of the season for Minnesota against Boston in 1967—with the two teams tied for first—and the Red Sox won the pennant by hitting balls in front of the plate on Chance. As for Arnie Thorslin, three years after Hofmann's prediction the big right-hander came down with a sore arm that ended his career.

I was later asked a number of times if I grew upset when my views on Chance were ignored and he went on to such great success elsewhere. No, I wasn't because the logic behind the decision was irrefutable and the consensus of all the baseball knowledge in the room that day was right, year after year, at least nine times out of ten. Judging talent was the key to the Baltimore organization, to its success, and to mine.

We've done very well in the minor-league draft, which some organizations don't go into. But Baltimore tries to keep spaces open on the roster for acquisitions. One year we drafted three players who went on to make the Orioles: Paul Blair, Dave May, and Curt Motton. Now there are almost never unanimous judgments on players. Some scouts said Brooks Robinson couldn't run fast enough to make the majors. Some said Boog Powell would never learn to pull the ball. Some said Dave McNally couldn't throw hard enough. Some said Belanger would never hit. Davey Johnson was the only player I had in the minors who *everyone* said would make the majors. Every other player had some flaw that, in the minds of one scout or coach or manager, would prevent him from going to the big leagues.

We drafted Blair after his first year in pro ball. He'd played for Santa Barbara, a Mets farm club, in the California League. He was on the roster of the Syracuse club and the Mets didn't protect him, perhaps because Blair had struck out 147 times in 122 games. Harry Dunlap, who managed our Stockton club in the California League, voted against drafting Blair because of those strikeouts. This was at our annual organizational meeting in which all the scouts and managers convene and go over every player in baseball. We'd have reports on each player from at least three people—a manager and two or three scouts. Freddie Hofmann had scouted Blair, as had Don McShane. When Jim McLaughlin asked if there were any players we should draft, Hofmann said, "Yeah, there's a kid in the California League who may be the best defensive center fielder I've seen since Joe Di-Maggio." Then Dunlap said Blair wouldn't hit. But McShane agreed with Hofmann and we got Paul for $12,000.

The Oriole management was clearly pleased with the way I handled youngsters. In the fall of 1960 I was asked to manage our Instructional League team in Arizona. It was made up of all the outstanding prospects in the organization. I had to give up my job at Liberty Loan and the $2,300 I earned there winters. I was moving in baseball. I loved the profession and felt like I was making an important contribution to my employers. Paul Richards also asked me to help out in the major-league camp in February, where I would put in a month or so before the central spring training camp opened. All together, I was now earning close to $8,000, which paid the bills as long as I watched my in-season expenses, even if I couldn't buy my wife many fur coats.

The Instructional League started in October and ran through December 2 as we played some forty-five games. The league was designed to provide special instructions for potential stars who needed to work on a particular aspect of their game. I was the youngest manager in the league, going against veteran organizational men like Charley Grimm. And if they planned to have a pitcher throw eighty pitches, he did so no matter how many hits or walks he gave up. I got in all our instructional work—with the help of other minor-league managers like George Staller and scouts like Billy Hunter—but I played the games to win. I was the only manager to do so. If my pitcher started getting hit hard, I sent in a reliever right away just as if we were playing a regular-season game. If you were going to learn how to play baseball, you might as well learn how to play it to win. That's the only way to play the game, and that was why we had the best record in the Instructional League.

But managing in Arizona wasn't an easy job. I'd be up at 6:30 and out on the field by 8:30 if Richards wanted to watch Thorslin throw or someone hit before our workouts began. Then after the game, Richards often wanted to look at another player hit or field or whatever. I also functioned as business manager of the team and had to spend a couple of hours several nights a week doing the paper work and paying bills. Richards, of course, would go off and play golf after his morning visit. I'd put in a full day hitting groundballs, throwing batting practice, managing a ball game, and keeping after the kids. Richards would show up again about 5:30, check out a player, then say, "Let's go over to Lullabelles and get a draft or two." I was so tired that I'd have one beer with him and my head would start drooping toward the table.

But a lot of nights with Richards were real treats for a man of my means. We lived like millionaires, it seemed to me. Richards would say, "How much money do you have, Earl?"

"About fifty dollars," I'd say.

"Well write yourself a check for two and a half," he'd say. "We're going to The Mountain Shadows tonight."

Paul Richards was an entertaining guy to be around. His mind was always working, and he was well known for bending the rules of baseball if he thought he could get away with it. He once played a high school kid under a fictitious name in an Oriole exhibition game. He liked the kid and signed him, but when the truth emerged the commissioner made the youngster a free agent.

At this time when I was managing in the IL Richards had a plan that I couldn't go along with totally. Chuck Hinton was a hard-hitting outfielder on the Orioles roster whom we figured to lose in the expansion draft. I knew Hinton's ability, having managed him at Aberdeen, and I was all for keeping him in the organization if possible.

But Richards came to me and said, "Earl, I want you to tell Hinton that he's got a chance of playing for me in Baltimore this season and I don't want to lose him. I want you to tell him to run into the left-field wall, hit it easy but make it look good, then fall on the ground like he's separated his shoulder. We'll run right out and help him off the field and release a story that he's hurt pretty bad. It might discourage the expansion teams from drafting him."

"Paul," I said, "I can't in all honesty tell him he might play for you next year." I knew that was an awful long shot, and a manager always has to be for his ballplayers first. I had never lied to a ballplayer, and I wasn't about to start. You lie to a ballplayer and the word soon gets around, and you might as well look for another vocation because you can no longer command respect from the people who win or lose for you.

"All right," Richards said, "I'll tell Hinton myself."

After the game that day Richards had Hinton shagging flies in left. I fungoed a ball high off the wall, Hinton leaped and crumbled to the ground. He was helped off the field with his arm dangling, and the story went out that he had separated his shoulder. He was sent to his home in California with his arm in a sling. But someone there must have pointed out to Hinton that if he was selected by one of the expansion clubs he would almost be assured of a job in the majors. A California newspaper soon reported that Hinton had not been injured, the Senators drafted him, he made the team, and in 1962 he batted .310 with 17 home runs.

I followed Chuck Hinton with some interest because I had wondered if he would ever learn to hit a curveball, which he hadn't been able to do with me. The old baseball theory for youngsters is: "Look for the fastball and you can always adjust to the curve." I didn't buy that. Common sense tells you that if you're going against a good curveball pitcher, that's what he's going to throw you. You go to the ball park looking for the curve, but somehow this idea is hard to impart to young players.

Hinton eventually became a good curveball hitter, good enough to last ten years in the majors. Few guys who can't handle both pitches survive that long, though I once heard Eddie Mathews say that he looked for the fastball every pitch throughout his big-league career. He hit over 500 home runs and I wondered: Did he hit *all* of them off fastballs? I know from my experience with Bobby Bonds in the majors that you can throw him 137 curveballs and have a chance against him, but if you throw him one fastball it'll go right out of the ball park. That is a fact you try to communicate to your pitchers. But I haven't always succeeded, even with a talent like Jim Palmer. I went out to see how Palmer was feeling after he'd thrown a fastball that Bonds had hit into the stands, and Jim said, "Well, what did you want me to do, walk him?"

"No, Jim," I said, "let him hit it out of the park."

Another time after he had walked Bonds late in a game, I went out and Palmer said, "What did you want me to do, let him hit it out?" Jimmy likes to cover *every* possibility.

chapter
six

Jim McLaughlin had a number of spring seminars to aid his managers in their relationships with team owners, community leaders, and the press. One of the seminars that McLaughlin advised me to attend was taught by an instructor from the Dale Carnegie organization. The two-night seminar focused on sales techniques and interested me, but I was so busy with my team that I told Jim I would read Dale Carnegie's book, *How to Win Friends and Influence People*. I read it carefully (though certain umpires might suggest that I missed a point or two) because I would be trying to "sell" various ideas to players. Such as: Stop swinging at the low, outside curveball when you can't hit it.

I would have a million messages to convey to youngsters and I knew from my playing experience that getting these across to the point where players acted upon them was one of the most difficult tasks facing a manager. What made a great teacher was his or her ability to reach a student's mind. And the area of the mind that absorbs and retains and translates information into action is the subconscious. That was the key, and I wanted to acquire every tool that could possibly help me stroke the subconscious.

I had become interested in the powers of the human mind in 1956 when I read the book *Bridie Murphy*. It was about a woman who, after being hypnotized by a doctor, allegedly regressed into a vividly recalled previous lifetime. I don't know if this is true, but I do know that during regression certain people have total recall. I can remember in great detail things that happened to me as far back as when I was two years old. For example, I remember being carried into a prison at age two to visit my Uncle Red, my mother's brother and the son of my Grandmother Zastrow who lived with us. Uncle Red was imprisoned in Detroit for involuntary manslaughter, having killed a man in a fight. I did not know that. The only thing any member of my family ever said about Uncle Red was "he's living in Detroit." But I recall driving to Detroit with my Uncle Bud and Aunt Irene Bochert as well as my grandmother and grandfather. They took me because my parents were so busy at their dry cleaning business. They carried me into a building with bars on every window and door.

A couple of years later, when Uncle Red's name came up at the dinner table, I asked what he did in Detroit. They said he worked in a bank, and that satisfied my curiosity, perhaps because tellers stood behind bars.

But when I was fourteen my grandmother received a letter from Uncle Red and abruptly my visit of a dozen years earlier came back to me. "Is Uncle Red in jail?" I asked.

My grandmother burst into tears and demanded to know who told me. I said I remembered visiting him. They said I could not remember such a thing from age two, that I must have overheard them speaking of Uncle Red in an unguarded moment or that I had read one of his letters. I had done neither. The accuracy of my recollection was acknowledged when Uncle Red came home at about the time I signed my first professional contract. He went to work as a steam fitter and did well for a year or so, then suffered a fatal heart attack.

That recall experience led me to read *Bridie Murphy,* and one fact in the book fascinated me: People use only 7 percent of the mind's capacity. I started reading all kinds of books on the mind, various volumes on hypnotism, works by Edgar Cayce, and articles on ESP experiments that had been conducted at Duke University. I tried to learn everything about what could be gotten out of the human mind. Hypnotism is nothing more than the power of suggestion on the subconscious, as Dale Carnegie is nothing more than the power of suggestion on the conscious. But it is easier to reach the subconscious because there is so much debris around the conscious.

I was amazed to learn how easy it is to hypnotize someone and have him act on the power of suggestion. In 1956 when I was still a player for Knoxville I tried it on a teammate—and he went right into a trance. I followed one of the tests to see if a person is truly in a hypnotic state, saying, "Put your right arm straight out. Your arm cannot be bent. It is like a steel bar. Now raise your arm overhead. It will not come down for ten minutes." No one can hold his arm aloft that long, but under hypnosis I've had people do so for 25 minutes—the duration of the trance.

In another test that checked out from the beginning on many hypnotized subjects, I had them stretch their bodies stiffly between two chairs, with the head on one seat and the heels on the other. Then I would have someone, say a 200-pound man, sit on the hypnotized person's stomach. Years later, when I did this to my second wife, Marianna, she did not believe me after awaking from her trance. "I wasn't even hypnotized," she said. I hypnotized her again and had a photo taken of me seated on her rigid body between two chairs. "I can do that any time, Earl," she said. Then she attempted to, and her backside plummeted to the floor.

It was almost frightening to realize what the human mind could accomplish. I knew that people are intelligent enough to talk themselves into doing things that ordinarily they are incapable of doing. In a hypnotic state you talk yourself into doing things, but you are assisted by suggestions.

There are four hypnotic states, the deepest of which is the somnambulistic. Only one out of four people can reach that state: Total loss of memory—but complete control of the mind. At this level you can give post-hypnotic suggestions and the subjects always follow them. I've put people in a trance and told them they will call me at a certain hour the following day. Though they would awake without recalling my order, at the prescribed time the phone would invariably ring.

In the early years I used all the tests because I wasn't certain that a subject was truly hypnotized. But now I'm almost always certain, having hypnotized hundreds of people over the past twenty-five years. I used to hypnotize people at parties, particularly at the home of a Baltimore attorney named Russ White.

I never hypnotized a ballplayer to get a message across, but I have tried to reach the subconscious by planting suggestions in any manner, shape, or form I could come up with. You can't reach the subconscious with everybody, but the object is to keep trying to get inside the mind. You know what a given player has to do to become successful in the major leagues. And you've got to get that thought in his head before he can act upon it. You have to plant the belief that *he can do it*. It's all trial and error, because you have to come up with the words and strike at the right time. You try so many things that often you don't know which words at which time have finally implanted the thought that the player has then applied to his performance on the field.

A number of baseball players have reportedly helped themselves through hypnotism. I believe that Jackie Jensen and Maury Wills both reduced their fear of flying. And one of my pitchers in Baltimore, Jimmy Hardin, saw a hypnotist while pitching winter ball in Puerto Rico in an attempt to sharpen his performance. He even learned self-hypnosis. The next season was his best ever in the American League; his control had never been better, and he won eighteen ball games for the Orioles.

In June of 1973 I suggested to Paul Blair that he might benefit from seeing a hypnotist in Baltimore, Dr. Jacob Conn, who had built a good reputation. Paul had been having trouble with outside curveballs since 1970, when a pitch from California's Ken Tatum had caused serious eye and facial injuries that put Blair on the disabled list for three weeks. After that Paul stood so far off the plate that he couldn't judge certain outside pitches, and as a result he got into a lot of unnecessary arguments with umpires. I'm not questioning Paul's courage because survival is the first law of man, and every individual deals with it in his own terms. Paul tried everything to overcome his problem—including switch-hitting for a short and unsuccessful time—except setting up closer to the plate.

Then Paul decided he might as well try the hypnotist. And after only one session with Dr. Conn our impeccable center fielder became a very strong hitter again. I congratulated him and said that I hoped he realized that hypnotic suggestions needed to be repeated regularly or they would disappear from the subconscious. Paul said he had gotten all of Dr. Conn's suggestions, that he now knew what to do himself. Besides, the doctor charged fifty dollars per session. I told him I would ask the ball club to pay the fees. Paul wasn't interested, and to his credit he went on to hit for his highest average, .280, since the year before he was beaned.

Initially he credited the doctor's help, but then Paul renounced the aid in the papers, saying, in essence, that he had little regard for hypnotism and its ability to improve one's performance on a baseball field.

Two years later Paul reverted to standing so far off the plate that he couldn't judge much less hit pitches on the outside corner. Then he wanted to see Dr. Conn again. But the doctor said he had read of Blair's disregard for the effectiveness of hypnotism and that, sadly, a person with such beliefs could not benefit from hypnotic therapy. Dr. Conn would not see him again, and Paul Blair never hit with authority again.

Early in the 1980 season Jim Palmer was having some serious personal problems concerning his future and where he was headed. He was confused and seemed to be having trouble relaxing. I called him in and told him there was a hypnotist in Chicago who had worked with a number of ballplayers. Mort Cohen was his name and he had helped players relax by implanting suggestions of positive thinking in their minds. I asked Jimmy if he would see the man, saying I would arrange for Cohen to meet us in Milwaukee on our upcoming trip there.

The only reason I suggested this was in the hopes Cohen could help put Jimmy's mind at ease as to his off-the-field concerns and maybe help with a problem he was having on the field finishing ball games. The latter might simply be physical after all the innings Jimmy had pitched, though the fact that he was thirty-four had nothing to do with it . . . not with Palmer's great body and fluid motion.

Well, Cohen met with Jimmy and I'd have to say that he went into a trance, even though Palmer denies it. But afterward Jimmy seemed much more relaxed to me. It may have been just the words Cohen said to him, but I know the session helped him.

Jimmy saw Mort Cohen again when we got to Chicago. And

everything good that had been done the first time was unraveled the second time. Mort's suggestions were wrong. I'm sorry I didn't brief Cohen beforehand on what the problems were and what suggestions should have been made. Jimmy struggled along and managed to work out his personal problems himself, though he couldn't solve his problem of not completing games.

Still, just because I believe in the potential benefits of hypnotism does not mean that I expect everyone to open their minds enough to do so. Some people never change their beliefs. I came into baseball bearing all of the beliefs and prejudices of a kid from St. Louis. I had little experience with black people and none with Hispanics, yet I had no problems discovering that good people were good people, whether they attended your church or voted for your candidate or dressed to your style or danced to your music. Baseball gave me the opportunity to open my mind and expand my experience—and it was a wonderful experience.

Some of the basics of hypnotism—suggestions that aid the ego in balancing the id and the superego—have helped me in dealing with players. I've always believed in boosting my players, in flattering their egos through the powers of suggestion: "You can lay off that pitch." "You can develop that change-up." "You can put this guy in the seats." *You can do it.*

As Reggie Jackson said after playing for me, "Earl makes you think you're better than you are. He always builds you up."

And I was amused in May 1981 to read something Frank Robinson said when Eddie Murray returned from a debilitating virus and had his problems at the plate. "Being around Earl taught me patience," Frank said. "It also taught me to have confidence in your people, to know what they're capable of and not ask them to do what they're not capable of. The best example of that is Eddie Murray right now. He's in a terrible slump. But I'll bet Earl has been telling the writers that come the All-Star break, Eddie'll be up near .300 with his 15 homers and his 50 ribbies. Earl stays with him."

That's exactly what I was telling the writers.

The year 1960 was the first in which I began earning my living from baseball year round, and the resultant lengthy separations from my family did not please my wife. I returned home from the Instructional League in December, then joined the Orioles in February, which meant I didn't see my wife and kids—who now numbered three, Michael, Rhonda, and Theresa—again until school let out in June. Thus, I was with my family for about two and one half months summers and only two months during the winters. But this was my job, the profession I had chosen, and I had no choice. Besides, I felt like I was learning and advancing.

In 1961 I was named director of our central spring training camp and given the responsibility of setting up a program of techniques and fundamentals to be used by every club in our organization below Triple-A. I introduced a number of my ideas and modified some of Paul Richards' in developing the program, which the major-league team subsequently adopted and has been following ever since. I take pride in the fact that the basic system of rundowns, relays, cutoffs, et al. that I introduced at age thirty is still alive and well regarded over twenty years later in Baltimore.

The work was very hard, managing all season and again in the Instructional League, working with the Orioles in Miami and then at the central spring training camp. The hours were long and exhausting much of the time for me and the other career baseball men who worked virtually year round. We were the physical laborers who ran the pitching machines in the spring, pitched BP, hit groundballs or flies by the hours, and were the catalysts for every repetitive drill from dawn until dusk.

But it wasn't all work, as I described in the Instructional League. We always found ways to enjoy ourselves in the off hours, such as they were. Although there were meetings and seminars at the Thomasville, Georgia, camp several nights a week, on the other nights we had fun at the only game in town: the Elks Club. As we didn't have any expense money coming in until the season started, it was incumbent upon us to find ways to cover the cost of our drinks. Billy DeMars, who managed in our organization until he became a Phillies coach in 1969, and I devised a simple system that allowed us to stay ahead of the slot machines at the Elks. We would chip in five dollars apiece and stand by the machines waiting for one to hit a stretch of no payoffs. Then we would take turns shoving half dollars into the "live" machine until it turned up three of something and a jackpot. As soon as we got lucky we quit and used our profits to pay for the drinks we carried from the bar into the Bingo game room, where we usually also had good fortune. There was a Happy Hour prior to Bingo and all drinks were half price: twenty-five cents. One night Billy and I hauled twenty-seven drinks from the bar to our Bingo table, seven for colleagues and ten apiece for ourselves. We had decided to go for a Happy Hour record, and we got pretty happy setting it.

On Sunday mornings four of us always played an early round of golf, the stakes being a dinner ($5.00) at the Elks Club. I had started playing golf at age sixteen with my Uncle Bud, and I still had the aged set of wooden-shafted clubs he gave me. They didn't look like much, but I managed to hack out a lot of free dinners with them. Our game was "play 'em down"—you had to play the ball no matter where it landed. In a drinking fountain. In the crook of a tree. In a water hazard. I once saw Harry Dalton take eleven strokes to get his ball out of a creek, as George Staller stood there loudly counting each swing. It was a real accomplishment to break 100 in this game. Our average score was about 110.

In Miami, after I began working with the Orioles, the golf was even better, as were the living conditions. I loved to bet at the dog tracks and at the Thoroughbred races at Hialeah, Gulf Stream, or Calder, to which we usually could wiggle passes. Miami, I immediately decided, was where I wanted to live when I retired, if I could ever accumulate the finances.

In 1961 there was no way we could replace all the stars we lost at Fox Cities and we finished fourth. Still, I again moved up, taking over the Class-A Elmira Pioneers in the Eastern League and putting together another damn fine ball club in 1962. Among my players I had Steve Dalkowski again—and a better view of this flawed talent. The previous fall I had convinced the organization to allow me to give all of the players on our Instructional League club the Stanford-Binet IQ test. I had grown more and more concerned about players with great physical abilities who could not learn to correct certain basic deficiencies no matter how much you instructed or drilled them. I must have seen Paul

Richards put a curveball in Dalkowski's hand two hundred times, yet Steve had never consistently broken them off effectively. Now, my time was not worth much in those days, but I wondered if Richards wasn't just wasting his time. The test indicated that Richards had wasted his time. For Dalkowski finished in the 1 percentile in his ability to understand facts. Steve, it was sad to say, had the ability to do everything but learn. It had been my experience that the more you talked to Dalkowski, the more confused he became. Now I knew why.

In 1962 I finally made Dalkowski understand one thing when I told him for the one millionth time: "Steve, if you don't throw the ball over that white thing and if the batters don't swing—you lose." In the final 57 innings he pitched that season Dalkowski gave up 1 earned run, struck out 110 batters, and walked only 11. He had a great fastball and a vicious slider, but the following spring he hurt his arm as he again tried to follow instructions and learn a curveball. It seemed a shame to me. If a ballplayer has one strength and simply can't add another—go with that strength. Hell, if Dalkowski allowed just one earned run in fifty-seven innings with two pitches, let him keep throwing those two pitches until he gives up two earned runs. Baseball is that simple. Steve Carlton demonstrated the truth of that principle in the 1980 World Series when he didn't get three curveballs over in one game. He went with what he could get over the plate—mainly his high fastball—and won. Sandy Koufax had a great curveball, but he couldn't negotiate five strikes with it in the last Series game he pitched against Minnesota some years back. On two days' rest he won the seventh game 2–0 almost exclusively with hard stuff.

I'm not criticizing the judgment made on Dalkowski. Many decisions in baseball would be changed in retrospect. I feel Andy Etchebarren might have become a better hitter if I hadn't rushed him from the rookie league to A ball. I became convinced when I had him in the Instructional League that he could compete at that level. In fact, I had such belief in Andy's bat that I played him against the toughest pitchers in the league and played another youngster, John Griffin, against the weaker arms. Came July, Etchebarren was batting .200 and Griffin .300. I reversed the roles in the second half and both ended up hitting

.250. Still, Andy had a good stroke and if he had started in a lower classification and built his confidence at the plate, his lifetime average might have been higher than .234.

For all the talent at Elmira in '62, we couldn't match Williamsport, which had perhaps the finest hitter I had seen to that time. Richie Allen hit every ball *hard*. We finished second during the regular season but put it all together to win the Shaughnessey play-offs.

Shortly thereafter I received an offer I couldn't refuse to manage winter ball in Venezuela: $3,600 for three months' work. Jim McLaughlin had moved to the Cincinnati Reds at this time and Harry Dalton had been elevated to farm director. I went to the Oriole offices to tell Dalton that I would not manage the Instructional League team. My overall salary with the Orioles was now $8,600 and Dalton said, "Well if we're going to lose you for two and a half months, Earl, I'll have to cut you back to $7,000."

"Hold it, Harry," I said. "That's *way* too much. I've been managing in the organization for six years. I've got a wife and three kids to support. You cut me below $8,000 and I'll have to quit baseball."

"I'll go in and talk to Lee," he said, referring to Lee MacPhail, as if Dalton needed the Oriole GM's approval to cut me "only" $600.

Dalton was in MacPhail's office for what seemed like an hour, though it was probably no more than fifteen minutes. I began to worry: Maybe they'll tell me to go ahead and take a hike.

Dalton came back shaking his head.

I stood up, saying, "So that's it, huh. Well, if I'm not worth at least $8,000 to this organization at this point, I'm better off out of it."

"Wait a minute, Earl. Just wait a minute. Lee's in there thinking. I'm going right back in and see if I can get him to come up."

He returned quickly this time. "You've got $7,800 right now, Earl."

"It's $8,000 or I quit, Harry."

"I'll be right back," he said.

Dalton came back nodding. "You get the $8,000, Earl, I'm happy to say."

"Harry," I said, "Elmira's being reclassified from A to Double-

A next season, as you well know. I'll be the only manager in baseball who's moving *up* and taking a cut in salary."

"Yeah, Earl, but you add the $3,600 from winter ball to your $8,000 and you have your best year ever: $11,600."

"Thanks, Harry. I guess I should say it's a pleasure being cut by you."

I managed in the lower of the two Venezuelan leagues, for an owner named Antonio Harerra. He always wore a big white hat and a white suit with baggy pants, like a fugitive from an old Warner Brothers movie. Harerra didn't speak English, but his GM translated. There were only seven Americans on the club, the rest local players who couldn't understand me. I arrived early for their spring training and began trying to teach my system of rundowns, cutoffs, relays . . . everything. I would give instructions to an interpreter who would screw them up, which annoyed hell out of me. The more excited I became, the longer we stayed out and worked—and the less the Venezuelans accomplished. I kept working them, along with the seven minor-league imports, until I realized the Latin players were all scared and the American players were there mostly for a vacation. I decided to adopt the local philosophy of *mañana,* and everyone relaxed.

Every time we lost, though, the fans threatened to kill us, the fans throughout Latin America being very emotional. My best relief pitcher was a big left-hander named George Stepanovich, but the first two times I brought him in he gave it up and we lost. The American players and myself would all stay together going out at night, and bands of kids would follow us shouting, "Stepanovich sonabitch! Stepanovich sonabitch!"

We got straightened out, though, and finished right behind Luis Aparicio's Maricaibo team. We lost the Caribbean play-offs, and I didn't get home until late-January. The kids were happy to see me. My wife did not express glee.

Less than a month later I was off to the Oriole camp, then to spring training with my club, then into the season. I phoned home at least once a week to see how things were going or to see if our checking account could cover the check I needed to write. I was operating on a budget of $75 every two weeks, and I could often stretch that if things went right on the golf course or if a scout came through and bought me a dinner or two. But in May

1963 I ran a little short and when I called home there was no answer. I dialed again every hour until midnight and heard nothing but rings. I grew more and more concerned because Jane was always home with the children. Something had to be wrong. I went to bed, awoke, and phoned at 3 and at 6 A.M., and still there was no answer.

At 10:30 in the morning, my wife finally came on the line.

"Where the hell have you been?" I asked. "I've been calling all night."

"The phone was broken," she said.

"Bullshit!" I said. "It was ringing."

"It didn't ring here."

"Well never mind. I have to write a check for $25."

"There's no money in the checking account."

"I sent you $3,600, Jane, so go to the bank and transfer some money from the savings account."

"There's no money in the savings account."

"What the hell are you talking about?"

"We're getting divorced, Earl. That's what I'm talking about."

"Now just hold it, Jane," I said. "Don't do anything. I'm on my way home."

"Earl," she said, "the only thing worse than you being gone is you being home."

I sat right down, thanks to my Liberty Loan experience, and wrote to the companies with which we had credit cards: please cancel. From then on I split my checks with Jane, but I kept worrying about the kids. When she demanded that I make the various appliance payments, I was about to until my lawyer said, "You send her half your earnings and pay all the bills, you're never going to get a divorce." I not only stopped paying for the appliances, I notified the store to pick up the washer and dryer and sell them at auction for the unpaid balance. After that the divorce went through with alacrity. On September 23 it was final. I gave Jane the house in St. Louis so she could stay there with the kids, as well as the furnishings and the car.

The divorce sent me right down the drain emotionally. I had to really buckle up and watch the beer because I was depressed and feeling a ton of guilt about the loss of my three kids. They had grown so much in the last few years and it seemed like I had hardly been with them. I felt like I had never done enough for them.

What I did that fall of 1963 was make a serious mistake by moving to St. Louis with my parents so I could see the kids. I'd pick them up after school and take them for a hamburger or to an early movie . . . or any place just to spend time with them. We bowled on Sunday afternoons. They were damn nice kids and it was great to be with them despite the gnawing guilt feelings that refused to dissolve.

I signed on with an insurance company and went through a four-week sales training course. By the time I finished I didn't believe in any of the malarky. I wasn't about to go out and lie to old people for a buck. Or young people either. So I just sat around my parents' house like a bum all winter. Finally I phoned Harry Dalton and asked him to send me out for the last few weeks of the Instructional League season. I got my board and expenses . . . and a chance to clear my head. Baseball made me think about something other than my own anguish.

In 1963 I had fielded another exciting team in Elmira. We finished second in a tight race, then won the pennant on the final day of the season in '64. By then I had my emotions in firm control again, and a huge factor here went far beyond baseball—I began seeing Marianna Osgood, the beautiful woman who would become my second wife in September 1964. I had met and dated Marianna a number of times the previous season, and knew I needed her and that she needed me. Marianna, the mother of a young daughter, was also going through a divorce. Once I got through that painful winter after my divorce, Marianna and I were always together when the Pioneers played at home. She did wonders for me.

Right after our wedding we bought a house in Elmira, where I was becoming something of a celebrity, and I decided to forego baseball that winter. First of all I was deeply in love and wanted to stay with Marianna. I also wanted to make as much money as I could to cover my rising child-support payments. An Elmira car dealer told me I could do very well selling for him. He didn't know how right he was. I was an ideal used-car salesman, after having read Dale Carnegie and having been trying to reach the subconscious of ballplayers for some nine years. The art of selling cars was similar to but easier than selling players on a new way of doing something.

Elmira, New York, in the winter is a city in which people devote more time to shoveling their cars out of snowbanks than driving them. Of course, there were persistent starting problems, so potential buyers came by looking for vehicles that would turn over on frigid mornings. All I had to do was say, "This car was *made* for you! You gotta have this car! I wouldn't sell it to anyone but *you!* Get behind that wheel . . . yeah. You want this car, and you're *definitely* gonna have it!"

Then a little diversion, to send the prospective buyer's mind onto another subject while the car simmered in the subconscious: "You know, I think we're gonna put together another pennant winner this season. You like baseball, I hope." Whether he did or did not was beside the point as long as the conversation proceeded for some minutes before the guy decided to make a deal on a car—which was why he had dropped by in the first place—or decided he needed a little time to think about it. You hit him again: "Well this is your car all right—no two ways about it. You want to drive it away now?"

If the guy went home to consider the car deal, he'd actually get involved in something else, like reading the paper or watching television. But suddenly the thought that had been nesting in the subconscious would fly to the conscious: *I want that car!* And the guy would get right on the phone to me or come back immediately. I said to myself: No wonder subliminal advertising is not allowed on television.

In the month of January alone I sold over twenty used cars and earned $1,700 in commissions. The year before, when my first wife left me, I had been driving an old Chevy that had no reverse gear and had to be hand pushed backwards in certain parking situations—and now I was making good money and had the use of a company car.

I held that job two winters and loved it. I knew I'd found a profession I could step right into if I had to leave baseball. That didn't hurt my confidence. And with Marianna working as a secretary and making a pretty good salary coupled with my baseball and car-sales income, I was suddenly in better financial shape than I had ever known.

Early in the 1965 season, on May 8, the Elmira Pioneers participated in a little baseball history—the longest game ever played in pro ball at that time. It was a home game and rain delayed the start until 3 P.M. Neither team had scored a run by the twentieth inning, the lights were turned on, and the scoreboard was cleared, there being no more space. By then it was 7:30, the starting time for night games, and a few dozen people bought tickets and came into the park not knowing that the first inning they would see was actually the twenty-first.

The Springfield Giants scored in the top of the twenty-sixth, but we tied it 1–1 and then retired the side in the top of the twenty-seventh. Johnny Scruggs led off for us with a triple and I called to the hitter from the third-base coaching box, "Make it go through!" The Giants had of course drawn in their infield. But the hitter struck out. I whispered to Scruggs, "I don't care where the ball's hit, even if it's back to the pitcher—you try to score. We gotta end this damn game."

The ball was hit to the shortstop, who came up with it and threw to the Giants' catcher. Scruggs slid into the waiting ball. The umpire hollered, "Safe!" Then he ran as fast as he could into the clubhouse, followed closely by the screaming catcher and Springfield manager, Andy Gilbert. But the game was finally over. The exhausted umpire had made a judgment call . . . and those rascals are *never* changed.

We didn't repeat as pennant winners at Elmira in 1965, but finishing second extended my consistent streak. In the preceding seven seasons my ball clubs had finished below second only once, and we'd won two pennants and a play-off. Harry Dalton was impressed. He wanted me to take over our Triple-A Rochester club. Frankly, he said, Red Wings owner Morrie Silver was leaning toward hiring a "name" manager who might bring more people into his ball park.

In truth, I wasn't all that keen about moving to Rochester. I was well established in Elmira. We owned our own house there, Marianna worked there, and her daughter, Kim, was now in school there. I thought I might be better off staying in Elmira for a couple of more years before advancing to what appeared to be pressurized big-time baseball in a city that sent over 300,000 people to games annually. Hell, I had never even competed in Triple-A ball.

But I drove to Rochester and had a nice lunch and then dinner with Morrie Silver. By the time I got back home, he'd made his decision. I was the manager of the Rochester Red Wings for the 1966 season.

Morrie Silver proved to be a warm and generous man, treating me to fine dinners twice a week all through the spring. Morrie was not a baseball person, but he was a good person who loved the game. The Red Wings had problems for the first two months of the season, as youngsters like Mark Belanger, Larry Haney, Mike Epstein, and Jimmy Hardin adjusted to Triple-A ball. One day when we were still in sixth place, Morrie came to me with the league batting averages and said, "Earl, pick someone out of here who can hit and I'll get him. I don't care what we've got to pay for him."

I shook my head. "I know these kids can play, Morrie, and they're better than anyone we could acquire for the second half of the season."

We soon began climbing the standings, to fifth, fourth, third, second . . . and on the last day of the season we won the pennant. Silver Stadium was packed with nearly 10,000 fans that day, as it had been for virtually every game once we began our charge. We took a 10–2 lead into the top of the eighth inning, and when I went out to the third-base coaching box the fans rose as one and gave me an ovation the likes of which I hadn't heard since I was a spectator myself in Sportsman's Park. It was unbelievable, all those people on their feet clapping and cheering and whistling for me. And after we had won and gone into the clubhouse, those people stayed at their seats and loudly insisted that I come back out for another ovation. When I stepped out of the dugout on that empty field and heard that noise and, waving my arms, looked around into all those ecstatic faces, for a moment I couldn't breathe. It was as if all of the oxygen had been sucked out of that ball park, but it didn't matter. I was inhaling pure joy.

Marianna was almost as excited as I was. We'd had a wonderful summer together. She had taken a leave from her job in June when Kim completed the spring semester and that winter we enjoyed a three-month, well-paid ($6,000) vacation in Puerto Rico. The owner of the Santurce team, Hiram Cuevas, hired me and it was the most delightful winter I'd ever spent. We enrolled Kim in school there, found a beautiful place to live near a glistening beach, and, as we played only four games a week, had plenty of free time to relax and enjoy ourselves. And on my club I had players like Orlando Cepeda, Tony Perez, Dave Johnson, Paul Blair, Juan Pizarro, and Reuben Gomez. We finished second during the regular season and then won the play-offs.

The most important thing about that club in Puerto Rico was that it introduced me to a catcher named Elrod Hendricks. When I arrived on the island, Hiram Cuevas said we needed a catcher. Hendricks, he maintained, was a good hitter who couldn't catch. Well, as soon as I saw Hendricks behind the plate in workouts I knew he needed some instruction on fundamentals. He had been born in the Virgin Islands and had played seven years of minor-league ball without receiving a lot of coaching. But he was agile and he worked hard, and despite the fact that everyone said he had a rainbow arm because he threw like a girl —somehow the ball got there before the runner. In workouts he was throwing out everyone. Still, the owner wanted another catcher so I brought in Larry Haney and used Hendricks as a pinch hitter.

Early on Elrod yanked a couple of pitches over the fence, and the Puerto Rican fans started screaming, "Play Hendricks! Play Hendricks!" They didn't have to. Anyone with a home-run bat like Elrod Hendricks' was going to play on my team. Once he became a semi-regular the home runs came regularly. I looked up his record and saw that Hendricks had hit 26 home runs during the '66 season and 35 the year before that for Jalisco in the Mexican League. I got right on the phone to Dalton.

"Harry, I got a ballplayer down here you won't believe! Elrod Hendricks, a catcher who hit over fifty home runs in the last two seasons in the Mexican League. Why don't you look him up and see who owns his contract. I'll hold."

Dalton came back on in two minutes and said Hendricks belonged to the Angels, that he was on the roster of their Triple-A club in Seattle. "We'd have to draft him at the major-league level, Earl. That's $25,000."

"Well for God's sake *draft him,* Harry. We ain't gonna find nobody like this SOB—a catcher who can hit over twenty home runs a years. If Hendricks doesn't make the Orioles, he'll hit a pile of home runs for me in Rochester with that 310-foot fence in right."

The Orioles had won the World Series in 1966 and Dalton couldn't find a place on the forty-man roster for Hendricks. I was distraught when we didn't draft Elrod, who would have hit sixty-five home runs for me in Silver Stadium.

Still, we had another fine team in Rochester in 1967, and we battled for first place all season. In late August Morrie Silver had a ceremony before a game and was kind enough to present me with a check for $5,000, which stunned me. We went on to finish the International League season tied for first, then lost a one-game play-off. That was, amazingly, the fifth successive season in which my club had been involved in a pennant race that was not resolved until the final game of the season or in a play-off. In '63 we lost the pennant on the final day, in '64 we won it on the final day, in '65 we lost it on the final day, in '66 we won it on the final day.

Hiram Cuevas invited me back to Puerto Rico and gave me a $1,500 raise in 1967, and we won the pennant going away. I caught Elrod Hendricks almost every game because he swung the bat with authority all season. The Orioles had tumbled from World Champions to sixth place, and now I had no trouble convincing Dalton to send a scout to check out Hendricks. The night Frank Lane arrived, Hendricks hit two home runs. Afterward Lane said, "You like this guy, huh, Earl?"

"Frank, you just saw him smack two over the fence in one game. How many catchers you know who can do that? You're damn right I like Hendricks. People say he's a horseshit catcher, but he's not. He's a competent catcher who will improve."

"All right, Earl, you've got my vote."

On November 18, 1967, the Orioles drafted Elrod Hendricks.

Shortly after we returned home to Elmira, Dalton phoned and asked me to come down to Baltimore. At the Oriole offices he took me in and introduced me to Jerry Hoffberger, the team owner. Hoffberger congratulated me on my managerial record and we sat around talking baseball for a while, then Harry thanked our employer for his time, I said it had been my pleasure meeting him, and we went to the general manager's office. Dalton's official title was director of player personnel, though in fact he was in charge of all *uniformed* personnel, managers, and coaches.

To the best of my recollection of our private meeting, Dalton was very disappointed in the Orioles second-division finish in '67 and in manager Hank Bauer. Dalton had been overjoyed the previous year, his first as GM, but a gap had opened between him and the manager when Bauer had gone over his head and negotiated a two-year contract with Hoffberger. The Oriole policy had been one-year contracts for managers. And Dalton felt that Bauer did not respect his baseball ability because Harry had never played professionally. Dalton said he had asked Bauer during the season what was wrong, what if anything they could do to improve the club. Bauer had virtually the same players who had beaten the Dodgers four straight in the '66 World Series, and he had insisted that they would start winning again in 1968.

Then Dalton said to me, "I think one problem is that we've got a playboy club here." That wasn't true, from what I had heard, but I didn't say anything. "Earl, if you were the Oriole manager, knowing as you do the personnel in our organization, who would you have as coaches?"

"Well I'd keep Billy Hunter," I said, "because in my mind he's one of the best third-base coaches in baseball. I know you can't be happy about all the sore arms on the staff, so I'd bring up George Bamberger [the minor-league pitching instructor] to handle the pitchers. George Staller would be my choice as first-base coach because I have nothing but respect for his baseball knowledge. And I'd make Vern Hoscheit the bullpen coach, because he's a mean SOB and a former catcher who would keep everybody on their toes."

Not long thereafter Dalton announced that, with the exception of Billy Hunter, the entire Oriole coaching staff—Harry Brecheen, Gene Woodling, and Sherman Lollar—had been fired. The new staff would include all the men I had recommended to Dalton except for Staller. I was to be the new first-base coach!

When Dalton called me with the news, I thanked him, then hugged Marianna and shouted, "I'm finally going to the major leagues!" It was a great opportunity, I told her. I would no longer have all the responsibility of managing, and if I did a good job—which I damn well *would* do—I could coach in the big leagues for at least five years and qualify for a pension. I think every man who reaches age thirty-seven without having a pension begins to worry about that fact, and now I could stop worrying. The only thing that bothered me was how Hank Bauer would react to having all his coaches fired and new men brought in without his consent or even his foreknowledge. As I muse on this now, over a decade later, I wonder if Bauer should not have done what Dick Howser of the Yankees did after George Steinbrenner summarily fired Howser's third-base coach, Mike Ferraro—for sending in a runner during the 1980 play-offs that any outstanding coach would have sent home. Howser negotiated a settlement of his contract and gave up his job as manager. I know I would never allow *anyone* to name my coaches without my approval.

Until I reached the International League I never gave a thought to the possibility of managing in the major leagues. Then I saw Dick Williams, whom I had beaten in '66, move from Toronto of the IL to Boston in 1967 and win the American League pennant. Damn, I said to myself, I know I can manage in the majors now. Of course, I had to admit that I couldn't think of a soul who would ever have the nerve to give me a chance, so I put that thought out of my mind. But now I was going to be a coach in the major leagues, and after twenty years in the minors that looked just fine to me, thank you.

I was really looking forward to spring training and my new role. Marianna had been to Florida with me only once before, and I was certain we were going to have a good time. During our other stay I had been allotted just enough expense money so that we barely squeezed by. But now I was making $15,000, the expense money was better and I was going to be working with coaches I had been associated with for some ten years.

We checked into the hotel the evening we arrived in Miami, had a nice dinner, and the next morning I went to the ball park fully expecting Hank Bauer, as any manager would with a new coach, to greet me and designate my duties, tell me exactly what was expected of me. Hank Bauer didn't tell me anything to do, because Hank Bauer didn't tell me anything at all. He didn't speak to me after he gruffly said hello. The days went silently on as we moved from workouts to exhibition games, and it was as if I wasn't even present. I later confided this to a friend, trying to describe what it was like, and my friend asked, "Did Bauer treat you like some insignificant minor-leaguer for whom he had no respect whatsoever?" And I said it was worse than that. It was frustrating, demeaning, and embarrassing. Bauer not only wouldn't talk to me, he wouldn't speak to Marianna. So this is the big leagues, I thought. After all those years of working like hell to get here, suddenly Aberdeen, South Dakota, and those twenty-hour bus rides didn't seem so unpleasant.

But even the other new coaches were reluctant to talk to me. They appeared to be fearful, because Bauer seemed to be ticked off at all of them, too. Vern Hoscheit didn't say two words to me all spring, and George Bamberger was careful to speak to Marianna and myself only on the side. "These people were always so friendly and nice to us before," Marianna said. "Something's wrong here." I said, "Marianna, you're right—something *is* wrong here." I was thankful for the presence of Billy Hunter. He wasn't at all intimidated by Bauer's attitude or anything else. I had most of my conversations with him and with Marianna. But since I like to talk all the time, it wasn't easy with so short a supply of conversationalists.

Evidently Hank Bauer, like most managers, was afraid for his job. Now everyone knows that any manager who stays around long enough will be fired, unless he happens to be named Connie Mack and owns the ball club or Walter Alston, who had so much success that he managed twenty-three years and quit before he could be fired. But a manager who doesn't make use of the experience and knowledge possessed by his coaches, who doesn't seek their counsel and solicit their suggestions . . . that manager has no chance at all for longevity. That manager is asking to be fired unless he is a helluva lot smarter than Walter Alston and Earl Weaver and Connie Mack combined. Hank Bauer sought no advice from any of his coaches. Apparently he was too upset over the fact that the coaches who had helped him win a

World Championship only two years before had been fired out from under him and a damn minor-league manager named Earl Weaver had been shoved onto his staff as a threat to him. When the Orioles were wallowing in the second division in '67 there had been considerable media speculation that if the team did not bounce back into contention this season, Billy Hunter would replace Bauer as manager. Well, Billy Hunter wasn't looking for Bauer's job and I wasn't either. We were organization men and our assignment was clearly to help Bauer keep his job by contributing to the Orioles' success. This is the ultimate goal of every manager, coach, and scout in the Baltimore organization—to assist the major-league team in winning ball games.

I must say that I felt for Hank Bauer, who had been put in a tenuous position by Harry Dalton, though the position would reverse itself if the team started winning. But I also understood that Dalton was in overall charge of a ball club he felt had everything that was needed to win. It is the general manager's job to assemble the players and hire the manager who can meld them into a winning team. Dalton thought he had improved the ball club by providing more depth to a team that had won it all two years before. Hank Bauer's major flaw seemed to be his sense of loyalty to the players who had won for him in '66. He refused to platoon or replace those players whose performance fell off the next year. Loyalty is a good trait, but it is not a good job-keeping trait if it results in your staying with players who can no longer do their jobs on the ball field as well as they had in the past. As a manager, your obligations are to the team you work for and the hell with the people who did things for you yesterday. A manager must live by that hard-hearted cliché: What have you done for me today?

So I didn't know what to do all spring except coach at first base once the exhibition games began. And it was apparent in the games that the Orioles had one crucial weakness—we needed to score more runs. The team had scored 101 fewer runs in '67 than it had in '66, losing 21 more games.

I knew how we *could* score more runs. We had three particularly weak spots in our batting order against certain pitchers. Left-handers just ate up left-fielder Curt Blefary, a left-handed hitter. Right-handers, particularly those with good sliders and hard curveballs, owned right-hand-hitting catcher Andy Etche-barren, and Paul Blair, another right-handed hitter who also hap-pened to be the best defensive center fielder in the league. But that winter the Orioles had acquired an outstanding switch-hit-ting lead-off man from the White Sox named Don Buford. He knew how to get on base, how to run the bases, and how to steal thirty bases a year. Buford had played the infield, and not very well, for five years in the majors, but I remembered him as a damn fine center fielder for Lincoln in the Three-I League in 1960. As it would turn out, Buford never became a good defen-sive outfielder in the majors. He was capable, though, and it didn't matter to me if he occasionally gave up a run—I knew he would manufacture a lot of runs if he got a chance to play.

My idea was to play Buford full time, sitting down Blefary against southpaws and Blair against right-handers, with the switch-hitter playing left field against the former and center against the latter. I didn't approach Bauer with this thought be-cause I was scared to death. How could I, a thirty-seven-year-old minor-league manager, tell a man who had been major-league Manager of the Year what *I* thought when the man wouldn't even speak to me? I did approach Donny Buford, though, and told him to shag as many balls in the outfield as he possibly could, saying that if the manager saw that he could go get the balls out there it just might convince Bauer to play him. Buford applied himself every day, hustling in the outfield, but it didn't seem to impress Bauer.

The other bat on the bench I liked, of course, belonged to Elrod Hendricks. But Bauer wouldn't even look at this guy. Ellie tended to bug everyone except me. He was black and he had a big mouth, even though the steady stream of words were nice and spoken with a calypso lilt. Every time Hendricks appeared, preceded by those good-natured words-without-end, Billy Hunter moved away shaking his head. And Vern Hoscheit, who instructed Elrod in the fine art of catching, immediately hated him. Hendricks would work like hell at blocking balls in the dirt and doing everything he possibly could to improve his tech-niques. But Hendricks had his own style, and some players you have to leave alone and just let them play. What difference does it make if a player is awkward or even spastic if he gets the job done?

When we assembled to discuss the final cuts, at a Miami restaurant called The Mousetrap, Harry Dalton presided over the meeting and the first name he brought up was Elrod Hendricks. None of the coaches said anything until Bauer said, "Screw 'im— send him back to the Mexican League, or wherever he came from."

"No," I said, "don't do that. We'd be making a mistake to—"

"Earl, be quiet," Dalton said. "I'm conducting this meeting."

"Yes, but Hendricks is the only left-handed—"

"Shut up, Earl. I want to go around the table."

"We need his bat—"

"Earl, I told you to shut up. I want to go around the table."

"*I'm* at the table and—"

"Shut up, Earl."

"I haven't had my say and—"

"Look, Earl, if you don't shut up you're going to have to move to another table and pay your own bill."

"All right," I said, standing up. "But you shouldn't get rid of a guy who can hit like Hendricks. I'm telling you I had him in Puerto Rico and he hit some tough major-league pitchers, and he'll do that for us and he's the only left-hand-hitting catcher we got, and that's all I have to say."

I walked over to another table, sat down, ordered another drink and my bill. The waitress brought both, I paid the bill, knocked down the drink, and then left, thinking: Screw 'em. If they can't see Elrod's value—just screw 'em!

I went home to Marianna with tears in my eyes. I couldn't help crying over the mistake we were making. I knew what Hendricks could do and I knew what Etchebarren and Larry Haney could do because they had all played for me. The left-handed bat in that trio would make it potent. Without Hendricks we would have two right-hand-hitting catchers who would get 80 percent of their base hits off lefties . . . and we would have no options. It was ridiculous.

When the decision was finally made to keep Hendricks, I was overjoyed. Apparently, though Bauer was never convinced that Hendricks was worth a spot on the twenty-five-man roster, there were enough positive words on him from the other coaches—coupled with the fact that the Orioles had paid $25,000 for Elrod and that there was not a lot of interest in him from other teams. Still, Hendricks went north with us and Bauer ignored him in game after game, far too many of which we lost 2–1, 3–2, or 4–3. We just weren't scoring enough runs. When Bauer finally played Hendricks in a game at Yankee Stadium, with its short fence in right field, Elrod hit 2 home runs.

We left New York and Hendricks resumed his seat on the bench. And Donny Buford did little more than occasionally pinch hit, too. Meanwhile, Blefary, Blair, and Etchebarren kept struggling at the plate trying to get their batting averages up over .200. Frank Robinson wasn't doing much better as he continued to suffer from double vision. In '67 he had slid hard—Frank *always* slid hard breaking up double plays—into White Sox second baseman Al Weis and cracked his head on Weis's knee. But all any manager could do with a Frank Robinson—the only man ever to be named Most Valuable Player in both leagues—was play him as long as he could swing a bat and pray for his health to return. To make matters worse, Frank Robinson came down with the mumps and was sidelined for almost three weeks. My sympathy for Hank Bauer had long since died as I watched us lose so many ball games in which he didn't even attempt to make use of all the weapons at his disposal.

We were 12 games behind the Detroit Tigers by the All-Star break, and I was damn glad to get away from the ball park for a few days. Marianna and I had rented an apartment in a complex called The Colony, and we decided to just lounge around the pool and get some sun. Kim had stayed with her father in Elmira, where we still owned our $12,000 house, and we talked about starting to look for a house in the Baltimore area. You couldn't go wrong owning real estate no matter where baseball might take you.

The apartment manager came out and said I had a long-distance phone call. "The party would not give his name, but he said it was very, very important."

The first thing I thought of was that something had happened to my children. I hurried to the phone. "Earl," Harry Dalton said, "we've made a decision. We're going to change managers. I want you to become manager of the Baltimore baseball club. But don't say anything to anybody. I haven't told Hank yet. I'm leaving from the All-Star Game for his home in Kansas City to tell him. You and Marianna check into a motel, because there will be a thousand calls. Come over to my house tonight around eight and we'll have dinner and talk."

"Okay, Harry," was all I could say.

I told Marianna I had been named manager of the Orioles, and she looked up in that innocent way of hers and said, "Is that good?"

I laughed. "Well, I got a good ball club and we'll make more money."

That night Dalton said that Jerry Hoffberger had finally agreed with him that Bauer had to go—a move that Dalton had wanted to make before the season started. "We should do better now, Earl," he said, "and we *need* to do better." Attendance had fallen from 1.2 million in '66 to 860,390 in '67, and the projected total for this season was even lower. In Baltimore the baseball team has to win to attract fans.

Then good old Harry tried to beat me out of about $6,000. My $15,000 coach's salary and the $7,500 I was to earn in Puerto Rico would give me $22,500 for the year. Dalton pointed out that major-league managers could not manage winter ball, and proceeded to offer me less than $22,000 to take over the Orioles. I told Harry I was not interested in the job at that rate. I don't know if I'm a good businessman or if I was indispensable to Harry at that point, but I said I wasn't going to manage for him for less than $28,000. That was what I got on a one-year contract, which would take me into the next season.

I was still probably the lowest-paid manager in the majors, but I couldn't have cared less. I was the manager of a major-league ball club, and I was going to win with it.

At the press conference Harry Dalton cited my record and said, "In short, I think Earl Weaver is a winner. He is very aggressive. He is a battler for the team, a battler for his organization, and a battler for what he thinks is right on the ball club."

I hoped I wouldn't have to battle *with* any of my players, but I knew that the regulars I was going to sit down against certain pitchers were not going to be happy. I called a team meeting and told everyone I thought we had a contending ball club, saying, "I think by scrambling a little more—stealing a base, bunting for a base hit, trying anything that might get us an early run —we may be able to take a little pressure off our pitchers in the early innings." With this in mind I made Don Buford our full-time lead-off man, with Blair sitting down against right-handed pitchers and Blefary against left-handers. And Hendricks would now platoon with Etchebarren.

I looked hard at Curt Blefary when I said he would be a part-timer. Some weeks earlier Bauer had finally benched Blefary for non-hitting. A week or so later I was sitting in my usual spot on the end of the bench when a frustrated Blefary had come clomping down to me. Suddenly he grabbed the front of my shirt and said, "Listen, you little asshole. If you ever become manager of this ball club and don't play me, I'll kill you."

"Settle down, Curt," I had said, removing his hand from my shirt. "You'll probably be in the lineup tomorrow." I had just tried to smooth things over, knowing that kind of talk would not do Blefary or the ball club any good. I liked Curt, who had helped me win a pennant at Elmira four years before. But I wouldn't stand for a repetition of that kind of shit from Blefary now. And I was glad to see he had smartened up because my announcement drew an expression of acceptance, not animosity, from Blefary.

I told everyone that I expected the grumbling that had been so prevalent under Bauer to stop. "My door will be open all the time," I said. "If anyone has a complaint, come see me and we'll talk it over in private."

The only player who walked into my office after the meeting was Frank Robinson. The best player in all of baseball said, "If there's anything I can do to help, let me know." I appreciated that.

I also thought of something. Frank had stopped signing the baseballs which the team used as souvenirs. He'd had an argument with the Oriole executive who was in charge of this bothersome but necessary task. "Frank, the first thing you can do is start signing the balls again," I said. "And if anybody asks you why you're doing that, just tell them, 'I'm helping the ball club. What are you doing to help?'"

Frank went into the clubhouse, sat down at the table on which the boxes of balls were stacked, and began signing. One of the players saw him and said, "What the hell are you doing, Frank?"

"Just trying to help the ball club."

I also posted a sign in the clubhouse that announced a credo of mine: "It's what you learn after you know it all that counts."

That night we were tied with Washington 1–1 in the ninth inning with one out and Frank on third base. Brooks Robinson hit a shallow flyball to left field. Frank tagged up and slid headfirst into home to score the winning run. Dave McNally pitched that game and came to me afterward saying, "I'm not gonna lose another game this season, Earl." He lost one, but finished with a 22–10 record.

Andy Etchebarren was the first player to enter my office with a complaint. "How am I ever gonna make any money in this game if you keep platooning me with Hendricks?" he asked.

"Andy, I ain't worried about you getting a raise," I said. "I'm only worried about you being a catcher on the Baltimore Orioles who contributes to our success. That may not get you more money, but it'll help you keep a job."

I believe in total honesty, and what I said to Etchebarren was the final figure, my guiding philosophy, and it went for every man on the ball club. Etchebarren was among the eight players on the team who, having played for me, were familiar with my philosophy. Although honesty often bruises feelings, it gets everything out in the open and lets every player know exactly where he stands. I placed no restrictions on the players' honesty, either, even though what they might have to say about me would very likely be no more complimentary or considerate of my feelings than my honest assessments of them. I've always felt that players should have the right to express their opinions about the manager. I know that as a player I would have released a lot of inner tension if I had been able to tell certain managers, without fear of retribution, exactly what I felt. I had made a pact with myself from the start of my managing career never to hold a grudge or let a player's personality warp my perception of his abilities.

As Frank Robinson later said, "Nobody can chew you like Earl can chew you, and it's plenty tough to take. But the instant it's over, it's forgotten. The man never carries a grudge. He does the best job of any manager I've ever seen at keeping twenty-five ballplayers relatively happy."

After a few weeks of platooning, Blefary came into my office, closed the door, and said he was sick of it. He had been a regular in 1966 and 1967, had hit forty-five home runs in those two years and felt that there was no longer any point in staying with the Orioles as a part-timer. "I want to be traded, Earl," he said angrily. "The sooner the better."

"If we can make a deal for you that will benefit this ball club," I said, "we will. I don't know if we can do anything until the season ends, Curt. This is an expansion year. But we won't try to hold you back. As I've told you, I'm using you in a way that I think is best for the ball club." Actually, I didn't think Blefary would ever learn to hit left-handers consistently, and I had already thought about trading him, possibly in an off-season deal for a left-handed starting pitcher.

Another system I had introduced when I took over the Orioles was to allow all my pitchers to call their own games. Many years before I had read that Roy Campanella sat down with his pitcher before each game and found out what the man wanted to throw to each batter. Then Roy would call for whatever the pitcher wanted to throw. That made sense to me. The pitcher knows what kind of stuff he's got on any given outing and what should work best on each batter. A catcher might know that a curveball is the best pitch against a certain hitter, but if the pitcher's curveball is hanging high or bouncing in the dirt he's got no chance with the pitch that day. The first year I started managing I told my pitchers to call their own games.

The Oriole pitchers were all for this idea. But a number of them were not as confident with Hendricks behind the plate as they were with Etchebarren. Andy was excellent defensively. They came to me, one after another, and said, "Earl, I'd really like to have Andy catch me. I'm used to him, and he calls exactly the game I want to pitch."

"Well, I can let Andy catch you," I'd say. "But you're gonna lose 1–0 or 2–1 like you were doing before. Aren't you tired of that shit? Ain't it better to get a few more runs and win?"

"Yeah, but it bothers my concentration shaking off Elrod so much."

"Look, you go out there and pitch your game. And don't be blaming that guy behind the plate if he puts down a 2 and you want to throw a 1. Shake him off and throw the 1. I don't want to hear none of this 'I shoulda thrown something else' shit. You throw what *you* want and win some games for us. And Elrod Hendricks will help get you some runs to win with."

When I first started managing in the minors I saw my ball clubs lose a number of games in which I thought of making moves that might have altered the outcome, but I didn't act on my instincts. I soon decided that if I was going to lose, I would rather do so making a move than just sitting there watching the defeat. I arrived in the major leagues bearing the reputation of a strong handler of pitchers, and I was proud of it. I had learned much in this area from two managers for whom I had played, Andy Cohen and George Kissell. Their theory was that you *never leave your starting pitcher in to lose a game* if you can help it. A 1–0 loss, for example, you can't help. But say your guy's pitching a one-hitter in the ninth inning of a scoreless game, he's gotten one out and then there's a bloop hit. You can't pull a pitcher in that situation. But if he gives up a line single, I'll go get him right there except in rare circumstances (such as a next hitter coming up who hasn't hit my guy in their last twenty matchups).

Now, if you go into the ninth with a 2–0 lead and your pitcher walks the first hitter, you've got to make a decision. You know that walking that lead-off man was the last thing in the world the pitcher wanted to do. It tells you he's tired, losing his steam. You go out and see him, and if he insists he's got plenty left, that he can get the next hitter, you may let him pitch to one more batter. Or you may yank him right then because if the next batter can hit one out, you don't want to stay with a man who has pitched a helluva game for eight innings and allow him to end up with a 2–2 tie in the ninth. A tired pitcher is just likely to lay one in there. And if you do give the starting pitcher one more hitter and he gets on—you go right to the bullpen. You don't let the starter pitch to the winning run.

Fans don't understand this move, particularly in Baltimore. They get pissed off when I pull a starter in the ninth. Jim Palmer may have two men on and only one out in a 2–1 game when I go get him, and the fans will boo me. He may be dying out there, his arm hanging, but if I leave him in I'll get a standing ovation. The fans think you're breaking the pitcher's heart. They're sentimental. If I leave him in and we lose, I don't even get booed in Baltimore.

At times I've even heard a lot of noise from the media for relieving a starting pitcher. In a nationally televised Monday night game in July of '79, at Milwaukee Stadium, Steve Stone pitched the finest game of his career to that point—8⅔ innings of 1-hit ball. The only hit was a home run, but Al Bumbry had hit a 2-run homer for us. Stone got the first two outs in the ninth, then suddenly walked Don Money with left-hand-hitting Cecil Cooper on deck. The instant that fourth ball hit the catcher's glove I had left-hander Tippy Martinez on his way in from the bullpen. Tippy got Cooper on a fly to left.

Some members of the media suggested that the removal of Stone when he had a one-hitter and only one out to go for a complete game was precipitous on my part. Others said the move was ballsy. I say the removal of Steve Stone in that situation was the only *responsible* thing to do. It was. We won.

In 1968 I was intent on producing the best record in the American League for the second half of the season. We had an abundance of strong arms in the bullpen—Eddie Watt, Moe Drabowsky, and Pete Richert among them—and I called on them often. Several times I used three separate men to get three outs, which kept everyone sharp.

My nickname became "Captain Hook," and I would not have minded it if I had been called "Captain Bligh" as long as we kept playing solid baseball. Initially, I thought we could catch Detroit after we won our first six games and reduced the Tiger lead to six. But the Tigers had a very strong club and our lack of hitting cost us dearly (we finished with a .225 team batting average). At one point we won eleven of fourteen ball games and *lost* a game in the standings. I kept trying new combinations. My regulars were Frank Robinson, Brooks Robinson, Boog Powell, Dave Johnson, Don Buford, and Mark Belanger. But Mark never got his batting average over .210 all season, and a number of times I played Davey Johnson at short and used Don Buford at second base. Buford became the best lead-off man in the league, batting .282 with 15 home runs and 27 stolen bases. Frank Robinson hit .300 for the balance of the season, yet still ended up with only 15 home runs and a .268 average. The fire with which he played—diving for balls in the outfield, sliding hard on the bases every time out, stealing a base any time we needed a man on second in a late inning—set an example for everyone on the ball club.

I talked with my coaches before and after every game, trying to come up with ways to improve the ball club's performance. I was pleased to have outstanding coaches like Hunter, Bamberger, and George Staller. I had made George my first-base coach when I replaced Bauer.

Hunter told me of his disappointment when he didn't get the manager's job. I said I could understand, Billy having been with the team for over four years. I begged him to stay because I wanted Hunter to be second in command. He agreed to do anything he could for the Orioles, as he always had. He also enjoyed playing pinochle, and eventually we convened a game nightly on the road, though more baseball was talked than cards were played. It was another opportunity for me to hear the views of my staff.

From the start I felt there was no better pitching coach anywhere than George Bamberger. He had pitched in the minors eighteen years and served as the Orioles' minor-league pitching instructor four years. George knew how to throw every pitch, including a knuckleball, screwball, and spitball, though the latter is far easier to hit than legend suggests. The Orioles would have voted unanimously to face any number of spitballs or other "trick" pitches rather than Sam McDowell's fastball that season.

George not only knew all the pitches, but he could teach them. He didn't know anything about Dale Carnegie or the subconscious or the superego. Yet George always found the right words to reach his pitchers. He was such an honest, loving person that most players just opened their minds and accepted his prescriptions.

I would sit down with George and tell him what I wanted, what a given pitcher needed to do, what pitch to improve or add and George would see that it was done . . . at least by those pitchers who were successful. Some pitchers had no discernible subconscious to reach, only a conscious wrapped in stubbornness or self-destructive instincts. My one constant request was based on an unwavering belief in the value of constantly changing speeds: "George, teach him any kind of slow, off-speed pitch. Your slow curveball would be perfect."

Later, after we'd had some success—and Bamberger had seven twenty-game winners in the next three seasons—George would begin a lesson by saying, "Look at how many twenty-game winners we've had here." If the pupil was reluctant and said something like, "I never did that before," George would shrug.

"Well, if you don't want to win twenty, it's all right," he'd say. "If you do, that's all right, too. There are a number of guys here who *do* want to win twenty, though."

My approach with the reluctant was more direct. Say a pitcher wouldn't want to cut his curveball to develop the slider he clearly needed, telling me he had just never done it before. I would reply, "Well you never won twenty games before, you dummy, but you can with this club if you'll listen."

The Oriole front office listened to an idea I'd had for a very long time: I asked that someone start compiling statistics on the performances of all our players against everyone in the league, how each of our pitchers had fared (every pitch thrown) against each batter and how each of our hitters had done against each pitcher. I asked that the stats go back to the preceding season wherever possible. The stats would make selecting a lineup and batting order much simpler and more effective.

By September, having played almost .700 ball, we leveled off in second place ten games behind the Tigers. When we went into Boston for our final series Harry Dalton wanted me to play Larry Haney. The Red Sox were looking for a catcher and Dalton figured that if Haney did well at Fenway Park a good trade could be arranged.

"I don't want to play Haney," I said. "I still have a shot at the best won-lost percentage in the league for the second half of the season."

"Earl, if you want to have the best won-lost record *next* season —play Haney now," Dalton said. "Let's see what we can get for him."

"Ray Culp's pitching for Boston and Haney couldn't hit him in the minors."

"Play him. Anyone can pop one off that Green Monster in Boston."

Dalton, of course, was right in that we didn't have any plans for Haney and the best we could do was try to acquire a player for him. I just couldn't see showcasing a batter against a pitcher he couldn't hit even if the left-field wall was right behind third base. Sure enough, Haney still couldn't do anything with Culp, striking out three times and hitting into a double play. The Red Sox no longer had any interest in Larry Haney.

We finished with a 91–71 record, and I felt we were a much better ball club than that and would show it next season. Frank Robinson, Brooks Robinson, and Boog Powell were all swinging the bat better. Buford and Dave Johnson were very solid hitters, and I figured to get a lot more production out of Hendricks. We had also brought up outfielder Merv Rettenmund from Rochester for thirty-one games and he'd hit .297 with power and played excellent defense. Merv, Blair, and Robinson would give me as good a defensive outfield as there was in the league. Boog Powell lacked a little range at first base, but our infield was superb defensively.

Harry Dalton asked me what we needed to win the pennant in 1969, and I said a solid starting pitcher would do it, in my estimation. He said he'd start working on it right after the expansion draft.

Seattle and Kansas City were coming into the league and we would be allowed to protect only fifteen players from our forty-man roster. When one of our players was selected we could then protect three others, until we lost a maximum of six. Naturally, we put the names of all of our regulars on our protected fifteen, plus a young pitcher named Mike Adamson we were high on and a Triple-A player named Don Baylor who we thought would become a great hitter in two or three years. But I was worried because we had to make available an awful lot of talent, including our best relief pitchers—Watt, Richert, and Drabowsky—plus such future stars as Rettenmund, Bobby Grich, and Jim Palmer. After winning fifteen games for the Orioles in 1966 Palmer had developed arm trouble that he had been trying without much success to overcome ever since. I still break out in a sweat every time I recall that we could have lost a pitcher who went on to win three Cy Young Awards. Drabowsky was our only real loss in the expansion draft.

But I felt we still had a solid bullpen and that we'd gotten off easy. Our top starters—McNally, Hardin, and Phoebus—had won fifty-five games among them and figured to improve. The only concern was Phoebus, whose inability to field or hold runners on base forced me to relieve him in close games even when Tommy still had good stuff. The worst-fielding pitchers usually can throw accurately to a base if they manage to catch a groundball or pick up a bunt. But Tommy tended to get excited and throw the ball past everyone. And he permitted runners to take such long leads that even the lame and decrepit could steal on him.

So we needed another starting pitcher, and the man we wanted was Mike Cuellar of Houston. A sore arm had limited Cuellar to only 171 innings in 1968 and he'd finished with an

8–11 record. But our scouts had watched him closely and said his arm was now sound, as his 2.74 ERA indicated. I had managed against Cuellar in Puerto Rico and had been much impressed with the left-handed technician's ability on the mound, particularly his murderous screwball.

Frank Robinson, who had replaced me as manager at Santurce that winter, also liked Cuellar. Frank had informed me of his interest in the managing job when we were in New York near the end of the season, and I'd told him I would speak to Hiram Cuevas on his behalf. Marianna had joined me for a few nights out in Fun City and we had a dinner reservation at 8 P.M. But I had to stay in the hotel room phoning Cuevas until 11 P.M. before I reached him.

"Here I am," I said to Marianna, "making $28,000 a year blowing a dinner reservation trying to get a winter job for a ballplayer who's making $115,000 a year." Then I winked. "Of course, Frank's worth every penny of that and more because he's gonna help us win the pennant next year."

Frank Robinson wanted the job to begin preparing for a future as a major-league manager, even though no black man had ever been hired for such a position. If that seemed to be a slightly ridiculous circumstance, it was also right in line with the forward thinking that had always been prominent in the upper echelons of baseball. Even my limited exposure to Frank Robinson told me that if he acquired some experience, he could do a good job managing. (I hated to lose Frank as a coach after the 1980 season, but I was happy for him that he did well managing the San Francisco ball club.)

At the winter meetings we traded Curt Blefary to Houston for Mike Cuellar, who would go on to win 23 games and the Cy Young Award in 1969. Blefary was traded to several other teams in the next few years and then dropped out of baseball.

The World Champion Detroit Tigers were favored to win the pennant again in '69, with the power-packed Boston Red Sox picked second by most experts. But I felt that we had the talent to improve enough in every category—hitting, pitching, and defense—to emerge at the top of the final standings. All I had to do was make the most effective use of the available talent, and I went to spring training tingling at the opportunity before me.

I had developed a detailed training schedule over the winter in which every minute of our workouts was utilized and no one had to stand around cooling off and wasting time. I had also drawn up, with the help of my coaches (Hunter, Bamberger, George Staller, and Charley Lau, who replaced Vern Hoscheit), a sort of manager's manual of fundamentals that would be used throughout the Oriole system. We would now teach the same plays—pick-offs, cutoffs, how to defense the bunt, how to defense the double steal, etc.—at every level from the Rookie League to the major-league team. The manual was over a hundred pages long to give you an idea of the details we went into—everything was covered thoroughly, both offensive and defensive plays. We worked harder on defense in the spring because it takes more time to practice all the variables on such plays. Once you can execute these complicated disciplines perfectly, you can use them to get a crucial out that can win a ball game. If you can devise five plays in which you can get, say, three game-winning outs on each over a season, that gives you fifteen ball games that you wouldn't otherwise have won. Fifteen "extra" victories in a season can certainly mean the difference in a pennant race.

I knew one play we were going to learn that would definitely make a difference. Early in the '68 season the opposing team worked a double steal on us that ended up costing us a game, and afterward the Baltimore writers told me they'd never seen the Orioles stop that play. I'm talking about base runners at first and third—the man at first breaks for second, the throw goes down there from the catcher, and the runner at third scores. I was stunned at what the writers had said, but two other times that season teams worked the double steal on us. In high school ball we hadn't made the throw to second, giving up the base to prevent the run. But in pro ball you couldn't afford to concede the opposition an extra base. The problem in the lower minors was that the throw would go to second, the runner at third would dash toward home, and the ball would be thrown back to the catcher too late. The play scored so many runs in the low minors that we came to regard the runner on first base, not the batter, as the RBI threat. Because the runner at first simply had to race toward second, then stop halfway, and even if he was tagged for the final out, the runner at third would have scored beforehand. So the runner at first had, in effect, driven him in.

When I started managing I decided there had to be a way to stop that double steal. The solution was as simple as the execution. When the runner at first broke, I told my catcher to look at third and hold that runner before releasing the ball to second base. If the runner at third didn't stop, the catcher had him cold. If he did stop, the catcher still had time to whip the ball to second and get all but the swiftest runners, and those guys were going to steal second over half the time anyway. So we were conceding nothing. If on the throw to second the runner at third tries to score he won't make it. Once he's stopped, no runner is fast enough to start again and beat a return throw from second.

So we worked on this play for hours in the spring until we perfected it. The first three times opponents tried the double steal on us in season we stopped the run and got the runner from first, once getting a double play.

Then we had a problem on one particular double steal. Ellie Hendricks executed well. As the man at first broke, Ellie glanced at third and held the man there, then whipped the ball down to Davey Johnson at second. The runner, who was fifteen feet from the base, stopped dead to get in a rundown. He hoped that would allow his teammate at third to score before he could be tagged in the rundown for the third out. As Davey chased the runner back toward first, the man suddenly dropped to the ground and the runner on third dashed for home. "Reach down and tag him!" I yelled. But Davey, normally a very heads-up ballplayer, lost his head. He *leaped over his runner* and made an off-balance throw home that was wide of the plate. But from midseason on and for years afterward, no team successfully pulled a double steal on the Orioles.

We also did a lot of work on our rundown plays that spring because they occur so often in games. And I'd seen so many clubs blow them as a result, I felt, of not practicing the numerous complications that turn up. If you don't have good rundown plays that get a man quickly, you can't keep other runners from advancing a base. I followed a Paul Richards' tenet here: You should be able to get a man in a rundown with *one* throw. For example, in picking off a man at first, Boog Powell would chase the runner toward second as fast as he could to drive him toward Johnson. Once the runner was in full flight, Johnson, who had been trotting toward him, would start running. That was Boog's signal to throw him the ball, because Johnson's momentum would carry him right into the oncoming runner, who would be moving too fast to stop and retreat. If the runner was not going at full speed, trying to avoid the trap, Powell would simply fake the throw and make the tag himself. In either case, the out was made quickly and any other runner would have no chance to advance.

We became very proficient at defensing the sacrifice bunt with a man on first and with men on first and second, and we worked hard on our pick-off plays: with a runner on second, with runners on first and second in a sacrifice-bunt situation, and with a runner on first in a sacrifice-bunt situation. The pick-off plays require precise timing.

Say I signaled Brooks that I wanted to try a pick-off at second. He would then relay the signal to everyone else. Or any of the infielders could put on the play themselves by signaling the catcher, who in turn would signal the pitcher. If Belanger rubbed his hand across his chest to start the play, everyone else would signal a response and the pitcher would go into his stretch watching the catcher. The latter would not give the sign for a pitch, but would be awaiting Belanger's move. When the runner edged to his farthest lead, Mark would take two steps in, which cut the distance he had to cover to second without his actually moving toward it. That also told the catcher to flash the sign to the pitcher (by opening his hand) that Mark was about to break for second. When the hand opened, the pitcher would whirl and throw to the base and the ball would arrive there just as Mark did—and before the runner if the deception and timing were crisp.

In my first spring training as a major-league manager I also made clear to everyone my offensive philosophy. Basically, I liked to get a couple-three men on base and have someone hit the ball out of the park. But I knew that some of my beliefs ran counter to those of other managers that my players had known. Some managers liked to try a squeeze bunt or suicide squeeze almost any time they found themselves with a man on third, less than two outs, and a mediocre hitter up. I disagree, because a slow groundball or a flyball can get that run in, so why give up an out when you've got the chance for a bigger inning? I don't believe in giving away an out at any time. (You've only got 27 in a 9-inning game, why cut that number?) The only occasion that might call for a squeeze bunt is late in a game when your hitter is known to strike out a lot against the pitcher on the mound.

The sacrifice bunt should be used very discriminately, too. The fact is that it is easier to score a man from first with no outs than it is to bring him home from second with two outs. I also believe you can score a runner from second with none out easier than you can score him from third with one out. The only time to sacrifice is when the hitter appears to have no chance of advancing the runner.

I do believe in trying to bunt for a base hit. And I told the Orioles when they saw the bunt sign to try and lay the ball down in an area where they could beat the throw to first. If the first baseman and third baseman both charged, the bunt was automatically off and the batter could swing away. You get any kind

of wood on a ball that's driven at a man charging from a corner
—and you are very likely to cause considerable havoc.

Everyone worked very hard in spring training, and I was very
pleased to see that Cuellar looked good and that Jimmy Palmer's
arm was strong again. Winter ball in Puerto Rico apparently had
helped Palmer's back and shoulder ailments. Right after Jim first
suffered those injuries, early in 1967, he'd been sent to me in
Rochester. I knew he had been through hell trying to come back.
I remember one game in Rochester in which we were leading
10–0, then Palmer gave up a hit and two walks. He was tenta-
tive, trying to pitch too fine. Johnny Bench was the next hitter
up and I went out to the mound. "What's the trouble, Jim?" I
asked.

"My arm hurts."

"You want to come out?"

"No."

"Well if your arm's sore and you continue to pitch, it's gonna
hurt. But you gotta get the ball over the plate or they'll score a
lot of runs without a hit. Throw the ball down the middle to this
next guy. If he hits it out of the park, you're still winning. But
we ain't gonna *give* them no runs."

Bench stepped in and hit the ball over the fence. Palmer
blamed me, but I was just trying to make a basic point that applied to him and every other pitcher in the world: If you don't
get the ball over the plate, the batters will keep walking around
and stepping on it.

Palmer had finished the '67 season in Miami and spent all of
'68 in the minors, bouncing from Elmira to Rochester and all the
way down to Miami again. In a total of ten starts he compiled an
0–2 record. But Jim Palmer refused to give up. He had been the
youngest pitcher, at age twenty, ever to throw a shutout in the
World Series when he beat the Dodgers in '66, and he was determined to regain that form.

I was pulling like hell for Palmer, who had a 90-mph fastball
and all the moxie you could want on the mound when he was
right. But I couldn't manage in my first spring the way I wanted
to and did once I had achieved some success. With our spring
games being reported prominently in the Baltimore papers, I felt
I couldn't afford to leave pitchers in to get all their work when

they were giving up a lot of runs. The Orioles attendance had been under 900,000 the last two years. We had to win to draw fans, and a winning record in the spring would stir interest in the season.

In Palmer's initial preseason start, he was pitching into an 80-mph wind, which is standard for Miami in March. Palmer walked the first batter. He walked the second batter. He went to a three-and-two count on the next batter and I was twitching in the dugout awaiting the next pitch. Ball four. "Settle down, Jim!" I hollered. "Get it over."

Then he walked in a run. I shot out of the dugout and ran to the mound. "For chrissake, Jim, throw the ball over the middle and see if anyone can hit it out against this wind. You got to get the ball over the plate."

"No shit, Earl," Palmer said, a phrase I was to hear from him a dozen times over the years.

"No shit, Jim," I said. "How can you be a major-league pitcher if you can't throw it over the plate?"

"Earl, you pitch," he said, turning his glove palm up and offering me the ball.

I didn't take it. I said, "I ain't gonna pitch, Jim. But one thing I know is I got a lotta kids here begging for a chance to get out on this mound. Now you get outta here and I'll bring one in."

I brought in Dave Leonhard, who happened to be a very good friend of Palmer's. Dave threw the ball over the plate, got us out of the inning, and put in a strong four innings. At game's end, Palmer was steaming in the clubhouse. I led him into my office and I called in Leonhard, too.

"Jim, here's a guy," I nodded at Leonhard, "who's begging for a chance to pitch in the big leagues. He knows that to do so you've got to throw the ball over the plate. That's what he did out there."

Poor Dave sat there looking at his friend not knowing what to say as I went on with the same message and watched Palmer become more and more subdued. That may have been one of the few times in our fifteen years together that Jim Palmer said to himself: Earl Weaver's right. I say again: *may* have been. And the run he'd given up that day may have been the only one he allowed all spring. He went on to outpitch everyone in camp and earn a spot in the starting rotation with Cuellar, McNally, and Phoebus.

I also continued to make extensive use of my bullpen once the season opened. But I remember one game in which "Captain Hook" hesitated. With a 4–2 lead in the ninth inning at Yankee Stadium, Palmer gave up a walk, retired the next two hitters, then gave up a single. The left-hand-hitting Jake Gibbs was coming up, and I should have yanked Palmer, who was tired. But Jim had handled Gibbs and I went against my cardinal rule by allowing him to pitch to the potential winning run. Aware of that fact, Jim pitched too carefully and walked Gibbs. I brought in left-hander Pete Richert to face lefty Roy White, who promptly singled to tie the game. We lost in the fourteenth.

I went into the clubhouse muttering to myself and Palmer called across the room, "What's the matter, Captain, got polio?"

Palmer won 9 of his first 11 decisions, then tore a shoulder muscle late in June and had to go on the disabled list for 42 days. In his second start after returning, Jim pitched a no-hitter against the A's and went on to finish with a 16–4 record—the top winning percentage in the league. He couldn't stand losing those four games, which were the result of his injuries or my bad managing, as far as he was concerned.

I finally realized early in the season how to correct something that had bothered me throughout the previous year. Mark Belanger had the best range of any shortstop I'd ever seen when he played for me in the minors. But in Baltimore he had not been executing as many remarkable plays, darting into the hole and making spectacular backhanded stops that would have been beyond other shortstops. Then I saw that our infield grass was so long that hard-hit balls were being slowed just enough so that Mark didn't *have* to lunge and stretch for them. He had too much time to get into position.

I had our groundskeeper mow our infield grass to within an inch of its life. The balls that we hit began shooting through the infield in bunches—and Belanger and Brooks Robinson began making one spectacular stop after another. The opposition would open an inning, say, with a single and a walk. Then there would be a shot hit to third and all of a sudden there was a cloud of dust, Brooks was winging the ball to second, Davey was sending it on to first, and we'd gotten two. Or there was a shot into the hole at short and Belanger glided over and knocked off the lead runner at third so fast that Brooks had a play at first or second. Brooks started three around-the-horn triple plays in four years, from '69 through '73.

Our defense had to be terribly discouraging to opponents and not only in the infield. Paul Blair was regularly taking shots off the top of the center-field wall. And I don't know how many times Frank Robinson read a sinking liner into right, dove six feet through the air, slid on his belly, and snared the ball off the grass.

Frank Robinson was the leader of the club, and he had come all the way back from his physical problems of the previous two years. Nobody has ever had more guts at the plate than Frank, who had resumed the death-defying batting stance he'd always used before suffering double vision. He actually curled his upper body and head over the plate and dared pitchers to hit him. Thirteen of them did so in '69. He usually took it out on the pitcher the next time up.

Frank got off to an incredible start in April, setting what was then a major-league record by hitting 12 home runs in that month's abbreviated schedule. In one doubleheader against the Yankees he went 6-for-8 with 8 RBIs.

He had great, great baseball instincts and tremendous physical attributes that allowed him to do everything right on a ball field. Frank still had very good speed at age thirty-three in 1969, but I would love to have seen him in his early years with Cincinnati. He could steal a base whenever we needed it, and he was almost never thrown out. It's sad to say but Baltimore will never have another Frank Robinson, not only because of his all-round abilities. No one will ever hit 49 home runs in a season in that big ball park, as Frank did in '66.

Frank was also an enormous plus for the ball club because of his manner and attitude. He never bitched or griped and he was always willing to counsel any younger players who sought his advice. At times I know he counseled a few who didn't seek him out when he heard them complaining. "That's enough!" he'd holler. "Don't rock the boat!"

Right after the '69 All-Star break, with the team comfortably in first place, the players decided to mete out a series of funny dollar fines for any indiscretion whatsoever as long as the man who brought the charge had a witness to support it. Naturally the judge was Frank Robinson, who got himself a mop for a judicial wig. He presided and ruled on all cases, no more than three of which were heard on a single night. But all charges went on the calendar and were heard eventually when the court was in session. That was only after victories, of course. And anyone who couldn't prove the charge he brought had to pay the fine.

I was among the first—and most consistently—fined because my coaches ganged up on me. I remember a doubleheader in Cleveland in which I rested Belanger in one game, then put him in for defense in the late innings. Mark made two errors. In the clubhouse afterward the Kangaroo Court was called to order and Billy Hunter stood up and said, "Your honor, I'd like to charge Earl Weaver with misguided managing. He sent in Belanger for defense and Mark made two errors."

"Guilty!" everyone yelled even before Hunter could call his witnesses.

"Earl Weaver, how do you plead?" Judge Robinson asked.

"Guilty as charged, and I'll pay the fine," I said.

The next night Belanger played the entire game without making an error and my fine was returned. But in that game I got George Staller, the first-base coach. We were on the bench with the Indians hitting and when we got the second out Staller started to get up to go to the coaching box. He raised his butt off the bench and reached out a foot to rise when he realized no one else was moving. George snapped his butt back on the bench, but I said to Hunter, "Did you see that, Billy?"

"Oh yeah. He didn't know how many outs there were."

"Make a note, Billy. That'll cost you a buck in court, George," I said.

You could literally be charged and fined for anything, which was why the court was so much fun and a real boost to team spirit and morale. Brooks Robinson was once fined for yawning on the bench.

"Your honor, a major-league dugout, I submit, was not made for sleeping," Merv Rettenmund said. "Players should get their sleep in bed. Yet I saw Brooks yawning on the bench and I have Dave Johnson as a witness."

"Did you see Brooks yawn on the bench?" Frank asked.

"I did, your honor, and it was a huge yawn," Johnson said.

"Brooks, do you have anything to say in your defense?"

Brooks had closed his eyes and was feigning sleep.

The guys even charged one of our radio announcers with making a mistake on the air and to plead his case he sent a "counselor" who was actually a double-talking bartender. The doubletalker rattled on for five minutes and nobody understood a word he said. George Bamberger was sitting next to me asking, "What'd he say? What'd he say?"

In addition to fines, the Orioles also periodically gave out various awards to players for giving up long home runs, for baserunning mistakes, for weak swings . . . We also had the Chico Salmon No-Touch Award for bad fielding plays. Salmon was our all-purpose utility infielder who filled in at all four positions and even provided some offense with his .297 average in 91 at-bats that year. But Chico sometimes had trouble handling groundballs, occasionally not touching them at all. In his very first game in the field for us Salmon made two errors, but he later topped that in a game in Washington. Trailing by a run entering the ninth, Brooks led off with a single and I sent in Salmon to run for him. We went on to score two and take the lead, and Salmon stayed in as Brooks' replacement for the last of the ninth.

Warner Wolf, who is now a $400,000-a-year television sportscaster in New York, was then the play-by-play announcer for the Senators, and his broadcasts were picked up in Baltimore as well. Wolf got very excited. "What's this, what's this?" he cried. "This crazy Weaver's making a defensive replacement for *Brooks Robinson!* I've never heard of anything like this!"

He obviously had not been paying attention, either, which can be said of various members of the media who at times report before they check their facts. I would suggest that it doesn't take an overabundance of common sense to know that *nobody* would replace Brooks Robinson for defensive purposes. But I subsequently received a number of angry letters from Baltimore fans who thought I'd done just that, thanks to keen-eyed Warner.

Anyway, the first ball in the ninth was hit to Chico, who

fumbled it. After we got one out, another grounder skipped down to Chico, and he booted it. We got the second out, and the next batter drove a *shot* at Chico. He scooped up the ball on the short hop as Brooks would have done and threw the man out. Thank goodness. But he was in no danger of having his name removed from the No-Touch Award.

Any player who had a particularly bad night at the plate was eligible for the Weak-Swing Award. It was a broken-off bat handle that, on presentation, often encouraged suggestions from teammates as to where the recipient might store the trophy.

In truth, we had no weak swingers on the '69 Orioles. We increased our team batting average from .225 to .265, our home runs from 133 to 175, our RBIs from 534 to 722, and our runs scored from 579 to 779. Boog Powell was our production leader with 37 home runs and 121 RBIs, followed by Frank's 32 homers and 100 runs batted in.

Every player has at one time or another what we call "a career year," and we had two such players that season, Mark Belanger and Paul Blair. Belanger batted .287 and gave a lot of credit to the instruction he received from coach Charley Lau, who went on to become the best-known hitting coach in the game at Kansas City. But what works for one hitter does not for another. If Charley could teach everyone to hit .300, we would have a lot of awful long baseball games.

Paul Blair hit 26 home runs and would have batted .300 if it hadn't been for a prolonged slump the final month of the season. Everyone rooted and cheered for Paul, one of the most popular guys on the club, and it was extremely depressing observing Paul's facial anguish as his slump reached 3-for-38. Still he finished at .285, and when you added in the 26 homers, 76 RBIs, and a team-leading 20 stolen bases, Paul had a fine season.

Brooks Robinson also concerned me because he kept getting down on himself over his lack of hitting. Brooks was one of the slowest runners in the majors. He and Powell continually competed in the who-will-hit-into-the-most-double-plays? competition. Brooks was the champ even though Boog had to carry some 270 pounds with him from the batter's box to first base. Brooks would come to bat with a man on first and less than two outs and we'd holler, "Uppercut, Brooksie—uppercut!"

Yet Brooks almost never got thrown out stretching a single into a double or a double into a triple. He was an excellent base runner once he got rolling, and he had a keen sense of exactly where a batted ball would land. Brooks was also a tremendous clutch hitter, a guy who batted over .400 through most of his career from the seventh inning on. Nobody was better at driving in a man from second base with two outs. With Frank or Boog coming up behind him, pitchers always challenged Brooks, which amazed me, because he would get his bat on the ball and just stroke it over the infield for the run.

In 1969 Brooks did have a poor average, finishing at .234. The problem with his batting average stemmed partly from his lack of foot speed, which prevented him from beating out infield rollers and high bouncers. But the main problem was that whenever Brooks started slumping he would forget about his strike zone and swing at bad pitches. I mean everything from fastballs at the shoulders to curveballs that broke outside in the dirt. The harder he struggled, the further his average would plummet. Despite this, he still hit 23 homers and drove in 84 big runs.

We also got effective offense out of Don Buford, who batted .291 and scored 99 runs, and Ellie Hendricks, who had 12 home runs while platooning. No doubt our hitting—and everyone else's —benefited from the lowering of the mound and the reduction in the size of the strike zone that season. I felt our pitching staff was markedly improved over the previous year, yet our team ERA increased from 2.66 to 2.83. That was still far and away tops in the majors.

We won the pennant by 19 games, finishing with 109 victories, only 3 less than the major-league record set by the 1954 Cleveland Indians. I really wanted to go for that record, and I'm sure we could have beaten it if I hadn't rested my regulars toward the end of September. This was the first season of divisional play in the majors, and we were concerned about the play-offs and wanted to be certain we had no injured or fatigued players. We felt a three-out-of-five series could be even more hectic, tension-wracked, and demanding than the seven-game World Series. If you stumbled in the latter, you had a little more time to regroup and battle back, as well as call upon all of your depth that had helped you win throughout the season. That's why I think the play-offs should be extended to seven games. A weaker team that has little depth can get hot and win three straight, which is unfair to fans everywhere who expect to see the best team in each league in the World Series. We had a better ball club than the Minnesota Twins, but I went into the play-offs frankly scared.

I was relieved when Twins manager Cal Ermer named Jim Perry as his opening pitcher. Perry had a better record (20–6, 2.94 ERA) than Dave Boswell (20–12, 3.23). But my stats revealed very clearly that Boswell had been much more difficult for us to hit. As Minnesota was primarily a left-hand-hitting team, we would start Cuellar in the first game and McNally in the second, both in Baltimore.

Cuellar didn't have full control of his five pitches—fastball, curveball, screwball, slider, and change—but he gave up only 2 earned runs in 8 innings. The problem was the Twins also scored an unearned run, and we went to bat in the last of the ninth trailing, 3–2. Then Powell led off with a home run, and I finally relaxed a bit and began to feel we *were* going to the World Series. But it wasn't easy. We hadn't hit a ball hard off Ron Perranoski through 3 innings of relief, but Belanger led off our twelfth by singling. Etchebarren sacrificed Mark to second, and Buford moved him to third with a ground-out. Then Blair—whose slump had now reached 3-for-42—laid down a bunt that the Twins couldn't even play. Belanger scored standing up.

The next day it took us only 11 innings to win. McNally, who had thrown a one-hitter against Minnesota while he was winning his first 15 decisions of the season, went all the way and gave up only 3 hits, no runs. Powell led off the eleventh by working Boswell for a walk. Brooks bunted him to second and, after Johnson was intentionally walked, Curt Motton pinch hit and drove in the deciding run.

The following day in Minnesota, Palmer gave up a first-inning run and another in the fifth. It didn't matter. We scored 11 on 18 hits. Paul thumped his slump with a homer and 2 doubles among his 5 hits.

Afterward we had a victory celebration in the clubhouse and learned that the New York Mets had also swept their play-off with the Braves. Good, I thought, the teams with the highest winning percentages in baseball would be meeting in five days to decide the World Championship. We had won nine more games than the Mets during the season; we should win at least one more than them in the postseason.

I didn't think for a moment that the so-called "Miracle" Mets would be easy opponents in the Series. Their pitching was too good, particularly that of Tom Seaver and Jerry Koosman, whom I had managed against in the minors. I remember Seaver's first professional start, for Jacksonville against my Rochester team in 1966. I had figured he would be a cinch, a kid right out of college starting against a top Triple-A club. I couldn't recall anyone having done that successfully.

But it was apparent in Tom Seaver's pro debut that he was ready for the majors. He had an excellent fastball and slider, and he put them precisely where he wanted to, in and out on the black of the plate, mostly knee-high. After Jacksonville beat us, I phoned Harry Dalton and said Seaver was going to be sensational and the Orioles could give up a piece of the franchise and do well to get him. I was right. Seaver had gone 25–7 in '69 with a 2.21 ERA.

Still, we didn't have a lot of trouble with him in the '69 Series opener. In fact, Don Buford hit his first pitch into the stands for a home run and we scored 3 more runs in the fourth. Meanwhile, Cuellar gave up only 1 run and pitched a complete game.

I felt confident going into game two. McNally was starting and he hadn't given up a run in postseason play dating back to the '66 World Series when he'd shut out the Dodgers. But in the fourth inning Donn Clendenon slapped a homer off Dave. And we didn't get a hit off Jerry Koosman until the seventh, when

Blair singled and we managed to eke out a run on a steal and Brooks' single. It wasn't that Koosman was that difficult, because the guys kept saying his stuff didn't compare to Seaver's the day before.

Our problem was not unusual for hitters in play-off and World Series games. They often become overanxious at the plate, especially your stars. They swing at pitchers' pitches instead of waiting for *their* pitches. They try so hard that they're not patient enough to look carefully at a 2–0 pitch or a 3–1 pitch, and they end up grounding out or popping out. Overanxiousness was to plague us through the Series.

We were lucky to be tied in the ninth. But a decision I'd made earlier cost us the game. The decision involved Al Weis, a weak-hitting infielder whom I had known in the minors and whom our scouts had advised us not to walk at any cost. Weis had batted all of .215 that season and if he walked, the pitcher could bunt him over for Tommie Agee, the Mets' RBI leader. So I told our pitchers not to worry about Weis, just fire the ball over the plate on him.

That's what McNally did after the Mets got two men on in the ninth—and Weis promptly singled in the winning run. That was the sixth hit off McNally. The hard-hitting Baltimore Orioles had 2 hits.

Still, we went up to New York feeling we'd take game three. The Mets were starting Gary Gentry, a rookie right-hander with a good breaking-ball, but one that could be timed, according to our scouting reports. They also said his fastball was not overpowering; he wouldn't get it by us.

Then the game started and Gentry's fastball crackled. It was one of those outings which a pitcher has once a season or maybe once a career—when his fastball suddenly has an extra three- or four-mph velocity and it moves up or down at the last moment, hopping crazily and keeping hitters off-balance.

Jim Palmer, our starter, had a good fastball too, but he was a little wild and gave up a run in the first. Then, trying to find his rhythm and control, Jim lightened up a bit in the second with two men on base and Gentry at bat, and the pitcher doubled in a pair of runs.

We didn't mount a threat until the sixth inning, when Gentry seemed to be losing some velocity. We got two men on and Ellie Hendricks lined one deep to center field that appeared to be a sure double high off the wall. But the wind was whipping in from left to right, and it held up the ball just long enough for Tommie Agee to race over and made a spectacular catch banging off the wall, and the Mets got out of the inning.

The next inning we loaded the bases with two out and Mets manager Gil Hodges replaced Gentry with a kid named Nolan Ryan, who blew two fastballs by Blair. Ryan had as much speed as I'd seen since Dalkowski. But Blair hung in there and connected with a fastball that leaped off his bat toward right center. Agee moved quickly to his left, but this time the wind kept driving the ball away from him. At the last instant he dove, the ball struck his glove, he tumbled over, and held on. Gil Hodges, who seemed to spend a lifetime in World Series with the Brooklyn Dodgers, said that those two Agee catches were the best he'd ever seen in Series play.

We couldn't touch Ryan in the last two innings. We had exactly 4 hits on the day and a 5–0 loss.

In the fourth game against Seaver we didn't do much better at bat, getting only 6 hits. But the reason our Series losses reached three had less to do with a player than with an umpire. Shag Crawford, the man behind home plate, literally stole that game from us.

I feared we might have some serious problems with Crawford, a National League umpire, when I first met him. That was in the suite of offices of Bowie Kuhn, the Commissioner of baseball, just prior to the Series. It was a meeting he holds annually with the managers from each team in the Series, as well as the six umpires, to clarify all the rules. During the meeting the Commissioner said he expected the umpires to make every effort not to throw anyone out of a game. This was baseball's annual showcase and certain rules could be bent in the interest of harmony. In the World Series, for instance, there is no time limit between pitches, and a manager can go to the mound more than once in an inning without having to remove his pitcher, as he has to during the regular season.

But when Kuhn asked that the umpires be patient with the players and their complaints, Shag Crawford popped to his feet and said, "What if Frank Robinson calls somebody a mother-bleeper?"

I was speechless, a rare occurrence indeed, and the entire room went momentarily silent. Even the Commissioner was taken aback. But he finally said, "Well, if anything like that should happen the man should be ejected."

"Excuse me, Commissioner," I said, holding in my anger. "I've never heard Frank Robinson use that word or say anything like that. I don't know what he was like in the National League, but Frank's never called anyone such a thing in the American League. So I don't know what that question was about."

I looked at Shag Crawford, who was obviously not pleased with my remarks. And I had no idea what he had against Frank, but it was something that had to have happened over four years before when he last played in the National League. For an umpire to hold something in his mind that long did not speak well of him or bode well for us.

Game four was the first in which Crawford was the plate umpire, and it was immediately apparent that the calling of balls and strikes was not his forte. In the second inning Cuellar had a 1–2 count on Clendenon, then came in with a third strike that Crawford called a ball. Hendricks, who was catching, protested and everyone on our bench hollered, too. When Clendenon hit the succeeding pitch into the bullpen, we really gave it to Crawford, saying the call he'd missed had cost us an out and a run. We were all shouting, as I said, because that is the Orioles style; if everyone is up the umpire can't single out one man. Crawford, in turn, gave us a long, hard look that seemed to say, "Keep it up, and you guys will pay."

Belanger opened the top of the third for us and fouled off a pitch, then took one that was no more than six inches off the ground. Crawford threw up his right hand and stared into our dugout as he hollered, "Strike!"

Again our dugout erupted in protest. Ellie Hendricks, still furious over the Clendenon call, was most vehement, out-yelling everyone. Crawford strode toward our dugout waving his finger. Not wanting to lose Hendricks, I hustled over in front of him. "That's enough, Ellie," I said to him, then I shouted at Crawford, "I guess we're not gonna get that pitch all day." I stepped out of the dugout to protect my players as Crawford said something. In all the noise from the Mets' fans, I didn't hear Crawford's words (though after the game he said the words were, "You better shut your goddamn mouth or out you go"), and when he turned back toward home I followed him to find out what he'd said.

"Shag," I called.

Crawford kept walking to the plate and I followed.

"Shag," I called again, and this time he turned around.

"You're out of the game for arguing balls and strikes."

I couldn't believe it, particularly after the Commissioner's request. No manager had been ejected from a World Series in thirty-five years; it just wasn't done unless there was some incredible provocation.

"I'm not arguing balls and strikes," I said. "I'm out here trying to find out what you said to our bench."

"You've heard all you're gonna hear," he said angrily. "Now get out of here."

"Well it looks like you're making us pay, all right," I hollered. "You've been out to get us from the beginning of this Series and you're doing it. And you may be showing me up right now, but in the long run you're showing up yourself."

I walked back to the dugout with my head up but my heart down around my great toe. It was the most embarrassing moment of my entire career, heading toward the runway before over 57,000 people in the stands and millions more watching on television. As player and manager I had been thrown out of a lot of ball games, including four that season, but never had I been ejected in such a manner before. It was a disgraceful performance by a major-league umpire, and the Commissioner couldn't have been too pleased by it because I wasn't even reprimanded.

But I had to watch the rest of the game on television in the clubhouse, and I kept thinking: I knew there were one or two umpires who were known to make revenge calls against people or teams that had offended them. In fact, that very season an umpire had done just that in our favor. He got mad at a player who was coming to bat against us, so he told our catcher, Clay Dalrymple, to sit on the outside of the plate. Clay, being no dummy, then called for outside pitches—six inches outside the plate. One, two, three pitches later and the umpire had called the batter out. Yet I still couldn't get over the fact that an umpire had made a revenge call in a World Series.

Billy Hunter took over the club in my absence and made every move I would have. In the ninth we rallied to get men on first and third with one out when Brooks came up and drilled a low liner into right field. Ron Swoboda, who was never known for his defensive ability, ran hard to his right for the ball, which appeared to be a certain hit. At first it looked like Swoboda was trying to backhand the ball on a bounce. Then he suddenly dove and with his body fully extended tried to catch the ball in the air. Somehow he backhanded the ball inches off the ground. It was one of the best plays any outfielder anywhere will ever make, and I could hardly believe it as the television replay was run over and over. We got a tie as the runner on third tagged and scored, but we should have had two runs.

Eddie Watt shut down the Mets and we failed to score in the top of the tenth. Hunter brought in Dick Hall to pitch the bottom half of the inning. Jerry Grote popped a high fly to left that Don Buford thought would carry deep, so he backtracked and then lost the ball in the sun. It dropped well in front of him.

With Rod Gaspar running for Grote on second, I sent word to walk Al Weis. He had been on base seven times in three games. And the intentional walk gave us a potential force at any base. Hodges sent up a left-handed pinch hitter, J. C. Martin, and Hunter countered with our ace left-hander in the bullpen, Pete Richert. We expected the sacrifice bunt, as that had been a key to the Mets' offense all season. Ellie Hendricks swears that Martin announced the bunt when he stepped into the batter's box, saying to Shag Crawford, "Give me the line." Ellie may have misunderstood Martin's words, but I have to believe Hendricks was quoting accurately in light of what followed.

Sure enough, Martin bunted down the first-base line. Richert got over quickly, but his only play was to first. Richert threw the ball and it hit Martin on the inside of his left wrist because Martin was running—*illegally*—well inside the base line to first. The ball rolled in to right field, and Gaspar scored all the way from second.

As I screamed at the TV screen—which indisputably showed

Martin running out of the base line—Hendricks heatedly protested to Shag Crawford and Hunter ran out trying to get the umpire to call interference. But hundreds of Mets fans had poured onto the field and Hunter never even got to Crawford, who took off. It takes special guts to call that interference play, which is missed often enough in season, but a World Series umpire should have the guts . . . or another profession.

At game's end Dalton protested to the Commissioner's office, sending along a newspaper photo showing Martin running out of the base line in violation of the rules, but nothing could be done despite the evidence. It was a judgment call.

We were beginning to suspect that the fates, gremlins, and even the Good Fairy were aligned with the Mets against us. But in spite of our 1–3 record, I pointed out to the team that we had won three straight games seventeen times during the past season and that we had lost four in succession only once. We were starting McNally, who had pitched very well in the 2–1 loss in game two, against Koosman, who had pitched well against us yet had needed two superb catches to win.

McNally shut out the Mets through two innings, then came to bat in the third with Belanger on first base. I knew the Mets expected a bunt and would therefore come in with high fastballs, the toughest pitches to lay down. McNally could hit the hell out of a high fastball, so I flashed the hit sign to Hunter, who relayed it. The left-handed Koosman, who could have handled the left-hand-hitting McNally with breaking stuff, threw a high hard one that Dave ripped over the right-field fence. We added another run on Frank's homer to take a 3–0 lead.

In the fifth Frank Robinson was hit on the left thigh with a sharp-breaking curve, but plate umpire Lou DiMuro ruled it a foul ball. I ran out to protest and asked him to get the opinion of another umpire.

"Earl, if I hadn't seen it hit the bat first, I'd ask. But since I feel like I saw the ball hit the bat, I'm not going to ask."

The ball never came close to the bat, but there was nothing I could do. I didn't want to watch another World Series game in the clubhouse. Frank made out and came into the dugout threatening to lower his pants to show his bruised thigh. We got a subsequent hit before the third out and I kept thinking we should have scored another run.

In the bottom of the next inning, McNally broke off a curveball that hit Cleon Jones on the foot and the ball bounced into the Met dugout. "Ball!" DiMuro called. But Hodges came out of the dugout bearing a ball smudged with shoe polish, which he showed DiMuro. He awarded Jones first base.

I ran out like a shot and said, "Lou, you called it a ball."

"I didn't see it."

"But you didn't see the ball hit Robinson and you called it against us. Now you didn't see the ball hit Jones and you still call it against us!"

He said he had seen the first and he had reversed his decision after seeing evidence on the second. I said, "But you weren't watching the ball when it went into the dugout. They could have rubbed shoe polish on any ball and brought it out here."

"Earl, I watched the ball all the way. The ruling stands."

I had been watching DiMuro, and he hadn't watched the ball in the dugout. He had no reason to because he had not known that Jones had been hit. Anyway, Jones was on first when Clendenon stepped in and hit a home run, his third in the Series, to win the MVP award given by *Sport* magazine. The next inning Al Weis (who else?) hit the only home run of his career in Shea Stadium to tie the score and earn major-league baseball's Babe Ruth award as Series MVP. I always felt Al should have sent me a thank-you note for that.

In the eighth we gave up two doubles, made a couple of errors and lost the game and the Series, 5–3. The Miracle Mets had beaten the best team in all of baseball because *they* had become the best team in baseball for four successive games by taking advantage of situations far better than we had. They got some breaks and used every one of them, which is what winning ball clubs do. They waited for their pitches and we did not. Baseball is a game of attitude and poise and the frame of mind you bring to the ball park; how much you want to play determines how well you'll do. No teams ever brought more enthusiasm to a Series than the Baltimore Orioles and the New York Mets did in 1969. But they scored 15 runs and we scored only 9. Our team batting average was a pitiable .146. With a lot of good pitching and a modicum of help from the Good Fairy, the Mets won the World Championship.

The loss didn't sit well on my stomach, and when I got home I threw up. Then I began thinking about the next season and how we were going to win it all.

And almost immediately the requests to speak at banquets started pouring in. It seemed that the losing manager in the Series, at least if he was a short, fat, funny man, was very popular. At $300 an appearance, I took every banquet I could fit in, and Marianna and I hopped around to over twenty of them in the month of January. That money combined with the nice raise the Orioles gave me made me feel, for the first time in my life, like one of the well-to-do.

We played equally tough baseball in 1970, winning 40 of the 55 games we engaged in that were decided by one run. All told we won 108 games, finishing 15 ahead of the Yankees. In the second half of the season I again cautioned everyone to avoid taking chances that might result in injuries. Naturally, that advice didn't mean anything to Frank Robinson.

In one game at Boston, we were losing 7-0 going into the sixth inning. Then Frank led off with a home run and we kept battling to score four more. In the ninth we tied the game at 7-7 and that score held into the thirteenth. Reggie Smith led off for the Red Sox, and Frank shaded him toward the line to prevent an extra-base hit. Smith lashed a shot down the line that looked like a home run. But Frank roared back, leaped, smashed into the wall, and made the catch. I told the writers later: "It's just such plays that give you an idea of what being super is all about."

But when Frank came down with the ball he lay on the field for five minutes grimacing and trying to regain his breath. I was scared silly. Although he stayed in the game, I later found out he was in severe pain from back spasms.

We loaded the bases in the fourteenth. Then Frank went up and, though I didn't know it, he couldn't even swing a bat. So he laid down a perfect bunt against a drawn-in infield, beat it out, and drove in what proved to be the winning run. That was the first time in his thirteen years in the major leagues that he had ever bunted. Still, whatever it took to win a ball game was what

Frank Robinson would do. I was damn happy that the back injury was not serious.

I had another little run-in that season with Lou DiMuro in Chicago, an incident I mention only because it shows that umpires are sometimes consistent. On a 2–2 pitch, Gail Hopkins of the White Sox clearly turned over his wrists swinging at the next pitch, but DiMuro ruled that he had held up. I ran out and asked him to check with first-base umpire Jerry Neudecker, who should have had a better view of the swing.

"I saw the play perfectly," DiMuro said. "I will not ask."

"It's just like last October," I said. "You won't ask for help." I went back to the dugout and continued to remind DiMuro that everyone could use a little help occasionally. A few pitches later he ejected me from the game. I ran out to ask him what I had supposedly said that was cause for me to be thrown out. But halfway there I was hit by a bolt from the blue. I hurried back to the dugout and asked for a ball, which was tossed to me. Then I ran back and asked DiMuro what I had said. When he had no logical answer, I reached down with the ball and rubbed shoe polish on it, then placed it at DiMuro's feet.

"Earl, you can take that ball and stick it," he said as I headed back toward the dugout.

DiMuro picked up the ball and flung it in my direction. It sailed over my shoulder and bounced off Billy Hunter's chest. He threw it back at the umpire but missed. Lou later told the writers that he was wrong to throw the ball, an honest admission. "That World Series gripe is old stuff," he said. "Umpires are supposed to forget past incidents and bear no grudges. Players and managers are supposed to do the same."

I told the writers, "We should all try to learn from our mistakes."

Our leading hitter in 1970 was again Boog Powell, whose 35 home runs and 114 RBIs earned him MVP honors. Brooks drove in 94 runs and Rettenmund batted .322 in 106 games platooning with Buford. Our pitching was again solid, with Cuellar and McNally winning 24 games apiece, Palmer winning 20, Hall winning 10 in relief, and Richert and Watt combining for 25 saves. We closed the season with 11 successive wins and went on to sweep the Twins again in the play-offs. Their pitching staff, with the exception of Jim Perry, whom we almost always hit, was hurting severely. We scored 27 runs in 3 games as Powell, Buford, Frank Robinson, Johnson, and even Cuellar homered. Dr. Longball held consistent office hours for us.

We were going up against a power team in the World Series, the Big Red Machine from Cincinnati, led by the home-run trio of Johnny Bench (45), Tony Perez (40), and Lee May (34). They had 381 RBIs among them. The Reds were the opposite of the Mets, against whom you worried about only one man, the pitcher. The Reds' pitching was anything but overwhelming, though the rest of their lineup certainly was, and odds-makers favored them in the Series.

I decided to open with Palmer against Cincinnati's right-handed power. He had been our best pitcher in the play-offs, and if the Series ran 7 games he would get 3 starts. Before the game, writers asked me how we felt about playing on artificial turf (no American League team had installed it yet). We had better infielders, so I said, "The turf won't bother us as much as the white houses beyond center field in Baltimore will bother the Reds." A little psychology can be fun at times.

Palmer's control was inconsistent initially as he gave up a homer to Lee May and three runs in as many innings. But Powell hit one out after Blair singled in the fourth, and Hendricks hit another off Gary Nolan in the fifth. I felt everyone was heeding my advice to wait patiently and not be overanxious. Brooks did just that in the seventh, hitting another shot that cleared the fence and put us ahead to stay.

The greatest play of the game was a diving stop Brooks made on Lee May, but the most interesting play was one in which Bernie Carbo tried to score from third on a ball hit off the plate that caromed high into the air. Plate umpire Ken Burkhart, unsure whether the ball would come down fair or not, positioned himself inside the base line as Hendricks looked straight up watching the ball's descent. Ellie caught the ball and dove just as Carbo came flying past from third. Burkhart was caught in the middle, but as he fell he saw Hendricks touch Carbo with his catcher's mitt and shouted, "Out!" Actually, Ellie still had the ball in his right hand.

Reds manager Sparky Anderson protested to no avail. That was fair enough as far as I was concerned. If Burkhart had not been in the way, Hendricks would have easily tagged Carbo, who never touched the plate anyway. And after those Shaggy calls in the Mets Series, I felt the fates might now be starting to swing toward us.

Cuellar started the next game, but it was cool and dreary in Cincinnati and Mike needed to break a sweat to get his screwball working. An error by Belanger led to three unearned runs in the first. Two innings later Bobby Tolan homered and Cuellar walked Bench. With May coming up, I brought in Tom Phoebus. May hit a rocket on a hop to third. Brooks lunged, speared it, and fired to Johnson at second, who relayed to Powell to take us out of the inning. Another standard Brooks spectacular; one of many that would combine with his .429 batting average to make him the Series MVP.

Boog started our fourth with a homer off Jim McGlothin, and the next inning we scored five runs. The final was 6–5, and we returned to Baltimore elated.

McNally pitched and batted us to a 9–3 win in game three. For the second year in a row he hit a homer off a high fastball in the World Series, the first grand slam ever by a pitcher in the Series. The Cincinnati scouting reports on McNally-at-the-bat weren't any more helpful than ours had been the previous year on Al Weis.

With Palmer going for us the next day, the Orioles to a man felt we were going to sweep in four and have our victory celebration that night. The champagne was on ice and our best right-hander was on the mound. But we lost 6–5.

I went into the dressing room with a sinking feeling in my stomach, and on the drive home that evening I actually felt queasy. One thought kept reverberating through my mind: The Reds are going to win it. Somehow I couldn't shake my conviction that everything pointed to them. Cuellar would be up again, and he hadn't looked good against either Minnesota or Cincinnati, the October weather being a definite disadvantage because of his need to break a sweat to be effective. Today's weather had been cool and dank, and the prediction for tomorrow called for more of the same. Shit. And despite our 3–1 lead we hadn't exactly throttled the Cincinnati power, the Reds having averaged over 4 runs a game off my 20-game winners and crack bullpen.

I had a few cocktails, ate dinner, then went to bed early, trying to still my mind. But the depressing thoughts kept compounding and ballooning and throwing me from one side of the bed to the other. I don't think I slept two hours. Finally, at dawn I gave up and arose. I couldn't even eat breakfast. After two cups of black coffee I jumped into the car and headed for the stadium.

I walked into the clubhouse expecting to have to turn on lights in the empty cavern. But several players were already there, among them Jim Palmer. He came right over to me. "Look," he said, "I know we're going to win today. But if we don't win it today, McNally will win it. You can bet your life on this. If neither Mike nor Dave win it, we'll win it in seven—because the Reds have scored their *last* run off me."

Well that sure as hell got rid of my negative thoughts! If Jimmy's words weren't enough, the comments from the players filtering in restored my confidence. "Final game," they said. And, "Today's the day." And, "Celebration tonight."

I stepped out on the field and it was overcast, but the temperature was headed for the low 70s and it was humid. As Cuellar took the mound I kept praying, "Break a sweat, Mike!"

But in the first inning Mike gave up 2 runs in between getting 2 outs, then gave up another single that scored a run. I think everyone expected me to go and get Cuellar and I carefully considered it. But Mike's stuff wasn't bad, two of the hits had been on damn good pitches and the next hitter up was not May, Bench, or Perez. Tommy Helms, a .237 hitter with little power, was up with a man on first. I bet Helms couldn't bring him around. Mike got a ground-out.

Then Mike, furious for the first time in the two years he'd been with me, stormed into the dugout and fired his glove against the wall. He was angry with himself, which was fine. Even more important were the beads of sweat standing on his forehead. All right! I had a feeling right then that Mike Cuellar and his five pitches were going to shut out the Reds the rest of the way. He did.

Frank Robinson stepped in with Blair on and hit a fastball

into the left-field stands, his second homer of the Series. In the next inning we added 2 more runs and another pair in the third. By the ninth our lead had grown to 9–3, and I said to myself, "Well what do you know, we're finally going to win it all!"

At game's end we let out a cheer and rushed into the clubhouse, where I hugged my father. I felt as much pride for him as the glowing pride for me that covered his face. The clubhouse was a madhouse of newspaper and television and radio people. They cornered me and fired questions which I answered for some 20 minutes. Unable to sit still any longer, I excused myself and said I would be back in a few minutes. It took longer than that for me to push through the mob of media and friends and major-league baseball officials as I made my way to each of my grinning, yelping, champagne-soaked players. But I had to thank every one of them for the way they had performed for me ever since I had been named manager of the Baltimore Orioles. Those two-and-one-half years had gone so fast, yet that July day in 1968 seemed so long ago.

After I had let each player know how grateful I was, I turned back to the press in my office. Then I saw several players grab Harry Dalton and, letting out shrieks, lift and carry him at chest height, his body parallel with the floor, toward the trainer's room. Arms immediately encircled my chest and legs, and as I was carried through the doorway I saw Dalton being tossed into the whirlpool tank. I was laughing—until I joined him in that water in which the champagne had been chilled.

But I popped up laughing even louder. I grabbed Dalton's hand and shook it, then saluted the players. They had made a short, fat, sassy, weak-armed former second baseman the happiest man on earth.

Earl "Class A tops" Weaver was a goddamn World Champion!

The 1970 World Series film appropriately highlighted the half-dozen or more splendid plays that had been turned in by Brooks Robinson, though those of us who witnessed his performance every day every season were not moved to extended bravos. We were spoiled.

Some writers felt the way the film had been edited made it look more like the Reds lost than the Orioles won, and they cited the fact that Sparky Anderson's comments were heard while not a syllable was heard from Earl Weaver. Well I had agreed to allow the film's producers to "wire" me for the Series only because the Commissioner thought it would benefit baseball. I said at the time that I did not think America was ready for my dugout vocabulary, adding that I was not about to change anything for anyone. Actually, I had tossed in a few extra dirty words because the producers like to include your dumb remarks as "entertainment."

The Associated Press Manager of the Year poll was won by Ralph Houk of the Yankees, who finished 15 games behind us. Many writers said I had been slighted, and I tended to agree. Two pennants in a row wasn't bad, and I must have been doing something right to win all those 1-run games.

I remember when Ted Williams had been named Manager of the Year in 1969 after moving the last-place Senators up to fourth. Ted said, "Those guys who voted must be some kind of nuts. Fourth place ain't even in the first division. There's not a nickel's worth of World Series money below third." There was no arguing with that logic. It seemed to me that winners should get the recognition. Of course, I figured that if I kept winning I had to receive some recognition eventually. Winning was the only thing I was really concerned about anyway. I now feel that only the four managers who win their divisions should even be eligible for Manager of the Year honors. Any manager who gets his club into the play-offs after 162 ball games has done the right thing day in and day out. The guy who doesn't win his division has not done everything he could have. The first time I won *The Sporting News* Manager of the Year award, which is voted by my fellow managers, I felt pretty good. Then I said to myself: Shit, this don't mean anything because you didn't even win your division in 1977.

Some newspapermen had begun calling me a "push-button" manager, and Curt Gowdy commented in the World Series film, "Once again Earl Weaver pushed the right button." That push-button label had annoyed me at first because I felt it tended to demean me. Then I recalled that the last man known as a push-button manager was the Yankees' Joe McCarthy. Exclusive company, I decided. More important: What else is a good manager but a guy who pushes the button that gets the right player into the ball game at the right time. That is simply the player best suited to accomplish what needs to be done to assure victory in a given situation, whether it be a pinch runner who can beat the double play or get you an extra base, or a pinch hitter who can deliver the runner, or a defensive replacement who can make the tough catch, or a relief pitcher who can get the big out.

A manager's daily job begins, of course, with the selection of his starting lineup. In 1970 I had gone through one stretch of more than 40 ball games in which I'd had a different lineup every day. Before every game, public relations director Bob Brown gave me a statistics sheet that showed in detail how each of my players had fared against the opposing pitcher. That was why Frank Robinson sometimes batted third, sometimes fourth, and at other times fifth, interchanging with Boog and Brooks on the basis of past performance and my desire to reduce our chances of hitting (Boog and Brooks) into double plays. If Frank had trouble with a certain pitcher, I would bat him ahead of

Boog. If the pitcher was a guy Frank handled, I'd put Boog ahead of him.

But I believe it is very important to play all of your ballplayers as much as possible, and right from the start of the season. The more they play, the less rust they'll have on them. You don't manage against opposing managers but against their bench, and by keeping all your tools honed you are in a better position to counter that bench. I recall something Frank Robinson said because it was a nice tribute from a star to a manager. "Earl Weaver knows how to use twenty-five men and get the most out of twenty-five," Frank said. "He isn't afraid to use the twenty-fifth man, and he isn't afraid to make a move because he might be criticized for it." I wasn't afraid of being criticized as much as I was afraid of losing my job if we didn't win. With a one-year contract, job security was not among my assets.

Our power fell off a bit in 1971 as we hit 21 fewer home runs and scored 50 fewer runs than we had the year before. But we had four 20-game winners in Cuellar, Palmer, McNally (21), and Pat Dobson, whom we'd acquired in a trade. And we again won over one hundred games (101), finishing 12 games ahead of Detroit.

We played good but not great ball the first seven weeks of the season, then there was an incident that really ignited us. Don Buford, after hitting two home runs in the second game of a doubleheader in Chicago, was drilled in the back the next time up by a fastball from Bart Johnson. Don charged the mound with the bat in his hand, but we all ran out there so fast that no blows were struck and both players stayed in the game. When Don went to left field in the bottom of the eighth inning, all kinds of garbage sailed out of the stands at him. Then, while Don was in the on-deck circle in the ninth, a fan in a box seat began calling Buford the most abusive names. As Don went over and challenged the man, another fan jumped on the field from the third-base side and attacked Don from behind. The entire Oriole bench went after that guy. He was escorted out of the ball park and Don was ejected—and I didn't mind getting him off the field at that point. We scored 5 runs in that inning and proceeded to win 9 games in succession. On June 5 we moved into first place and stayed there.

Before our next game against the White Sox after Buford had been plunked, I was asked if the Orioles might just accidentally hit one of their batters. I said no, our organization is adamantly against throwing at hitters. A baseball thrown at speed is a lethal weapon, and I could never live with myself if I were responsible for a ballplayer being injured. I never believed in trying to intimidate batters, and I still remember what it felt like to get hit in the head. The only time I ever asked a pitcher to brush back—not hit—a batter was when I managed Elmira in 1962. We chased Williamsport from a distance all season, and a major reason for that was Richie Allen. He crowded the plate much like Frank Robinson and there was no way to pitch to Allen. So I told pitcher Herm Starrette to move Allen off the plate. Starrette pitched him too far inside and nailed Allen in the back. Richie charged the mound, but catcher Andy Etchebarren wrapped his arms around him from behind. Allen flexed his arms and popped the six-foot-one, 200-pound Etchebarren off him like Killer Kawowski breaking a bear-hug. The delay averted a fight, thankfully, and from then on we tried to pitch around Allen and his 500-foot home-run power.

But a manager has to find ways to keep opponents from throwing at his players. Since I refuse to retaliate in kind, I insist that the umpires put an end to this dangerous practice. You can't afford to lose a player. That's why Kansas City manager Jimmy Frey got so upset in the 1980 World Series when a pitch went right at George Brett's head. I still don't know how Brett got out of the way. Jimmy ran out and made such a scene protesting to the plate umpire that the Phillies couldn't possibly go way inside on Brett again. That's how Jimmy and I, who worked together for years, both handle that situation because neither of us would ever tell a pitcher to throw at anyone.

I remember when Billy Martin charged that I had ordered Jim Palmer to throw at a Yankee batter, but those were just words. Billy knows me better than that. The incident occurred in 1976, the one year we had Reggie Jackson. Dock Ellis of the Yankees hit him under the eye with a fastball and sent Reggie to the hospital. I was incensed, but I wasn't at all sure that Ellis had thrown at Reggie and the umpires didn't report any intent. Still Jim Palmer, who was on the mound for us, was so angry that he hit Mickey Rivers in the shoulder the next inning. Now Jim did not throw his good fastball at Rivers. While I did not condone Palmer's action, the pitch was more a warning, a gesture.

Jim was fined $500 by Lee MacPhail and accepted it without protest, saying, "I don't believe in throwing at batters, and the only reason I did it was to protect my teammates. But I know two wrongs don't make a right."

No outstanding batter in the history of major-league baseball was hit by more pitches (198) than Frank Robinson. He took care of those pitchers himself by hitting the hell out of them. Frank refused to back off the plate for anyone. In 1970 the Brewers acquired a big relief pitcher named Bob Bolin from the Giants. Bolin had thrown hard at everyone in the National League for eight years. I wasn't looking forward to my players having to face him, and I think the first man to do so was Frank. He simply put on one of the special helmets with a flap that covered his left cheek and took his regular stance with his head sticking over the plate. If Bolin had hit him, there would've been a helluva fight. The Oriole players had decided to straighten out this guy right away. And Bolin threw no beanballs, thanks to Frank.

Frank Robinson had another fine season in 1971 and extended his achievements in baseball's annals. He was the MVP in the lone All-Star Game victory I managed, as Frank became the only man ever to homer for each league in the annual affair. Although free agency makes it possible, I doubt that there will ever be another player who earns MVP honors in both leagues, in the All-Star Game, and in the World Series as Frank did. I was so pleased when he made the Hall of Fame in 1982.

On September 13, 1971, in a doubleheader at home, with fans yelling, "Hit it now!" on every pitch, Frank joined ten other players who had hit 500 home runs in the majors. He hit number 499 in game one before 13,000 fans (the Orioles were not what you could call "a big draw" then) and number 500 before perhaps 800 spectators who hung in until almost midnight. A seminarian in the left-field stands caught the historic ball and kindly returned it to Frank. He hadn't saved many balls over the years, though he did have one autographed by Stan Musial. "Maybe I kept that one because I always thought Musial was the greatest player I'd seen," Frank said. But if I had my choice between a young Stan Musial and a young Frank Robinson, I'd have to go with Frank.

Duplicating the previous year's finish, we won our final 11 games. We also swept the play-offs for the third successive year, this time beating Oakland.

The odds-makers favored us over Pittsburgh in the World Series, and I heartily agreed. "I've got the best damn ball club in the universe," I told the press. A writer mentioned the push-button label I'd been given, and I laughed. "I've got *too* good a ball club," I said. "It just keeps winning. I've heard it said that anyone can manage this team. That's fine with me . . . as long as I get the check."

Dave McNally's wildness and throwing errors by him and Belanger helped give the Pirates 3 unearned runs in the second inning of the opener. Frank got 1 back with a home run. In the third Belanger and Buford singled ahead of Merv Rettenmund's shot into the stands. McNally then settled down and retired 21 of the last 22 batters he faced. The final was 5–3, our third victory in our last four games by that score.

It was a good omen, we felt. Baseball players love finding good omens because they are the most superstitious group in the world. For example, George Bamberger and I always alternated carrying the lineup card up to home plate, the winner doing so until he lost. We had now won 15 in a row, so George would again deliver the card to the umpires in the next game. I had been making out the lineup with a blue pen all through the streak and would continue to do so until we lost.

In those days I wore the same uniform throughout a winning streak. But the accumulated grundge finally forced me to change everything except my outer socks. Now I'll stay with those baseball socks even when we lose if we play well. Once we play bad ball, all the outer socks get washed.

I have a bunch of other habits, like never looking at the time in a ball park because I don't want to know how long a game is. I might tell a coach to bang a bat three times on the dugout floor when we're in a tight situation, and if we get out of it unscathed that coach knows what to expect in the next tight situation. All these superstitions are just silly fun, and I don't believe in any of them. But, of course, I would never test the fates by going against them.

Mike Cuellar probably had more superstitions than any player I knew. We faced a crisis one year when Cuellar was to start a game for us in Milwaukee. Mike had won nine straight games, but his "winning" baseball cap had been left behind in Baltimore. Mike told me the problem and I understood its gravity immediately. I've always regarded new caps as bad luck, I guess because they've always turned out to be. In the 1971 World Series writers were asking me about the battered, misshapen cap I had on, and I told them it had taken me months to break it in before I could actually put it on my head. I had been given a new cap for the Series and I threw it against the wall dozens of times trying to crack a seam and get it game worthy, but it still needed work.

So when Cuellar had told me he was in trouble without his game cap, I went to our traveling secretary, Phil Itzoe, who got right on the case. Getting the cap from Baltimore in time for the game was complicated. The cap had to be delivered to an airline representative in Baltimore, who had to pass it on to a colleague when the cap changed planes in Chicago. Then Itzoe had it picked up at the Milwaukee airport and delivered to the stadium. I was relieved when it arrived just before game time.

Cuellar opened the package and I was no longer relieved. "That's not my *game* cap!" he shouted. "They sent my *practice* cap!"

Mike got knocked out of the game early, not surprisingly. On his way into the clubhouse he paused in the dugout just long enough to fling his cap on the floor and stomp it. The cap, I noted, began to look more like a gamer.

The second game of the '71 Series, on Sunday, was rained out and rescheduled for Monday afternoon. Jerry Hoffberger asked Bowie Kuhn to make the Monday contest a night game. That made sense to me, when I thought of all the working people with tickets who wouldn't be able to use them on a Monday afternoon. The far-seeing Commissioner wouldn't consider such a thing. Now, of course, all the non-weekend Series games are played at night—some in near-freezing temperatures.

In game two Palmer had a helluva fastball (he struck out 10) and serious control problems (he walked 7), throwing 168 pitches in 8 innings. But Richie Hebner's 3-run homer accounted for the only Pirate scores, and by then we had 11 runs. Dick Hall shut out Pittsburgh in the ninth. Brooks and Frank each had 3 hits in our total of 14—all singles.

I told the writers, "I got my finger on that singles button and couldn't get it off."

Steve Blass started for the Pirates in game three and our scouting reports speculated that he might be having arm trouble. You can't put much stock in reports on pitchers in a short series, though. First of all, home plate is only 17 inches wide and pitchers stand 60 feet, 6 inches away from it, so they can't throw every pitch exactly where they want it. A pitch comes in a half inch off target and the batter hits it off the fence. The reports on the hitters give the pitcher a pattern on how to work each man.

Blass was good, but we had a helluva hitting ball club and should have gotten to him. The old overanxious syndrome gripped our guys again, and we didn't get a hit until Brooks singled in the fifth. Cuellar had allowed only 2 runs going into the seventh, and Frank hit one out to draw us close. But in the bottom of the inning Pittsburgh got two men on and Bob Robertson stepped in. I figured Pirate manager Danny Murtaugh would have Robertson bunt, and that's the way we played it. I was right. Roberto Clemente danced off first and he started waving madly at Robertson as he strode to swing. Robertson had missed the bunt sign and Clemente was trying to get his attention. I'm sorry to say that Roberto failed. Robertson swung away and hit a low screwball out of the park. That was the game, 5–1 Pittsburgh.

"The battery died and the push-button machine wouldn't work," I told the writers. "Look, Blass pitched a helluva game. That one's over. We forget it. Tomorrow's another day."

I overheard Jim Palmer tell a writer before the next game, "Weaver's the most optimistic man I ever saw. He programs his outlook and transmits it to you. He never gives up. Yesterday when we were down four runs, he said, 'Come on, come on! Let's go. If we lose we'll have to stay here another night.' We didn't figure to beat Blass by then and I'm sure Earl knew it, but he wanted us to keep trying. Now he's positive Dobson'll beat 'em tonight and McNally will end it tomorrow. And he's got the rest of us thinking that."

The approach was right but the execution was lacking. We lost game four, 4–3, and we weren't playing like the Orioles. We had committed eight errors in four ball games. We also had only seven hits in the last two games.

There seemed to be no way our hitting could get worse, but we found a way. We got two singles off Nelson Briles in game five and lost 4–0. We hadn't scored a run in 17 successive innings. Damn!

Still, there was no point in getting down. We were going home, and all we had to do was win two games in a row. "The thing is I pushed busted buttons," I told the writers. "I told Harry Dalton to get a guarantee when he bought that machine, so we're gonna return it to the manufacturer and get our money back. From now on, instead of depending on the machine, I'll figure out a game plan."

"Any changes in mind?" a writer asked.

"Only my underwear," I said. "But if we win Saturday, I won't change that."

I was so nervous before game six that I had chain-smoked almost a pack of cigarettes before I reached Memorial Stadium. For some unfathomable reason, attendance was over 9,000 below our first two games. I'll say this—the folks who stayed away missed a great World Series game.

Murtaugh used his sixth different starter, Bob Moose, and I went with my stopper, Jim Palmer. Jim gave up only two runs through nine innings; one a Clemente homer. Buford hit one for us in the sixth and we tied the score the following inning.

In the tenth Frank Robinson won the game for us with his head and his legs. With one out he worked Bob Miller for a walk. Frank's right Achilles' tendon was painfully sore, but when Rettenmund grounded a single up the middle Robinson flew around second and kept going. Center fielder Vic Davalillo's arm was not the strongest, yet his throw reached third just as Frank dove headfirst to the outside of the bag and beat the tag. He rose slowly, dusting himself off and rubbing his left thigh. He had pulled a muscle there.

Brooks then hit a fly to shallow center and Frank tagged as Davalillo came in under the ball. Frank broke and Davalillo threw in. The ball bounced once and then bounced higher. As Sanguillen reached for the ball and swung down, Frank slid under the tag—3–2 Orioles! The entire season was down to one game.

Before game seven I watched Mike Cuellar warm up and liked his stuff. I didn't figure Steve Blass could throw another three-hitter at us.

He didn't, giving us four. That was also the total Cuellar—who retired the first 11 Pirate batters—gave up. One of the hits was a Clemente home run. A Stargell single and a double by Pagan built another run. We got one back in the eighth, but that was it. We'd lost the seventh game of the World Series, 2–1. You can't get much closer than that, but we lost.

I trudged into my office past the unmanned TV camera, shook my father's hand, and shrugged, "Our best just wasn't enough." The press, mostly Baltimore writers and a bunch who needed a few words from the losers' locker room, came in. I ran my hands, which were shaking a bit, through my hair. My voice, hoarse from two hours of hollering, cracked with emotion and I fought back tears when I spoke:

"I'm proud—proud of the ball club, proud of the players, proud of myself. We'll be back next year."

I had thanked the players before the game and I had promised them that next season we would become the first team to win a hundred games four successive years. I tried to think about that promise now while answering the writers, whose questions were all about why we'd lost. After some forty minutes of this losing talk I said, "Fellas, I can't take anymore." Then I went into the shower and threw up.

President Nixon phoned and offered his sympathies, saying he knew what it meant to lose. That didn't help.

Thank goodness we took off for Japan three days later. We needed to get away, and it was a 31-day trip in which we played 18 games against Japan's best players and teams. It was a fantastic experience and we all had a helluva lot of fun.

No one enjoyed the excursion more than Boog Powell and his

wife, Jan, who are two of the most beautiful people I've ever known. Boog was such a good-natured guy and he purely *loved* life. Two of his favorite things were eating and drinking. He was not an abuser of alcohol, thanks to his enormous, virtually limitless capacity. We all had our fill of food and libations on that junket to Japan, but no one came close to matching Boog's intake.

His capacity was not outlandish when you consider that he weighed between 270 and 280 pounds in season. The front office was always after me to make Boog lose ten or twenty pounds. Even in 1970 when Boog was the Most Valuable Player in the American League I had gotten calls from Harry Dalton or Frank Cashen when a groundball went under Powell's glove because he couldn't quite bend over far enough fast enough to impede a ball that was all the way down there on the damn ground. This would happen all of four or five times a season, yet after each occurance my phone would ring and Dalton would say, "Make that SOB lose some weight, for God's sake, Earl! He can't get his glove on the ground with his goddamn belly in the way!"

So I'd put Boog on a diet, which meant he couldn't have his beer after games—and he was miserable. A lot of players liked their beer after playing in Baltimore's 95-degree heat and breath-taking humidity. But Boog *needed* his beer the way a diabetic needs insulin. Boog would give up his beer for three or four tortuous, agonizing days in which he'd lose ten to twenty pounds along with his edge at the plate, and I'd bring him a six pack.

Actually, Boog could lose fifteen pounds in a single ball game on a real hot night. He'd come into the clubhouse scarlet-faced and quickly take off his shoes, because his feet couldn't stand his weight bearing down on them. Next he would strip off his sopping uniform, grab a six pack out of the cooler, and plop down on his stool, which looked like a kiddy's seat under his bulk. Then Boog, leaning forward, his left elbow on his thigh, would raise a can of beer to his lips, tip it up, and hold it there until the can was empty. Putting the can down beside his stool with a sigh, he would take a deep breath and hoist another live can to his mouth. When that one was half empty he would pause to wipe his lips with the back of his left hand, then he would drain it with one more long swallow. On the third beer he took three swallows.

This entire ritual was performed in total silence amidst the chatter all around Boog, whose concentration was fixed on the crucial task of replenishing his dehydrated body. Thirty-six ounces of beer accomplished that to the point where he could negotiate the distance to the shower. Then the nice, freckle-faced giant would return to consume his other three beers in a more leisurely fashion, during which he would not only have the pleasure of tasting the brew but might even issue a word or two to those around him now that he was fully breathing again.

On the flight to Japan Boog thought he had boarded the good ship Cornucopia, as did quite a number of us. We left Baltimore about 9 A.M. and Boog immediately started on Bloody Marys, emptying a few of those before breakfast. Then he moved into vodka-and-tonics that carried him into lunch. That was served with wine and champagne with which Boog and Jan toasted one another several times. After lunch it was cocktail time, and the Powells opted for martinis and Manhattans. Marianna and I, who pretty much stayed with our gin-and-tonics, observed them with admiration.

"If you're having any trouble getting a drink, Boog," I said, "just ring for the stewardess."

"Thanks, Earl," Boog said. "No problem so far."

"Good. Wouldn't want you to dehydrate."

When we landed in San Francisco to refuel, naturally we stopped in the VIP Lounge for a drink or two, by which time many of the AL Champions were feeling *very* good. Yet Boog and Jan Powell, an attractive and statuesque lady who had a capacity that approximated that of her husband, looked like they had been sipping lemonade.

When we reboarded, the imbibing continued for the next leg of the trip to Honolulu. There, after all that quaffing, we spent the refueling time eating ice cream cones. But not long after we were back on the plane dinner was served, again with wine and champagne, and after dinner the Drambuie, Irish Mist, and Cognac flowed, and segued into such evening potables as scotch, bourbon, and Jack Daniel's. The Happy Hour was endless, as was the laughter, until darkness delivered a number of people into sleep.

I know I was still awake when all of a sudden, because we were flying East, the sun came up and sent slanting rays through the windows. The instant the sunlight struck Boog, his hand reached up and rang for the stewardess, who hurried down the aisle. "Yes?" she said.

"May we have two Bloody Marys, please," Boog said.

In Japan all they did was feed us and serve libations. Even during ball games waiters would march into the dugout wearing tuxedos and bearing napkins and china and all kinds of raw fish, cakes, and tea. I'd never seen anything like it and the chow was delicious. We ate only in the best restaurants, and all we had to do was sign checks. When we traveled by train to the next stadium we were given the most elaborate box lunches. I think Boog came back from this trip weighing 320.

Our Japanese hosts threw some fancy parties at which a huge gong was rung and massive Sumo wrestlers would tromp in carrying a casketlike box that was full of saki. At one of those affairs a Sumo demonstrated his strength by lifting me two feet off the ground with one hand. Some of my beloved players yelled, "Drop him! Drop him!"

We won twelve games and lost only two, but we played four tie games. That's right: ties. It seems the Japanese trains wait for no man, and if a late-running game threatened a team's making connections to the next opponent, the game was simply called. The Japanese fans would applaud and leave politely. I looked at the Japanese baseball standings and saw some teams had fifteen or sixteen ties. I thought at first I was looking at the National Hockey League standings. But it was a truly delightful trip.

When we returned home I cornered Boog briefly and advised him to please take off some weight. For four years I had seen him report to spring training weighing close to 300 pounds and then watched him struggle painfully to get down to 270 or so. I pointed out that a regimen like that was extremely hard on his body—on anyone's body—and might well shorten his career. Boog never lifted weights like the other players, never did anything to keep himself in shape winters. He wouldn't even squeeze a rubber ball as *everyone* else did.

Boog sat there silently as I talked, perhaps nodding occasionally, looking straight at me and giving a strong impression of attentiveness. But Boog Powell, the nice, big bear of a man, let everything I said go in one ear and out the other just as he always had and always would. He appeared to be listening, but he would close off his mind because Weaver's words were never important to him. I could have been chewing him out, preaching a sermon, or reciting the Gettysburg Address and Boog's bemused expression would not have changed a lick.

I have to wonder, though, what he might have done had he listened to a word or two, particularly in terms of the length of his career. Boog played fourteen years with the Orioles and two more with Cleveland under Frank Robinson. In fact, we gave up on Boog too soon after his home-run totals fell to 11 and 12 in 1973 and '74, because he popped 27 for the Indians in '75 and batted .297. Still, he was finished the following year at age thirty-four, and with all his ability I feel certain he could have played a few more years if he had ever toned his muscles and watched his weight just a bit. But Boog always insisted on doing things solely his way . . . and what he did was pretty damn good.

Boog, who owns a marina in Florida, was in Baltimore early in the 1981 season for a boat show. When he came to the clubhouse, I swear he had to turn sideways to step through the doorway. "Hey, you've gotta be *way* over 300 now, Booger," I said.

"It don't make no difference now, Earl," he said, smiling through his freckled tan. "I'm enjoying it."

"It never made no difference to you, Booger, and you *always* enjoyed it."

Not long after our return from Japan, I had to make the toughest decision of my life in baseball. Harry Dalton had become the Angels' GM, and the man who replaced him in Baltimore, Frank Cashen, along with others in the Oriole hierarchy, felt it was time to trade Frank Robinson. During his six years in Baltimore the Orioles had won four pennants and two World Championships. As Davey Johnson once said, "Frank taught us how to win." But Frank had reached age thirty-six in August 1971.

Just the thought of giving up Frank Robinson scared me to death. But a manager cannot let fear deform his reason. The fact was that we had a lot of talent in the outfield. Rettenmund had led us in batting average the past two seasons. Buford had 19 home runs in '71 despite missing 40 games. And Don Baylor was a young outfielder at Rochester who had batted over .300 and averaged over 20 home runs and 100 RBIs the past two seasons. We had to make room for him and for infielder Bobby Grich, another .300 hitter with power at Rochester.

I had rested Frank more in '71. He had played 133 games and I'd used him at first base in 33 of them. I felt he could do that again. Still, if he did start to slip, could Frank adjust to a part-time role? I didn't think that would be fair to Frank, after all his great years, or the team. Frank might well have another excellent year or two. But the concensus in the organization was to trade him a year too soon rather than a year too late. Another consideration: Frank was earning $130,000 a year and the

Orioles weren't drawing. So every bit of reason pointed to a trade of Frank, and on December 2, 1971, we struck a deal with the Dodgers. We acquired pitchers Doyle Alexander and Bob O'Brien, catcher Sergio Robles, and outfielder Royle Stillman for Frank and pitcher Pete Richert. As it turned out, our scouting reports were better than the performances of the players we acquired, except for Alexander. Frank had an injury-plagued season with the Dodgers, then hit 30 home runs for the Angels in '73 as a designated hitter. If the DH had come in a year earlier, I would never have agreed to a trade of Frank Robinson.

I went to spring training in 1972 and made the same speech I've given twice every year since I've managed the Orioles, the first when the pitchers, catchers, and early arrivals report, the second a week later when the balance of the team comes in. The speech is ad-libbed and spoken with enthusiasm and sincerity. "The object for all of us here is to get in shape to appear in the World Series this fall, because you wouldn't be here and I wouldn't be here if I didn't feel that we had the ball club that can win the American League pennant if we work at it. And the work starts right here and now." Then I run over our training camp schedule and what our goals are. "Our overall goal is to win as a team, because that's the only way you win. But if everyone has a good year individually—the kind of years you are all capable of—we will win."

I go on like that, speaking optimistically, because I honestly feel that way every spring. I was worried about the loss of Frank Robinson, but I still felt we had more than enough talent to win if the youngsters came through. Don Baylor, who could fly, resembled a young Frank Robinson, as I gauged it. But when the writers asked me if Baylor was our *new* Frank Robinson, I said, "This guy is not expected to take Frank Robinson's place. I don't think anyone will. But I do think Don Baylor can develop into an outstanding player in five or six years. You know, it took Brooks Robinson five or six years to become the league's Most Valuable Player, and it took Frank and Boog Powell that long to become MVPs. I'd say that by 1978 Don Baylor can become the Most Valuable Player in the American League." (As it would turn out, Baylor won the award in '79—when I thought Kenny Singleton should have won.)

But Don Baylor was not ready to play full time against major-league pitching in '72. In fact, a number of our veterans weren't ready either. It was a most frustrating season, as virtually the entire team slumped at the plate. Hendricks batted .155, Belanger .186, Etchebarren .202, Buford .206, Johnson .221, and Rettenmund .233. Brooks hit all of 8 home runs. Etchebarren and Hendricks had combined for 18 home runs in '71; they combined for 2 in '72.

I kept manipulating players and trying different combinations, hoping to put together one that could get us some runs. I played Bobby Grich—who led us in hitting with a .278 average and was second in homers with 12—at shortstop in 81 games, at second base in 45, at first in 16, and at third in 8. I kept "going to the books," as the players said, using every stat available that suggested a player might hit a certain pitcher. I sat down Boog in over 20 games even though, after a terrible first half, he led us in home runs (21) and RBIs (81). But there were certain pitchers, most notably Mickey Lolich of the Tigers and Jim Kaat of the Twins, he just couldn't hit. I think Boog was about 3-for-80 in his career off Lolich.

The one player I should have sat down more was Buford. Early in the season I saw he was no longer looking over pitches as he used to. The best lead-off man in the league the year before would now get a 3–2 count, the next pitch would come in at his shoulders . . . and Donny would strike out. I'd drive home after a game thinking: I play Terry Crowley in left tomorrow. Or Tom Shopay. Or Don Baylor. Anyone except Buford. He's killing us. He's not hitting. It's just not his year.

Then I'd get home and think about all the hits Buford had gotten in other years off the next day's scheduled pitcher. I'd recall the season in which, with a man on third and less than two out, Donny had driven in the runner nineteen times in a row! I'd dream about Donny getting on the next day, stealing second, and scoring the winning run on a sacrifice fly.

So I kept playing Donny, and he kept failing. Try as he might, somehow he'd lost it at the plate.

And every night on the road I'd confer with my coaches: Bamberger, Hunter, Staller, and Jimmy Frey, who'd joined us in 1970. We'd meet over pinochle or at the bar of the hotel where the team was staying (which was off-limits to the players; only myself, the coaches, and writers drank there), trying to come up with that elusive winning combination. After a streak of particularly bad games, the coaches would take turns drinking with me individually to listen to my bitching. They would have the same gripes usually, but the poor guys couldn't take listening to me every night when answers to our problems were not to be found. Fortunately for all concerned, we seldom got more than three drinks because hotel bars all close early. Many times we raced back to the Hollander Hotel in Cleveland after a game to find the bar had closed. Then the bitching grew louder. Some of us were in dire need of a couple of stiff drinks to cut the throbbing edge after a slovenly loss.

Our team batting average dropped 32 points from the '71 figure to .229. Our home-run production decreased by 58, and we scored 223 fewer runs—an average of almost 1½ runs per game!

For all of these inauspicious offensive statistics, our pitching staff turned in the best ERA in the league, 2.53, and no AL club had a better defense. These factors kept us in the thick of the pennant race with Detroit, Boston, and New York well into September. After a slow start we put together a nine-game winning streak in early June that thrust us past the Tigers into first place. We remained in first or second through September 3 and weren't eliminated from the race until the twenty-ninth of the month, four days before the season ended. We finished third, five games behind Detroit. And I had to admit that if we'd kept Frank Robinson—even if he had sustained the injuries with us that plagued him with the Dodgers—we would have won our fourth successive pennant. Frank's nineteen home runs would have won those six extra games we needed.

Given all of the lineup changes I made in '72, it was not unexpected when some of the Orioles expressed their unhappiness.

Dave Johnson complained to the press when I sat him down against pitchers he couldn't hit. "I'd rather be platooned than come to the ball park every day and never know if I'm gonna play or not," he said. But Johnson knew as well as I did which pitchers consistently picked his pocket at the plate.

Mark Belanger said, "When things are going good, a manager

tends to overlook things. But Earl has changed his idea—his whole personality has changed—because now he gets on our backs."

I had to chuckle at that coming from Mark, who had seen me get on any player all the way back to the minors, who was not playing up to his capabilities. I had called Mark into my office in 1968 and told him he wasn't playing up to the ability he'd shown in Rochester and that if he couldn't do better I'd have to get another shortstop. His play in the first half of '68 had contributed to Hank Bauer's losing his job and I didn't want to lose mine. Mark bounced back strong the next year. When he floundered again in '72 I was forced to play Grich at short half the season even though Bobby was a better second baseman.

I made it clear to everyone that any time we were losing as a result of individuals performing beneath their capabilities, I wasn't going to be as easy to live with. Case closed.

We tried everything we could to improve—extra batting practice, early workouts, more postgame meetings than ever to go over mistakes, innumerable lineup combinations, even bringing in new players. We brought up Johnny Oates from Rochester and used him at catcher most of the year. In mid-August we traded Elrod to the Cubs for Tommy Davis in hopes the former batting champion would drive in some runs. In November we resigned Elrod as a free agent and assigned Davis to Rochester, which meant any club could have acquired him. Thank God none did! Tommy became the best DH in the league in '73 (.306, 169 hits) and again led us in hits in 1974 with 181.

My efforts in the original acquisition of Elrod Hendricks, incidentally, paid off in many ways. He was always a good role player. He not only brought us Tommy Davis, but in 1976 was one of the players we sent to the Yankees for pitchers Rudy May, Tippy Martinez, and Scott McGregor, plus Rick Dempsey. At the end of that '76 season we again signed Elrod as a free agent, and he became a player-coach, then our full-time bullpen coach.

Davey Johnson had made a "play me or trade me" announcement during the '72 season, as Andy Etchebarren had been doing ever since Elrod came in. Andy was our top defensive catcher and too valuable to trade.

But Davey was definitely going. I had seen it coming two years before, after the 1970 season when he had arrived at the New York Baseball Writers annual dinner looking like Ralph Salvon, our 250-pound trainer.

"My God, Davey!" I said then. "How the hell much do you weigh?"

"About 220," he said, looking pleased.

"Your playing weight's 185," I said. "What the hell are you doing?"

"I want to hit some home runs next year."

He reported to spring training in '71 weighing about 205. I hit him a groundball, and this guy who had been so quick afoot suddenly couldn't move four strides in time to field the ball. We got him back down to 185 or so, but the effort that went into taking off all the weight cost him a step. Davey never regained all of his ability in the field. He did have his biggest home-run year in '71, hitting 18, but Grich had the second-base job for the future.

Our organizational meeting that fall was in Hawaii, and the first question that came up, naturally, was what the Orioles needed to win the pennant in 1973. "Well," I said, "we had a total of 19 home runs from our catchers the last time we won, in '71. This past season our three catchers had 6 among them."

"So you need a catcher who can hit the long ball," said Jimmy Russo, our superscout who was sitting next to me.

"Jimmy, you get me a catcher who'll hit 20 homers next season and we'll win it again," I said.

"I'll get you a catcher who'll hit 40 home runs," Russo said.

"Where you gonna get a guy like that? The American League home-run record for catchers in a season is shared by Yogi Berra and Gus Triandos with 30. You can get me a catcher who can top them?"

"That's right."

"Where?"

"Atlanta," Russo said. "Earl Williams. Hit 33 in '71 and 28 last year."

"Yeah, in that little ball park." I turned to Walter Youse, one of our regional scouting supervisors. "What do you think, Walter?"

"He's gonna hit a lot of homers, Earl. Williams can hit 'em a long way. He and Henry Aaron are the only players to put one in Atlanta's upper deck."

"The one thing, Earl, is Williams doesn't like to catch," Russo said. "But he's got great hands and you can make him a catcher."

I looked hard at Russo. "So you'll get me a longball-hitting catcher who don't like to catch."

Russo ignored that. "He's a little problem on a club, Earl, but you can handle him. You haven't had a problem with any player you couldn't straighten out."

"Well what the hell kind of problem *is* Williams?" I asked.

Russo looked pensive. "It's hard to say exactly . . . one thing, he doesn't like to run out groundballs. But on this club he will."

The next morning I opened the sports section of the Honolulu newspaper and saw a headline: "Weaver Says if O's Get Williams, They'll Win the Pennant." Jesus Christ! Jimmy bleeping Russo loves ink! He went directly from our meeting to the press and gave out a story! Now it's gonna cost us twice as much to get this guy Williams who don't like to catch or run out groundballs but who is gonna win the pennant for me.

As we began negotiations for Williams, we checked him out a little further and all the negative reports on him were confirmed. He couldn't catch too good, I heard, but then I told myself Elrod wasn't a finished catcher when we got him. Williams is trouble, I heard. All right, it's gonna be difficult, I told myself. But if Williams can hit twenty home runs—never mind forty!—for a team on which only one man had over thirteen the year before, I can put up with some discomfort.

On November 30 the deal for Earl Williams was completed. We also acquired minor-league infielder Taylor Duncan, but thanks to good old Russo we gave up a bunch of talent: Davey Johnson and catcher Johnny Oates, plus pitchers Pat Dobson and Roric Harrison. I wasn't overjoyed about losing Dobson, who had pitched better than his 16–18 record of '72 suggested. Still, I felt Doyle Alexander was ready to step into the starting rotation, and you have to make room for your youngsters or they don't develop.

At spring training in 1973 we brought in Jimmy Schaffer to tutor Williams. Schaffer had retired only a few years earlier to become a manager in our organization after sixteen seasons as a catcher. Williams had come up with the Braves as a first baseman-third baseman and had been a catcher for only two and a half seasons. I watched as Schaffer began working with him on fundamentals, throwing balls into the dirt in front of and to the sides of Williams. And it was apparent that this big man had unbelievable natural abilities—agility, quickness, soft hands.

Then Schaffer told Williams to get his arms out from between his knees so he could reach to either side faster. Jimmy threw a few more balls and Williams kept his arms outside his knees on the first two but didn't bother to on the third.

"I don't like this shit," Williams said.

Schaffer said, "You have to get down and in front of the low balls, Earl. Let them bounce off your chest protector. Just keep the ball in front of you."

"Am I supposed to use the glove?" Williams asked.

"No, you're supposed to get in front of the ball," Schaffer said, "and block it with your chest."

Williams removed the glove from his left hand and slung it ten feet away.

Well, I said to myself, the scouting report on this guy's discomfort factor is as accurate as the one on his catching potential. Now all we have to do is find a way to reach him.

When Schaffer checked out Williams' throws to second, the ball flew down there hard and true. I almost applauded his arm. And when Williams took BP, there was no question as to why Russo was all for this guy's bat. He drove one pitch after another on a line over 400 feet.

I started Williams in the first exhibition game, and by the third inning he was giving the signs on his knees—where a catcher should never be. It was easier on his legs than crouching, but any pitch off the plate was a lost cause. Pitchers break a lot of curves into the dirt in the spring, and Earl wouldn't even make an effort to move for them. Pitches were bouncing to the stands as if we were in a Little League game. I yanked Williams after four innings.

Figuring the point had been made, I started him again in game two. He hit a ball a mile . . . and gave the same desultory performance behind the plate. Every head on our bench was shaking. Etchebarren looked so disgusted I would not have been surprised to see him throw up.

I played Williams only three innings, and afterward called him into my office. "For chrissake, Earl," I said, "put a little effort into it out there. You can be one of the better catchers in the American League. The league home-run record in a season for catchers is thirty. *You* can hit thirty backing up, damnit. But to do that you've got to get in there every day. And in order for you to play—you've got to make an effort. Now start showing me what you can do!"

By this time Etchebarren and Hendricks were beginning to call me names in the Baltimore papers. With some justification. I hadn't been giving them a fair shake, trying to get Williams' act together, but I knew what they could do. I knew what Williams *should* be able to do . . . if I could get him to *want* to do it.

Williams checked the starting lineup before our third preseason game and made a sour face when he saw his name listed. "Aren't there any other damn catchers on this club?" he said to no one in particular, though the quote circulated throughout camp instantly.

Williams did not want to catch every day, or any day, but I had to use him as much as possible to teach him the position. Now our standard procedure calls for the starting catcher to warm up not the starting pitcher but the pitcher who's getting his work between starts. Say Palmer has started on Tuesday. He throws on the side Thursday, then starts again on Saturday. But Bamberger decided that Williams should warm up the day's starter so they could get used to each other. I agreed it was a good idea.

Bamberger went to tell Williams. "Get your gear on, Earl," George said. "We want you to warm up the starting pitcher."

"Let those goddamn bullpen catchers warm him up," Williams said.

Etchebarren happened to be standing within earshot, and he was furious. He strode over to Williams and said, "Listen, you asshole! Us so-called bullpen catchers have caught in three goddamn World Series. What have you done lately except give catchers a bad name? Yet you're trying to get our job. We don't think you're gonna do it—even if that other asshole's trying to give it to you."

Williams shrugged, as he did at most such comments from his new teammates.

I did give Williams the starting job, and once the season began Andy and Elrod got tired of doing all his work. They had been warming up his pitchers and picking up infield for him, but they got fed up. So one night they decided, the hell with it, if Williams won't warm up the starting pitcher, we won't pick him up during infield practice.

That night Andy and Elrod warmed up both the starter and the pitcher throwing on the side. Williams, who was late getting on the field as usual, came out of the clubhouse as Billy Hunter was ready to hit to the infield. Earl took the first round of infield, threw the ball down to second base, then turned looking for another catcher. He didn't see any, because Andy was in the clubhouse and Elrod was way down the left-field line signing autographs for fans at the railing, as was and is his habit; Elrod loves to sign autographs.

Williams tossed Hunter the ball and said, "Screw this." He walked into the dugout. Hunter was left standing there with a bat, a ball, and a full complement of infielders, but no one to catch the balls thrown home. Elrod saw the situation and raced in to get a mitt. Too late. Hunter was so angry he called off infield practice and walked away.

Earl hit five home runs in six games at Memorial Stadium from April 17 through 22, and he also vied with Tommy Davis as RBI leader even though Williams' batting average was in the .220s. Yet his lackadaisical attitude drew everyone's ire. The list of grievances against him grew to include: failure to run out groundballs, missing signs, and missing buses to the ball park, to which he often reported late for afternoon pregame workouts. I made trainer Ralph Salvon Earl's personal wakeup service on Sundays: "Ralph, Williams ain't at the park yet so get him on the phone." When we were on the road I'd watch the players board the bus for the park. If Williams didn't show I would have Ralph go back into the hotel and call on the house phone.

Williams was invariably late for batting practice even when he was at the park on time. I heard a couple of players griping about this fact in New York toward the end of June and warned Williams that I couldn't have one set of rules for the team and another set for him. A week later we were in Boston for a weekend series, and Williams missed the team bus to the Sunday afternoon game. As soon as we reached Fenway Park I told Ralph: "Get on the bleeping phone and tell Williams to get his ass here pronto!"

I was furious, as were all of my coaches. Here we had given up four major-league players to get a guy who wouldn't even get to the ball park on time. But I told myself to be calm. I sat down and made a list of all the things that Williams was doing wrong. I was going to ream him the minute he arrived.

The clubhouse was empty when Williams came rushing in. "Earl," I said, walking toward my office, "come in here!"

"*Now* what's wrong?" he said, following me in. "What the hell did I do now?"

I closed the door behind him. "Sit down. It's not so much what you do—it's what you *don't* do. You don't make the team bus. You don't read the signs. You don't warm up your starting pitchers. You don't stay with infield."

"I'm not taking any more infield," Williams said.

"What?"

"I'm not taking any more infield. I'm not going to let those guys get away with not picking me up."

I exploded. "I've had enough of your shit, Earl! Pack your bags and get out of here. This ball club doesn't need a malingerer like you. You're suspended."

"That's great," he said.

"Well get the hell outta here!"

Williams stuffed his personal items into a bag at his locker and calmly left the clubhouse. But he must have realized that he no longer had a hotel room or transportation because he carried his bag into the stands and sat down. Ten minutes later he returned and told the trainer he wanted to see me. Ralph Salvon came into the dugout and relayed the message. "Tell Williams I'll see him after the goddamn ball game."

Bill Lee, a left-hander whom Williams crushed, beat us 1–0 while Earl watched from the stands. Afterward Williams came in and apologized. He said he was "going to try and correct myself in all the areas in which I've been found to be deficient."

He made an effort for about a week. Then he went back to his same old routine. I kept calling him in, sitting him down, and chewing him out. Williams kept apologizing and swearing he would straighten out and conform to the rules. He would give me just enough encouragement for three days, four days . . . even a week . . . to make me feel he might change.

Earl was very well spoken and very convincing. Both with me and with GM Frank Cashen. Earl had a way of actually making you feel *you* were picking on him. More than once Cashen called me in and said, "Earl, I think maybe you've got this guy wrong."

I don't think to this day that Earl Williams has ever run out a groundball. He would hit a ball to shortstop, take two steps, drop his bat, and walk back to the dugout. Fans in Baltimore came running from all over the ball park to holler at Williams. "Go bleep yourself, Williams, you lazy bastard!" they would yell. "You no good SOB!"

Jerry Hoffberger sat right behind home with his wife and children and various guests. Fans would yell at him, "Why don't you trade that sonofabitch Williams! He's a rotten lazy bastard!"

The racists were the loudest, "You nigger motherbleeper!" They would come right down behind the dugout and call him unspeakable names, and Earl would jump out of the dugout to answer them.

Our dugout is one of the longest in the league and Earl would be at one end looking for his shin guards, say, because he never knew where they were. Wherever they were, his chest protector was someplace else. So he'd be looking for his gear when a voice from behind the other end of the dugout would shout, "You no-hustle black bleep!" Earl would run down there and holler, "Bleep you!" Then another voice would shout from behind the opposite end of the dugout. Earl would whirl and run down there.

We would sit there watching Earl move faster in the dugout than he ever did in a ball game, our heads swiveling as if we were at a tennis match. Someone always grabbed him before he could yank a fan out of the stands.

In one game in which Williams refused to run out groundballs his first two times up, fans really started getting on him when he went behind the plate. Suddenly Williams, down in his crouch, stopped giving signs. He kept turning his head to see who was calling him names. He stood up and stared at the stands. The yelling stopped and he went back into his crouch—then someone called him another name. Williams stood up and stared at the stands until he spotted his antagonist, and we could see Williams hollering back through his mask, which he was apparently too lazy to remove because he would only have to put it back on. Earl was adamantly against expending any more energy than was absolutely necessary. The fan comments finally moved Williams to charge the stands, but the plate umpire grabbed him.

Not long after this incident Cashen called me and said, "Earl, you've got to keep Williams from shouting 'Bleep you' over Mr. Hoffberger's box."

"Frank, I'm trying my best to stop him. If I could get him to run out groundballs the fans would get off him. But he doesn't understand that or doesn't care. I tell him every day that as long as he loafs, he's gonna hear from the fans."

"Maybe I'll have a talk with him again," Cashen said.

"If you find a way to get through to this guy, let me know what it is," I said. "I've never had a player like this one. Williams is in a class by himself—the terrible class."

Cashen spoke to Williams. Then, of course, Frank called me and said, "It's very possible we've misjudged Earl."

That night the fans behind home gave it to Williams, who yelled, "Bleep you!" back at them, the words floating just over the heads of Jerry Hoffberger and his family.

I called Williams into my office after the game and reiterated the request from Cashen. Williams said, "You're picking on me again. I'll go see Frank Cashen myself."

Later Cashen phoned me to say, "Are you sure you're not picking on Williams?"

Williams certainly felt we were, as did Tommy Davis, who egged Earl on all the way and kept saying, "They're picking on you." Tommy marched to a different drum, too.

Yet Davis was one splendid hitter, especially with men on base, going with the pitch and sending balls to all fields. He led the club in RBIs with 89, and Williams had 83 in almost 100 fewer at-bats. Earl's 22 home runs topped our No. 2 power hitter, Bobby Grich, by 10. Small wonder that, despite all the problems Williams presented, I used him in 132 games and would have played him more if he hadn't been sidelined for two weeks with an ankle injury. And the 4 passed balls and 6 errors he was charged with as catcher were not all that bad for a player of his limited experience. But he was better defensively at first base, where I played him in 42 games.

Still, I received a ton of nasty letters and comments from Baltimore fans for bringing in Williams in the first place—and particularly for giving up Davey Johnson. One fan regularly sent me reports on Johnson's home-run totals, which seemed to grow daily. Davey had hit exactly 5 for us in '72. He shocked the baseball world in '73 by hitting 43 for Atlanta.

Yet our readings on Johnson's decline proved accurate. The following year he could no longer get to groundballs at second base. Davey Johnson was soon out of the majors.

Donny Buford was also out of the big leagues in '73, and I was saddened when that came to pass after all he had done for me. But after Donny's poor '72 season the Oriole front office was going to cut his salary 20 percent. Buford was making about $70,000 a season. Then the Orioles received an offer from a Japanese club for Buford. He called me and asked what he should do, saying his salary in Japan would be $120,000 plus free housing and other fringe benefits. I advised him to take it, and he went on to have several good years there.

Buford might have had a difficult time making the '73 club. I not only had Blair, Rettenmund, and Baylor (who would bat .286), but two speedy young outfielders who had batted well over .300 at Rochester. Al Bumbry and Rich Coggins were two little left-handed hitters whom I used mostly against right-handed pitchers. Each played in 110 games, with Bumbry hitting .337 and Coggins .319. They finished one-two in the Rookie-of-the-Year balloting. Both could also run the bases, Bumbry stealing 23 and Coggins 17.

The Orioles were no longer a power-hitting ball club. Though in '73 we had the highest average, .266, of any Oriole team since 1954, we became a running club and a bunting-for-base-hits (we totaled 42) club. You manage according to the abilities at your disposal and don't ask anyone to do anything he isn't capable of. We had speed and we used it. I've always controlled the stealing on my clubs and let players run only when they had a good jump. I don't know how many times Belanger has been given the steal sign and then waited through two hitters while negotiating a jump before going. But I almost wore out the steal sign that season.

We ended up setting an Oriole record in leading the league with 146 stolen bases. Eight players had more than 10 steals, paced by Baylor's 32. The running helped us manufacture runs—235 more than we had scored the previous year. All of this led writers to ask, "Isn't it nice having all that speed?" To which I would reply, "I'd rather have more three-run homers. Then everyone can take their time and stroll home. I've never had a base runner thrown out once a ball's been hit over the fence."

As usual our pitching was the best in the division. Palmer was 22–9 and won the Cy Young Award, Cuellar won 18, McNally 17, and Doyle Alexander 12. In the bullpen, left-hander Grant Jackson was 8–0 with 9 saves; right-hander Bob Reynolds won 7 and saved 9.

On August 12 we started a 14-game winning streak that carried us into first place in the Eastern Division, and we were never really threatened thereafter. We finished 8 games ahead of Boston. Right after we clinched a spot in the play-offs I took my coaches out for a celebratory drink and to thank them for bearing up under the duress created by Earl Williams. I congratulated myself, too.

"Russo told me Earl would hit 40," I said. "But I only asked for 20, and Earl hit 22—and we *did* win the division. How many managers and coaching staffs do you think would be willing to slosh through that shit he put us through all season if they ended up with the division crown?" I laughed. "All 20 of them losers—that's how many!"

In game one of the American League Championship Series against Oakland we locked up the victory in the first inning as Williams singled in 2 runs, Davis and Belanger 1 apiece. Palmer shut out the power-hitting A's and struck out 12. Jimmy was now 4–0 lifetime in the play-offs.

McNally gave up 3 early bases-empty homers in game two. RBIs from Davis and Williams kept us in there until the eighth, when Sal Bando's 2-run shot into the stands settled things.

Williams' third RBI in as many games, a home run, put us ahead for seven innings in the opener in Oakland. And the way Cuellar was pitching I felt it would take a miracle for the A's to score. But in the eighth Matty Alou got a cheap hit off the handle, and after a sacrifice and a strikeout, Joe Rudi barely made contact on a pitch that also looped over the infield. That tied the score. Then Campy Campaneris led off the bottom of the eleventh with only the fourth hit off Cuellar, who had struck out 11. It was a home run. Campy had hit all of 4 homers in 151 regular-season games.

Many people thought we were dead in game four when we trailed 4–0 after six innings. But Williams led off the seventh with a walk, Baylor singled, and Brooks drove in the run with another single. Then Etchebarren hit a Vida Blue pitch over the left-field wall to tie the score and our dugout went berserk. Bobby Grich—who had set an all-time major-league fielding record for second basemen by committing only five errors in 945 chances—led off the eighth with a long, sweet home run off Rollie Fingers. Grant Jackson shut down the A's the last two innings, and we were still alive.

But crafty Catfish Hunter fried us in the finale, 3–0. We got eight men on base and none of them touched third. It was probably the closest ALCS in history, the A's and O's each scoring a total of 15 runs, the pitching staffs turning in identical 2.74 ERAs. We had more hits, 36 to 32, but the A's won the home-run contest, 5–3 . . . and the right to go to the World Series.

I didn't even feel any excitement when I was voted the AP Manager of the Year. It was nice to finally win it, but I would have rather won the pennant.

In 1974 we won the East again—in the most harrowing finish we'd ever had in Baltimore. It took us almost five months to get going, as on August 28 we were in fourth place, eight games out of first. Our record was two games below .500, 63–65.

We'd been struggling and again trying all kinds of different combinations hoping to hit on a winner. The ball club was virtually the same as the previous year's. Our only trade had brought us starting pitcher Ross Grimsley for Merv Rettenmund. Grimsley was an important acquisition. Palmer came down with arm trouble and was on the disabled list until August 13, and Doyle Alexander never got untracked. These two men who had won 34 games between them in '73 combined for 13 this season, though Palmer was strong at the end. Boog Powell's home-run production had diminished to 11 the previous year, and I had hoped that was only an off-season. But I had learned my lesson with Donny Buford, and by July I started pinch-hitting for Boog and resting him against more and more left-handed pitchers. I played Earl Williams at first in 47 games and Don Baylor there in 28 others.

Williams was even more recalcitrant in his second year as an Oriole. My coaches and I got so upset with him that we summoned Earl to a meeting. Each of us had written down all of the points we were going to make beforehand. We covered everything that Earl did wrong, how he aggravated his teammates and how he aggravated us. Jimmy Frey was the most incensed and vehement of the group, tearing into Williams for a full twenty minutes. As always, Earl was most apologetic about his transgressions and convincing in his expressed desire to change. But he never did for long.

I remember one game in which Williams gave the sign to Palmer, who shook his head on the mound. The next thing I knew Jimmy had his hands on his hips, staring in at Williams. Then Jimmy turned his back and refused to throw the ball. I went running out to the mound.

"What the hell's wrong, Jim?" I asked.

"Well, Earl, I'll tell you," he said. "It's tough to pitch when your catcher's making faces at you. This guy tipped up his mask after I shook off the sign—and stuck his tongue out at me."

Williams seemed to have no respect for anyone—and certainly not for authority. There was a series in Detroit in which we played a night game to be followed by a day game. I closed the hotel bar after the night game and boarded the street-level escalator heading for the main lobby at 1:45 A.M. As I was riding up, Williams was coming down on the adjacent escalator.

"Hey, Earl!" I said.

"Hi, Skip," he replied.

"Where are you going?"

"I'm going out."

"It's one-forty-five."

"I've got plenty of time," he said. "I don't have to be any-where until two."

I was almost to the top and he was almost to the bottom when I hollered over my shoulder, "Well don't be too long. We got a game this afternoon."

I stepped off the escalator and saw him wave and push through the revolving door into the night. Now I don't have rules on curfews because I respect ballplayers. Either they are responsible adults who know how to take care of themselves, or they don't last in the majors very long. But even those players who occasionally like to dip into the night usually have enough respect for authority to turn right around if they have been caught as Williams had been.

Yet in my desire to win ball games I continued to put up with Williams because of his potential at bat. His hitting had figured to improve in his second season in the American League, but in-stead it declined. While a number of his 14 home runs and 52 RBIs won ball games, those totals were a major disappointment. Tommy Davis, Bobby Grich, Paul Blair, and Don Baylor all drove in more runs than Williams.

Fortunately Boog Powell got torrid at the plate in the season's final three weeks, batting .351 with 4 home runs and 9 RBIs.

We began our rush for the division lead with that 63–65 rec-ord in late August by winning 10 games in a row. During that streak Grimsley and Cuellar pitched 1–0 victories over the Red Sox, who were tied with the Yankees for first. Then Palmer shut out Boston on 3 hits. Next McNally beat the Indians 2–0 and Cuellar won the second game of the doubleheader 1–0. Grimsley extended our scoreless string to 54 innings—a league record—before yielding a 2-run homer in the ninth against Cleveland.

It was the most amazing pitching performance by a staff that I have ever witnessed, and you can see from those 1–0 and 2–0 scores that the arms had to come through for our splintered bats if we were to stay in the race. On September 17 we went into New York for a 3-game series with the Yankees, whom we trailed by 2½ games. Palmer beat them 4–0, Cuellar won 9–2, and McNally pitched a 7–0 victory to move us into first.

On September 20 we beat Boston 2–1, winning for the nine-teenth time in our last 24 games. But we didn't finally clinch the Eastern Division championship until October 1 . . . the next-to-last day of the season. On the final day we won our ninth consec-utive game to finish two up on the Yankees.

I was never happier to see a pennant-race end. It had been so hectic I was worried that the Orioles might be drained going into the play-offs against Oakland. We didn't seem to be at all tired in the first game on the West Coast, though. Blair, Robin-son, and Grich all homered off Catfish Hunter—who had beaten us seven successive times. Cuellar and Grimsley combined to check the A's as we won 6–2. But after that we definitely looked drained, getting only 7 hits and no runs in the next 2 games and losing 5–0 and 1–0. In game four Cuellar and Grimsley combined to limit the A's to 1 hit. But Cuellar—who had never walked more than six men in a game in six years with us—walked 9 and Oakland won 2–1. Our pitching staff had given up only 7 earned runs in 4 games, but our hitters had driven in only 1 run after the opener.

Without question, we were going to have to go out and find us some people who could hit the ball. We had the arms, but it had been three years since we'd been paid an extended visit by Dr. Longball.

Earl Williams was scheduled to be history. Jerry Hoffberger had already told Cashen not to bring Earl to spring training under any circumstances. Well, I thought, a little sanity might be nice for a change. But we did win two division titles with Earl Williams . . . even though some said we did so *despite* Earl Williams.

During the 1974 World Series, A's owner Charlie Finley asked Frank Cashen for permission to talk to me about managing Oakland. When Cashen told me, I was flattered, though not surprised by the overture. In my last twenty years of managing, my teams had finished first or second sixteen times. But I had already signed a contract to manage the Orioles for the 1975 season, and I was happy with life in Baltimore.

Marianna and I had purchased for under $30,000 a nice little three-bedroom house in the Perry Hall suburb of Baltimore, which was less than a thirty-minute drive from Memorial Stadium. That was in September 1968, and the following spring we had added an in-ground swimming pool. And I was now earning more money with the Orioles than I thought possible for an aging kid from St. Louis.

Harry Dalton had gotten me at a closeout-sale price in '68, but I'd pushed him for a $12,000 raise my first full season as manager, to $40,000. Figuring I had excellent bargaining power after we won the pennant in '69, I'd asked Dalton for a two-year contract. I wanted some security. He wouldn't even talk about it, saying multi-year contracts were against team policy. I knew that, but I also wanted to double my salary and I told Harry, "Well, here's what you're gonna have to give me—$80,000 for 1970, and I'll agree right now to work for $5,000 less in '71." After some hemming and hawing Harry agreed to this arrangement. The second-year obligation was mine alone.

The important thing to me was getting the bigger salary first in case I got fired. The key to negotiating, I had learned years ago, was in deciding what you would be satisfied with. I was satisfied.

Of course, after we won the World Series in 1970, I had to think Harry would say, "Despite our arrangement, I don't want to give you a cut for next season, Earl."

Well think again, Earl. I worked for $5,000 less in '71—and we won the pennant again. I signed a contract for a $95,000 salary in '72 and again offered to work for $5,000 less the following year. This deal was made with Frank Cashen, who had replaced Dalton. Since we didn't do so well in '72, I didn't mind signing for $90,000 in '73. But when we won the Eastern title that season, I said the hell with those two-year deals. I was the 1973 Manager of the Year and had far and away the best record in baseball over the past five and a half years. I had now established my abilities and realized that if I kept signing one-year contracts I'd make a lot more money in the long run—assuming that we kept winning and there *was* a long run. I went close to $100,000 in '74, we won again, and I eventually moved up to around $175,000 per year.

I remember one year Cashen made me a contract offer, and I said, "Frank, I've got a higher figure in mind. I'll have to think about it and come back, because that figure wouldn't satisfy me." When I came back, Frank went up considerably. I told him, "That's $5,000 more than the figure I had in mind."

"Earl, that's what we're going to pay you," he said.

"No," I said, "just give me my figure and I'll be happy."

"We'll split the difference," Frank said. "I'll give you $2,500 over your figure and we'll all be happy."

I didn't sign a multi-year contract until 1978, which also covered the '79 and '80 seasons and had solid increases built into it. By then Marianna and I had purchased a beautiful home on a golf course in Hialeah, Florida. As we were thinking about retiring there, perhaps after the 1982 season, my most recent contract was for only two years.

But I have to say that I was lucky to have already signed with the Orioles before Charlie Finley expressed interest in me following the '74 season. Finley was known for making multi-year, high-salary contract offers that were not easily turned down. Every manager wants security. Billy Hunter left us in June 1977 to sign a multi-year contract as manager of the Texas Rangers. When he got fired he still had a couple of years' salary coming to him. A number of teams subsequently offered him very enticing contracts to become their manager, but it didn't pay him to accept them. Any money he earned in baseball would simply reduce the salary he already had coming from Texas. I really don't see how it's legal for a manager to be paid by two teams at the same time. Say I was making $200,000 with Baltimore and got fired, but signed with Oakland for $150,000. Baltimore would still be paying me $50,000 while I managed against the Orioles. It seems to me to be a conflict of interest, though it's within the rules of baseball.

Still, the idea is always to get what you can while you can. When I signed the three-year contract I think I was the highest-paid manager in baseball. But very soon others passed me by, as managers got fired and new men came in while salaries throughout the game were zooming upward. I *know* when I signed my last contract that it was for the highest figure ever paid a manager. The Mark McCormick agency that represents me got a list of manager salaries from the Players Association. In the old days the owners tried to keep salaries confidential so that players, managers, and coaches had no basis for comparison. Thanks to Marvin Miller and the Players Association all that has changed. I know I would never have been able to include a death-benefit provision (Marianna will be compensated should I die) in my contract if the ballplayers had not pushed improvements that aided all of us. I think Billy Martin has since topped me in salary, which is as it should be, the last to sign raising the top figure for all to shoot at. I would certainly move ahead again if I decide to manage beyond 1982.

The toughest negotiator I knew among the players was pitcher Dave McNally. Jim Palmer called Dave "the No. 1 mercenary." Jim labeled me "No. 2 mercenary" and himself No. 3. Bobby Grich qualified, too. Palmer quotes Mike Flanagan as having told Grich, "The only time you let loose of a nickel is to get a better grip on it."

But McNally would *never* bend in contract negotiations or

anything else that had to do with money. Near the end of the 1968 season Jimmy Hardin had eighteen wins. In our rotation he had only one more start coming up. McNally already had twenty-one victories and he had two starts remaining, including the season's final game.

I called McNally in and said, "Dave, would you mind giving up your last start for Jimmy Hardin? You've got your twenty. If Jimmy wins tomorrow he'll have a shot at twenty in the last game. But that's your start. What do you say?"

"Are you serious?" Dave said, and proceeded to tell me in no uncertain terms that he would not be bypassed. He wanted to win as many ball games as he could.

Then I found out why. McNally had a bonus clause in his contract that would pay him, in addition to his basic contract figure, $1,000 for every win over twelve. He went out and won that final game to earn $10,000 in bonus money. It also turned out that Hardin lost his bid for win number nineteen, so it didn't matter that McNally wouldn't give up a start.

But during negotiations for 1969 with Harry Dalton, McNally insisted on starting at a figure that combined his previous salary *and* bonus. Dave was coming off his first twenty-win season, having finished at 22–10 with a sparkling 1.95 ERA in '68.

"Oh, no, we can't do that," Dalton said.

"Well, we're going to," McNally said, "or I won't be pitching next year."

Every spring McNally was a holdout for ten to fifteen days. And every day George Bamberger and I would collar Dalton and say, "For God's sake, Harry, give McNally what he wants. We can't afford to lose a twenty-game winner and you know it."

McNally would be in Key Biscayne playing golf, refusing to even talk until Dalton agreed to discuss Dave's figure. McNally was the only player I knew who could consistently bring Harry Dalton to his knees. Dalton never once got Dave to come down even a nickel below what he felt he was worth. You have to remember that baseball salaries were relatively low in those days; the minimum was still about $7,000. Only a few years before this Ralph Houk, as GM of the Yankees, had fined Jim Bouton for every day he held out and refused to report to spring training. If Dalton had tried that with McNally, I'm certain Dave would have filed a lawsuit.

Once Dalton left, Frank Cashen inherited the annual problem of trying to sign McNally. Frank fared no better than Harry had. So when we began talking about trades at the organizational meeting following the '74 season, McNally's name came up. Dave was coming off a 16–10 year, but he'd had some arm problems. And the team we wanted to deal with, Montreal, needed a left-handed starter. I hated to part with a competitor like McNally, even though he'd once said in annoyance, "The only thing Weaver knows about pitching is that he couldn't hit it." He knew better than that. In each of my first four years as his manager McNally had won twenty games or more and had averaged nineteen wins through seven seasons with me.

The player we were after was outfielder Ken Singleton, a big, sharp-eyed switch-hitter. Only two years before he'd had over 100 RBIs, over 100 walks, 23 home runs, and a .302 batting average. Bamberger didn't want to give up McNally, either, but Montreal turned down the other players we offered. So we traded Dave, Rich Coggins, and minor-league pitcher Bill Kirkpatrick for Singleton and pitcher Mike Torrez.

I had decided I couldn't play Coggins and Bumbry in the same outfield. I did not want to have to keep running to score rather than watching balls fly over the fence. I felt Bumbry had more potential than Coggins, who was a nice polite fellow but a very different drummer. He liked to dress in pink suits, big straw hats, and knickers that he tucked into high boots. Every day he went to a florist and bought a boutonniere. Rich didn't last in the majors very long. I was surprised when I heard he had joined the FBI. Weren't they all plainclothesmen?

Neither Bamberger nor I liked the reports on Torrez, who had won fifteen games for a sub-.500 Expo team in '74 but had a history of wildness. George did a tremendous job with Torrez. I had him teach Mike the slow curve and I also had a number of discussions with him about the philosophy of pitching and how to concentrate and work on each batter. Mike tended to nibble too much instead of firing the ball and setting up hitters. He won twenty games for us in '75, the only time he's ever done so.

We acquired another big power-hitter that year, Lee May,

sending infielders Enos Cabell and Rob Andrews to Houston for him. May led us in RBIs with 99—the highest total on the Orioles since 1971—and hit 20 home runs, second only to Baylor's 25. The trade was a great deal, as was the one for Singleton. Singy soon developed into the most intelligent hitter I had ever seen. He knows how to work pitchers into giving him *his* pitch—or a walk. He had 118 bases on balls and a .300 average in '75.

We also traded Boog Powell to Cleveland for catcher Dave Duncan, who became my right-hand-hitting backstop. Etchebarren's wish was finally granted and he was sold to a West Coast team, the Angels. Duncan hit 12 homers for us and Hendricks had 8 . . . so I got my 20 without good old Earl Williams.

Williams was not invited to spring training. That didn't stop Earl, who showed up on his own. Cashen had been trying for months to deal off Williams. But every team knew about Earl the Pearl, and no one wanted him. Cashen told me, "He has to stay until I can get rid of him. I'll find some team. But I'll tell you one thing—Earl Williams is not going north with us."

That was fine with me. I certainly hadn't been able to reach Earl and had no hopes of ever doing so. He was the one player in the majors with whom I had totally lost. I took the big L.

Still, cut time came and Cashen had made no deal for Williams. "Give me two more weeks," he said to me. It wasn't until ten days into the season, on April 17, that Cashen finally unloaded Williams. The only team that would take him was Atlanta, whence he had come. "Nice going, Frank," I said. "You got them back for what they did to us."

Earl Williams subsequently went from Atlanta to Montreal to Oakland and was released after the '77 season. Then he took out ads in newspapers headlined: "Have Bat, Will Travel." After a couple of seasons in Mexico, I heard he was out of baseball at age thirty-two. One scout who saw him in the Mexican League said Williams told him, "I wish I had listened to Weaver." Etchebarren, who was second-string in Los Angeles and then Milwaukee before getting cut, might have decided he would have been better off staying in Baltimore, too.

Cashen was quite pleased with having relieved himself of two headaches in Williams and McNally. As it turned out, McNally became a historic figure shortly thereafter. Dave was earning

$160,000 in Montreal, but he came down with a shoulder injury, and after twelve starts (3–6, 5.26 ERA) he packed his bags and went home. "I'd have the hitter set up for a fastball," he later told me, "and I knew I had him out. Then he'd rip the fastball. So I told the Expos, 'I'm not worth the money. I'm retiring.'"

Expo president John McHale refused to believe McNally was quitting. McHale said it was "just a matter of talking green" to McNally and flew out to see Dave in Billings, Montana. McHale offered more money, but Dave wasn't interested. He could have just stayed in Montreal and collected his $160,000 doing nothing. I was not surprised that he didn't. Dave had too much pride. I knew about the man's character, and when he made a decision it was final.

Following the 1975 season McNally and Andy Messersmith of the Dodgers, with the backing of the Major League Players Association, challenged the reserve clause. (McNally had no intention of playing again, his fight being strictly a matter of principle.) Arbitrator Peter Seitz ruled that the option clause in their contracts bound them to their teams for only one year. Before issuing his decision, the impartial arbitrator informed the negotiators for both sides how he would rule and suggested that before he did so they settle the matter themselves. John Gaherin reportedly could not convince the owners to negotiate because their lawyers were certain the courts would overturn Seitz' ruling. The owners, who'd had everything their own way for a century, blew it by not sitting down at the bargaining table right then. A federal court backed Seitz, ruling that baseball's reserve clause was illegal, and free agency changed the old ball game after the 1976 season.

As for all those player moves that restructured the Orioles for the '75 season, they looked great in Florida. We won 18 of 27 exhibition games, then nose-dived when the regular schedule commenced. It was bad enough when we hadn't even achieved a .500 record by mid-May. Then we lost 11 of 12—including 7 in a row, our longest losing streak since '68—and fell to last place. We had the lowest batting average in the league, and our relief pitchers were 1–9 with a 5.25 ERA.

From that point on we compiled the best record in the league, 74–43, led by Jim Palmer, who won his second Cy Young Award.

Palmer was 23–11, with 25 complete games, 10 shutouts, and a
2.09 ERA. But this was the season Boston came up with two
rookies named Fred Lynn and Jim Rice, and we just couldn't
close the gap on the Red Sox no matter how hard we tried. We
finished 4½ games behind, in second place.

Even when the Orioles were winning pennants and division titles, certain members of the press corps in Baltimore were writing columns calling for the firing of Earl Weaver. Phil Jackman
of the *Evening Sun* wrote several such columns in 1973 when we
were going bad, but then we won the division. The next year we
had a bad streak and he wrote, "Quick, fire Weaver now before
he starts winning again." We did win again. That didn't deter
Jackman's campaign to get rid of Weaver. Early in '75 he wrote
a column headlined "Time for the Pink Slip." In it Jackman said,
"The last few years, the manager has mishandled, misused, mis-
arranged, mismanaged, miscued, misconceived, misapplied and
misbehaved, only to have the players save his bacon with a couple of stretch drives to the division flag." He went on to write,
"Weaver never wanted good backup personnel, because it made
handling them a tough job." That was plain stupid. The more
talent a manager has on his bench, the better his chances of winning. I kept reading Jackman and wondering why, instead of
covering a ball club, he wasn't switched to covering the garden
club.

Now any writer's words are only his opinions. The problem is
that most people who read those words in a newspaper accept
them as facts, believing the writer knows something about baseball. My own father read that column and asked me, "Why don't
you want good backup people?" My father had been around
baseball most of his life, he was intelligent, and should have
known better. But he believed that everything printed in a newspaper was the gospel truth.

I remember one time we had an 8 P.M. game in Baltimore and
the newspaper had it listed for 7:30. I could not convince my
own father that the newspaper was wrong. "Earl, it wouldn't say
7:30 in the paper if the game wasn't scheduled to start then."

"I'm the manager of the ball club and I have to turn in my
lineup card," I told him. "So I have to know the starting time."

"But look what the paper says."

I couldn't win with my father and I couldn't win with Jackman or a young reporter named Chan Keith, who covered the Orioles for the *News American* from '69 through '73. After we lost in 1972 Keith wrote a four-part series "dealing with the Decline and Fall of the Orioles." The essential reason why we lost, in Chan's view, was because we didn't bunt enough.

Keith was not the expert on baseball he thought he was. I recall a game in September when we were still in the race. We got the first two men on in a late inning and Tommy Davis came up and doubled off the wall to drive in two runs. We won 2–0. The next night we had a similar situation. Two singles, then Tommy Davis stepped up and hit into a double play. The next batter hit a flyball that would have scored a run had we called for a bunt that moved the runner over. We lost in extra innings. Afterward, Keith said to me, "You little idiot—if you'd bunted you would have won."

I angrily pointed out to him that the previous night we hadn't bunted in that situation yet had won. But my explanations never got into Keith's stories. There was nothing I could do about how badly he made me look in the papers, maybe even in the perception of my employers. Not that I was worried about losing my job, because I had already agreed to a contract for the following season when the series began on October 2. But the more I read Keith's series, the more it festered in my mind and the more I wanted to rap Keith in the nose.

We were in Cleveland for the last day of the season and Keith was in the clubhouse after we split a doubleheader. I saw him standing there and, to my everlasting shame, I lost control. I walked over and spit on him. Later, God forgive me, I spit on him again. I guess I was hoping Keith, who was much bigger than me, would take a pop at me and I could punch him back without fear of an assault charge.

But after I released the rage in me, I realized that as long as I was managing there would be writers like Keith and Jackman and Neal Eskridge, another Baltimore columnist who persistently denounced me as incompetent and demanded that I be fired. Such members of the media are simply another occupational hazard of managing in the major leagues. Players are subjected to the same hazard.

And not only from writers, but from certain radio and television interviewers, too. The worst is insult specialist Cliff Keane, who has a radio show in Boston in which he talks more than his guests. I find him kind of funny at times, but he won't have me on his program anymore. Keane's show is "live" and I once told him on the air, "You're unknowledgeable about baseball. You've been around the game for years without learning a thing about it. Why don't you shut up and let somebody speak who knows what he's talking about."

I thought Don Baylor was going to punch Cliff the first time they met. It was 1972, Baylor was a rookie, and we were sitting in the dugout before a game and this little guy came over spouting insults a mile a minute. Baylor had never heard of Cliff Keane when he walked up and said, "This team traded Frank Robinson for a parachute-arm player like you? You throw a ball, Baylor, and it arcs so high it comes down with frost on it." Baylor looked at Cliff like he was nuts for a few more minutes of his insults, then Don stood up and went for him. Someone stepped in between them and Cliff said, "Sit down, parachute arm."

Cliff Keane phoned me at Memorial Stadium in 1981 trying to reach Mark Belanger after Mark had hit his first homer in about five years. I said, "Are you still on the air with that nickel-and-dime radio show?" He told me what he wanted and I said, "Mark don't want to talk to you. A person would have to be stupid to pick up the phone and be insulted by you for fifteen minutes." The only time Mark talked to Cliff, Keane called him "a hotdog-and-Coke hitter." Mark asked what that meant, and Cliff said, "Every time you step up to the plate, the fans all go for a hotdog and Coke." Mark didn't appreciate that.

Now all members of the media aren't the same. Some of them have done as much for me as my 1,200 victories have. The kind words I always appreciated and I've thanked writers, in person and in notes I've written them, for stories that I thought were particularly well done. Some of those guys have studied baseball and it shows in their work. And there was no animosity toward any writer whose words on Weaver were negative but accurate in relating mistakes.

But I've pointed out to writers—just as I have to ballplayers and umpires all these years—their mistakes as well. I've torn stories out of the papers when they contained inaccurate or misleading information, brought them to the ball park, and told the writers where they had gone wrong and why. Some of them have appreciated the lessons. Others would just as soon Weaver take that story and shove it.

"What difference is it going to make if there's an error in a story?" they say. "Nobody's going to know tomorrow."

"Hell," I say, "when I make a mistake, you make sure *everyone* knows it tomorrow."

I don't think any manager in baseball has made himself more available to the press over the years than Earl Weaver. I arrive at the ball park early and see writers in my office and in the dugout or on the field pregame. I enjoy watching batting practice like any fan, but often I can't do so because I'm being interviewed, and I feel that is part of my obligations. I give them as much time as possible after games, too.

Of course, there have been occasions when writers have caught me at a bad time and I've hollered, "Get out of the office! Can't you see I'm busy?" But I've apologized to almost everyone I've hollered at. I've apologized to all of the Baltimore writers, because I've hollered at all of them over the years. I've apologized when I've been wrong, and I've apologized when I felt I'd hurt a writer's feelings unjustly. I refuse to carry a grudge. I even started speaking to Phil Jackman again after years of silence on my part.

I just wish I'd had my radio show—which I did not start doing until the 1980 season—from the beginning in Baltimore. Or at least from '72 on when the Weaver misrepresentations began. It always irked me that false information was going out to so many people who I had no way of reaching. Now when a writer misrepresents the facts, I don't mind refuting him on "Manager's Corner."

A newspaper story early in the '81 season really annoyed me. It was headlined: "Weaver-Martin Overshadow McGregor Performance." The writer started off the story saying something like: "It's a shame that whenever Earl Weaver and Billy Martin get together they have to act like rowdy schoolboys." Then he went on to say that my ejection from the game and Martin's pulling his team off the field had detracted from Scotty McGregor's beautiful pitching performance against Oakland. Well, in that game there was no Weaver-Martin shit. Some writers have been writing for years that we're always at each other's throats.

What the writer should have written about this Oakland game was that when Eddie Murray was ejected, Weaver became so incensed that he also was ejected and *then* he acted like a rowdy schoolboy. That was what happened in the second inning. I was in the office with my feet propped up watching on TV when Belanger subsequently tried to bunt our runner over. The ball got by the Oakland catcher and the runner was safe. But Martin came out claiming there had been a foul tip. The plate umpire said no and Martin argued for a while, then appealed to the first-base umpire. He reversed the decision. Cal Ripken, the Orioles' acting manager, and Belanger angrily argued that Mark had never touched the ball. This went on for some time—so Martin pulled his team off the field in protest.

I thought this was pretty funny. The umpire had to be saying to himself: "What the hell's going on here? Martin wins the decision and *he* pulls his team off the field." But the Baltimore writer's column gave the impression that *I* was still on the field causing the delay. He never said that I was already in the clubhouse, and that's what I took exception to and said so on the radio—the misrepresentation of the facts. I said this writer was not knowledgeable about baseball and that his columns were his opinions, which he was entitled to, but the reporting was not factual. Then I repeated some of the questions he had recently asked me, which showed that he didn't even know whether a particular hitter was left-handed or right-handed. That seemed to me ridiculous for a writer covering baseball.

Equally ridiculous was the treatment I had received at a Los Angeles television station two years ago. I agreed to be interviewed on the live evening news program when we were at Anaheim Stadium. It was bad enough that I had to stand there with a mike pinned to my chest while the sports report was pushed back farther and farther. When it finally came on, my interview was preceded by a four-year-old tape of me arguing with an umpire. "And now, a live report from the Big A with Earl Weaver," the anchorman intoned as the tape ended. The camera flicked on me as I was tearing off my microphone, declaring, "I already saw this picture" and stormed off. An ancient tape was not germaine to the 1980 season.

But overall I think my association with the media has been a good one. I've built up an excellent rapport with most of the baseball writers all across the country over the years. Most of them are good guys with whom I've enjoyed bullshitting, and I presume they have too.

chapter
Thirteen

With free agency on the horizon, everyone who would become eligible at the end of the 1976 season was playing out his option. They wanted to see what they were worth on the open market. We all knew it would be an enormous amount of money. Our unsigned players were Don Baylor, Bobby Grich, Mike Torrez, and Wayne Garland. The question was: Could we afford to keep them?

Hank Peters had become general manager, with Frank Cashen staying on to concentrate on the business side, and Oriole finances being what they were, it was a difficult time for them. The Orioles had lost several thousand dollars in '75 despite a rise in attendance to just over a million. In '74 the club's net profit was only $82,700, so there was no money to throw around. We always tried to hold down expenses in Baltimore, which is not a complaint but simply a statement of the reality we lived with. That didn't mean we wouldn't spend to stay competitive.

For example, almost as soon as I took over the ball club I'd had the Orioles go to the expense of filming our hitters, making a record of them when they were going good, then filming them when they slumped so we could show players what they were doing differently at the plate. I believe in using every tool available.

In 1975 I had a chance to try out, with the thought of buying a radar gun for the first time. I saw it would be an invaluable tool for us in clocking the speed of pitches and the speed of throws from the outfield. Without a mechanical device, you never know the exact answers to these questions. That was why scouting was imprecise. I remembered all those times we minor-league managers sat in the stands, and in different locations so that we wouldn't influence one another, and rated players. Often one of us would rate a player 1 while two others would rate him a 3 or a 4 in the same category.

Using the radar gun that spring of '75 I discovered why Ross Grimsley's change-up was so effective. His fastball clocked at 82 mph and his change-up came in at 62. That 20-mph difference was what really threw off hitters. If a pitcher had an 82-mph fastball, say, and his slider came in at about the same speed, that was no good. We could slow the slider to 72, because that would make the batter hesitate.

When I timed our outfielders' throws, Larry Harlow was faster than anyone on the Oriole pitching staff—92 mph. I decided right then that there would be a time when I would use Harlow on the mound. Every season you have periods when your pitching staff is thin and you're getting bombed out of a ball game in which you don't want to waste a pitcher. A couple of years later we were in just such a situation against Toronto, losing 19–6, and I brought in Harlow. The plate umpire initially said I couldn't, until I pointed out that this was within the rules. Hadn't Campy Campaneris played all nine positions in a game for the A's? Harlow came in and struck out the first two Blue Jays he faced, just blew them away. Then he walked three or four batters, so that experiment ended.

But the point is that the radar gun, which cost $1,200 then, would be a big plus for the Orioles. Unfortunately, Cashen said he couldn't squeeze the money out of his 1975 budget to purchase a speed gun. But in 1976 I convinced Hank Peters to buy a number of guns for our scouting staff and for the Orioles' use. We pay a former minor-league infielder, Charley Bree, to sit in the stands behind home plate in Memorial Stadium and clock the pitchers on both teams. Now there's no longer any such thing as an opposing pitcher being "sneaky fast." We know exactly how fast his pitches are and our hitters know what to expect. And since we got the guns we know that when one of our scouts reports that a prospect throws as hard as Jim Palmer, he's not guessing.

Peters and Cashen were most concerned, going into the '76 season, about signing Baylor, Grich, and Torrez. Wayne Garland was only 2-and-5 in '75. And there was some hope with Grich. But Baylor was represented by Jerry Kapstein, one of the most demanding agents, who was asking far more than Oriole management felt it could afford. I certainly didn't blame Kapstein for aiming high for his client, but I didn't want us to lose a player of Baylor's ability without getting something in return. There weren't a lot of outfielders around who could hit 25 home runs in Baltimore as Don had in '75. The feeling was Torrez would ask for a fortune, too.

So Peters worked out a trade with Oakland that brought us Reggie Jackson and pitcher Ken Holtzman, who were also in their option seasons, along with a minor-league pitcher. We gave up Baylor, 20-game winner Mike Torrez, and pitcher Paul Mitchell. The deal was made on April 2, and I couldn't wait to get Reggie—a better outfielder with even more power than Baylor. Our entire coaching staff was excited about Reggie; we needed another left-handed hitter.

But Peters couldn't sign him. Reggie didn't like the offer and he flew to his place in Arizona and said he wasn't going to play baseball anymore. Peters flew out there to see Reggie three times. Jackson was asking for a four-year contract at $250,000 per season. If we had foreseen the heights salaries were going to reach, we'd probably still have Reggie Jackson today—and he would have been the greatest thing to happen to Baltimore since crab cakes. He finally signed for one season, for about $185,000.

Reggie didn't report until May 2, but Oriole fans loved him from the go, giving him a standing ovation that first day. The O's had never drawn many black fans, despite the city's sizable black populace, but they started coming out for Reggie, who was always widely quoted in the papers and exciting on the field.

Reggie liked to get to the ball park early, because he loved to talk to the press. In fact, he was almost always still in the clubhouse talking to writers when batting practice started. I felt Reggie believed he was giving his time and selling the team in the newspapers to help attendance.

Still, I had to run in and get him for batting practice several times. "Reggie, you're two minutes late. Let's go."

"Okay," he'd say, and run right out and pop a few balls into the right-field seats.

The third time I had to fetch him for BP, I said, "Look, Reggie, I can't do this every day. You've got to be out there with the rest of the players when BP starts, because Reggie Jackson and Timmy Nordbrook are the same on this club."

"Who?" Reggie asked.

"Timmy Nordbrook. He plays shortstop and second base for us. Timmy's out there right now working his ass off."

Reggie didn't know all his teammates immediately, I discovered, but he tried to do everything he could for the ball club from the beginning. He's a good person. He was also right when he joined the Yankees the next year and said, "I'm the straw that stirs the drink." I know it caused him trouble, particularly with Thurman Munson, but the statement was accurate. Reggie is *the* leader.

The one small problem I had with Reggie concerned base stealing. He didn't understand why I do not allow players to steal on their own, which he wanted to do. He seemed to feel that I didn't trust his judgment. I told him that no matter how smart a player is or how hard he tries, it's impossible for a player to think about the whole team. But Reggie wanted to show me.

He was on first with one out and Lee May up against a left-handed pitcher. Reggie promptly stole second, which resulted in an intentional walk to Lee May. I had to send up a right-handed pinch hitter, and he made out. Reggie came in looking pleased with himself.

"Yeah, you stole," I told him. "That opened first base and naturally the left-hander walked May. I had the gun loaded with Lee. You took the bat out of his hands and forced me to waste another player. That's what your stolen base got us."

"Yeah, I see," said Reggie, who never stole on his own again.

Reggie Jackson had a fine year with us, hitting 27 homers and driving in 91 runs in only 121 games. He also stole 28 bases in 35 attempts.

I wished from the beginning that Ken Holtzman had come in with Reggie's attitude. When he reported, Holtzman told Hank Peters that if he didn't reach a contract agreement with the Orioles by mid-May, he wouldn't sign with the organization, period. Holtzman arrived with a bad attitude that got worse. He would argue about *anything*, from free agency to the general manager to his teammates and whatever may have fallen in between those subjects. I had *some* debates with him and very few of them lasted less than thirty minutes.

George Bamberger was not crazy about Holtzman as a pitcher, but I loved him. He had a good fastball that he moved around, and he changed speeds extremely well. He kept throwing fastballs low and outside and the batters kept hitting groundballs to the shortstop. He was stubborn, though. Holtzman would *never* throw over to first to hold a runner on base. And he insisted on throwing his dinky curveball over the plate instead of wasting the pitch. He'd throw three curveballs a game and give up three hits off them.

Holtzman showed me some guts on the mound. He pitched one game with a tremendously swollen ankle, though that may have been because he was pitching for next year's contract. And he pitched well: 5–4 with a 2.85 ERA. He had everything going for him, except for his stubbornness and surly attitude that led us to get rid of him.

On June 15 Ken Holtzman was the key man in one of the great trades in Oriole history. We sent him to the Yankees with pitchers Doyle Alexander, Grant Jackson, and Jimmy Freeman (from Rochester) and catcher Ellie Hendricks. In return we got pitchers Rudy May, Tippy Martinez, Scotty McGregor, and Dave Pagan, as well as catcher Rick Dempsey. It is rare when a team can acquire in the same trade two young pitchers with the ability of Tippy and Scotty and an outstanding catcher like Rick. As for Holtzman, Billy Martin stopped using him the following season, finally trading him away.

Despite all of our new talent, we were an up-and-down ball club for the first half of the '76 season . . . mostly down. In June we had a nine-game losing streak, the longest I had ever suffered through. When we got pitching, we didn't hit. When we scored some runs, we couldn't keep the opposition from scoring more.

Now the only difference between a nine-game losing streak and a three-game losing streak is that the former is three times as long. I kept trying different lineups, each of which I was sure was going to bring us a win. When it didn't, the anguish mounted in my gut. But I arose every morning *knowing* I was going to win that night. If you believe in your players, you just know you are going to win. Then a bloop hit beats you 2–1. And the next night a Jim Palmer goes into the fifth inning with a 5–1 lead . . . and can't hold it. You lose 8–7 and it's nightmare time.

During the streak, we played four particularly miserable games in Kansas City. The Royals were hitting singles to the outfield and sliding into second. In Mike Flanagan's first start they stole about seven bases on him in less than three innings. He just didn't know how to hold runners on, and he also took too much time releasing the ball to the plate, which allowed men on first to get enormous jumps. Two weeks later he went back to Rochester to work on these deficiencies.

It was in Kansas City that I thought I was being fired. Kenny Nigro wrote a story in which Hank Peters said things like, "We can't continue to play like this. The team looks like it hasn't played baseball before." I went right to Hank and said, "Look, damnit, if you want to fire me, go ahead and fire me. That's your prerogative. I've got too good a record—but go ahead if you want to."

I was happy he didn't, but I knew I wouldn't have much trouble finding another job . . . probably at a raise in salary, too.

We turned right around after losing nine straight and won seven in a row. Then it was back on the roller-coaster again, as several of my great veterans began that sad, inevitable slide into part-time roles. Brooks Robinson hadn't reached double figures in home runs since 1971, had batted only .201 in '75, so Doug DeCinces became my regular third baseman that season. There had been a story in the spring that Peters and Cashen had promised Brooks he would start the first month of the season, but of course that wasn't true. I had never made a promise to a ballplayer in my life and I never would, not even to an institution named Brooks Robinson. And Brooks accepted his new role gracefully, filling in on defense in late innings and saving us in several games with his glove.

Hank Peters got on me pretty good early in the season over Mike Cuellar's poor performances. But the Cuban-born left-hander had never pitched well in cool weather and as a result got off to slow starts virtually every year.

"Earl, are you sure he's still got it?" Hank asked.

"He's done this before and come on," I said. "Mike lost five of his first eight decisions last season."

"He's thirty-nine now," Hank said.

"He was thirty-eight then, and he ended up with seventeen complete games—five of them shutouts. Hell, he had two one-hitters, a two-hitter, a three-hitter, a four-hitter, and six five-hitters. I ain't giving up on Cuellar yet."

Mike Cuellar had won 139 games for me in seven years—an average of almost 20 victories per season—and he held the club record for complete games with 131. But his pattern was to give up runs in the first inning or so, then he would break a sweat and the hitter's backs. I'd close my eyes early and leave him in till he got out of the jams, and then he would take charge.

In 1976, though, it eventually became apparent to me that Mike could no longer be counted upon to extricate himself from first-inning troubles. I say eventually because I gave him a lot of opportunities, as his ultimate 4–13 record indicates. But, with runners on the corners and only one out, I had to start relieving him in inning one. I'd probably passed the point of common sense in keeping him in the rotation, letting my judgment be clouded by sentiment.

After I'd relieved him in the first inning of one game, Mike came into the dugout angry. "You give me no chance!" he shouted.

"Mike, I gave you more chances than my first wife!" I hollered back.

In late August I had to put him in the bullpen, which didn't make me feel good. Mike came to me and there was sorrow in his eyes when he said, "You used to call on me all the time."

"I'm sorry, Mike," I said, "but you know I gotta think of the ball club." We released him that winter.

Paul Blair was the third veteran whose playing time I was

forced to reduce because his batting average fell to .197. I started Al Bumbry in center field in over fifty games, knowing he was our future there. But Paul was still a phenomenal defensive player, and I used him in 145 games. He always found ways to contribute.

Yet Paul Blair was among the most underpaid players in the game. After eleven years, he was being paid about $80,000. And at season's end the front office tried to cut his salary $10,000 for '77. That winter as usual I played golf with Paul almost every day, and he kept asking me to trade him. I didn't want to. He was a tremendous asset to the club and I felt he would hit enough against left-handers.

Then he found out the Yankees were interested in him, and he begged me to trade him. "Please trade me, Earl. Please."

"Why do you want to go to New York?" I asked him as we rode in a golf cart. "You say I don't play you enough here, but you'll play even less there. You won't get 375 at-bats with New York as you got here."

"Just let me go, Earl," he said. "I'll play and I'll also make more money."

In January we traded Blair to the Yankees for outfielders Elliott Maddox and Rick Bladt. Paul signed a contract that guaranteed him $270,000 for two years. He batted 165 times the first year and helped the Yankees win the 1977 pennant with his defense. He was released the next season, but at least he retired with the best salary of his career.

Although the Orioles played .600 ball the second half of the '76 season, we never drew closer than seven games of the Yankees. There were a number of keys to our turnaround. Kenny Singleton, whose batting average was .185 on June 2, finished at .278. Lee May led the league in RBIs with 109. Jim Palmer won 20 games for the sixth time in the last seven seasons. And Wayne Garland, who won two games in '75, had 20 wins this season.

Garland had spoken about eight words in the two-plus seasons he'd been with us. But late in the season I picked up the paper one day and saw a story in which Garland—who was 15–5 at this point—said, "Earl Weaver mishandled me."

Goddamn! I thought, I wished someone had mishandled me the way I had mishandled him! Garland went on, "Weaver left me to rot in the bullpen. I could have helped the team in 1975, but instead he brought up Paul Mitchell and Mike Flanagan. He never gave me a shot." In '75 Garland had pitched more innings for us than Mitchell and Flanagan combined, even though they had both been more impressive at Rochester.

Garland also said that he would sign with the Orioles if he were offered a multi-year contract and if Rochester manager Joe Altobelli replaced me in Baltimore. I told the writers, "This kid is in a position to make a whole lot of money now, but that isn't good enough for him. He not only wants to make a million dollars—he wants to name the manager of the Baltimore Orioles! I shouldn't have to take this kind of crap from children!"

I cooled off the next day, as I always do after a player has made some foolish remarks. Garland was welcome to his opinions, but how he figured he should have been a starter on a staff with Palmer, Torrez, Cuellar, and Grimsley, plus Doyle Alexander, I don't know.

What we did know was that as a twenty-game winner, Garland was going to command a big contract. He was now also represented by agent Jerry Kapstein. Hank Peters consulted with me and asked what I thought of young left-hander Mike Flanagan, if he was ready to move into the starting rotation. Flanagan had won three games and lost six for us in '75 and '76.

From the first time George Bamberger saw Mike Flanagan though, he loved him. "Goddamn, Earl, this guy can pitch!" George said, and he was right. I told Peters, "Flanagan's got as much ability as Wayne Garland. So if we lose Garland, that leaves a spot open for Flanagan in the rotation. Flanagan's gonna be another Mickey Lolich."

Flanagan had also played out his option and had to be signed. But that did not appear to pose a serious problem—until he too became a Kapstein client. Then Peters had to come up with some pretty good money, $800,000 spread over five years.

If I had said that Garland was better, Hank would have made a strong effort to sign him. But I don't think Hank could have matched the contract the Indians reportedly gave Garland—$3 million for ten years.

As it turned out, Wayne had the misfortune to tear the rotator cuff in his right arm, an injury few pitchers return from. In the next three seasons Mike Flanagan won 67 games for us.

Had the Oriole coffers resembled those of George Steinbrenner, we would have been able to satisfy Bobby Grich's contract demands. Unfortunately, he signed with the Angels. With Grich I would have had much more hitting potential in the infield, as he could have switched to shortstop. I had tried to upgrade the hitting there by experimenting with Doug DeCinces at short during each of the previous two seasons, before finally making him the starter at third in '76. I wasn't worried about second because I felt rookie Rich Dauer, who had led the International League in batting with a .336 average, was ready to hit major-league pitching.

The so-called experts were really putting us down in the spring of '77, feeling sorry for the poor O's who had lost Reggie Jackson, Bobby Grich, and Wayne Garland in the re-entry proceedings. But I thought we had enough talent to be serious contenders, and that feeling increased during spring training.

I told the writers then, "This is potentially the finest set of arms since our four twenty-game winners in '71."

One of the writers repeated that to Jim Palmer, who said, "Is Earl serious?" Then Palmer thought a moment and mused, "Ross Grimsley didn't pitch anywhere near his potential last year. And you know Rudy May can throw the ball as well as anybody." In addition we had Palmer and three talented youngsters: Flanagan, Scott McGregor, and Dennis Martinez. McGregor had been 12–6 at Rochester and pitched well for us at season's end. He was a superb athlete, a better player than his teammate George Brett in high school, and he looked like a future twenty-game winner to me. Scotty is the man who taught Flanagan to throw his change-up with the same motion he uses releasing his fastball, and that pitch really gives batters fits.

Dennis Martinez was the young right-hander I liked a lot. He had become the first Nicaraguan to appear in the majors when he earned a victory in relief late in '76. Martinez had all the pitches—good fastball and slider, hard curve, slow curve, and change-up. He needed a lot of work on fielding bunts and holding runners on first base, but those refinements would come. I used him as a spot starter 13 times in '77 and he won 6 of 9 decisions. In 29 relief appearances, Martinez was 8–4 with 4 saves. After going 45–19 in three minor-league seasons and 14–7 as a major-league rookie, we felt Dennis Martinez could be a great one.

Our most impressive first-year player in the spring of '77 was Eddie Murray, a powerfully built first baseman. He was only twenty-one years old, had played just half a season of Triple-A ball, and had been a switch-hitter for all of one season. A natural right-hander, he hit the ball from the left side even better in '77 (.297). Overall, Eddie batted .283 with 27 home runs and 88 RBIs. He drove in the winning runs in 5 of our 8 victories over New York. He also won the AL Rookie of the Year award.

Murray was always better in a game than in practice, and as a result I used him at first base in only 42 games, DHing him the rest of the time. I didn't want to put undue pressure on the youngster by using him regularly in the field where he might make an error in a situation that would bring boos raining down on him. I came to realize that he was a good fielder at first with far better range than veteran Lee May, and I switched their roles a year later. May also hit 27 home runs in '77 and drove in 99 runs. Kenny Singleton matched that RBI total and had 24 homers to go with a .328 batting average. Those three made the Orioles' lineup formidable in the middle, and with Al Bumbry batting .317 leading off and Doug DeCinces smacking 19 home runs, we had our best overall hitting club in some years—including 29 more homers than we had with Jackson and Grich, who left with 40 between them.

Two other role players made significant contributions at the plate in '77—young Andres Mora and veteran Pat Kelly. Mora had shown considerable power but little consistency during trials in '76. We recalled him in June of '77 and he was amazingly consistent with men on base, driving in 34 runs with his first 37 hits. He finished with 13 homers and 44 RBIs.

We had acquired Pat Kelly from the White Sox in a trade for Dave Duncan in the off-season. After going virtually o-for-April, Kelly went berserk in May, batting .356 with 5 home runs in 6 games. He also put together a 19-game hitting streak, longest of the year in the AL. Three of his 10 homers won games for us in extra innings. In addition, Pat stole 25 bases.

Kelly was one of the sweetest men I ever met. He was a Born-Again Christian who was very active in the Baseball Chapel program, and he was always pushing religion. I happen to be a religious man myself, the result of my Lutheran upbringing. I went nine years without missing Sunday School as a youngster and I would never disparage anyone's religion. But I don't push my beliefs and I have to be honest when anyone presses theirs on me.

One day Pat said, "Skip, don't you want to walk with the Lord?"

"Kell," I told him, "I'd rather you walk with the bases loaded."

Another day Pat came into the dugout all excited after hitting a home run and said the Lord had been looking out for him.

"Yeah," I said, "and what about that poor sonuvabitch on the mound who threw you that high slider? We better not be counting on God. He always knows who's gonna win. We're just acting it out so 26 million people will pay to get through them ballpark gates."

We had eight rookies on the club and they all contributed . . . except for Rich Dauer through the initial six weeks of the season. He started the first five games at second base and went hitless. Then I played switch-hitting Billy Smith, whom we'd signed as a free agent. Billy got 17 hits in his first 36 at-bats. When he tailed off, I platooned him and Dauer. Poor Rich still couldn't hit. I called him into my office.

"What do you think your problems are, Rich?" I asked.

"What problems?" he said.

"For chrissake, kid, you're 1-for-41! Your batting average is .024! I've had pitchers who could hit better than that!"

"Hey, just let me play—I'll hit."

In the meantime, I was practically losing my job by playing him, which Rich Dauer or no other player ever thinks about. I've had slumping veterans say, "Stay with me, Skip." I've said, "I'll stay with you, but if you don't snap out of it somebody else may be here with you before the end of the season."

I thought about sending Dauer down—but very briefly. All the scouting reports said he'd hit, and I didn't want to chance crushing him. He got hot in June, and batted almost .280 for the balance of the season.

Writers have praised my patience with a player in a slump, but the patience is really guesswork. Knowing when to get a guy out of the lineup is one of the most important and toughest parts of managing. If a guy goes hitless in five games and you take him out, did you make a mistake only the last time you played him, or were you wrong about him from the beginning? Or are you making a mistake now because he's ready to break loose? Getting a guy out of the lineup at the right time is important and the stats are helpful there—but having a guy *in* the lineup at the right time is even more important.

Mike Flanagan also got off to a poor start. On June 27 he was 2–8 with a 4.69 ERA. I got mail that asked, "How can you keep starting that bum?" And several writers raised similar questions. I told them, "If this kid can't win, nobody can, and I would bet my paycheck on that." In a sense I *was* betting my future salary on Flanagan by staying with him. But I asked my coaches if I was wrong in doing so, and they all said, no, Mike can get them out.

From June 27 on Flanagan was 13–2 with an ERA of 3.11. He had 15 complete games.

Flanagan felt I did make a mistake with him, according to a story a few years later. "Earl's been good to me," he said. "He stuck his neck out for me, but the human factor isn't there. In '77 when I was 2–8, he made it tougher by not really encouraging me, telling me he saw good signs. Jim Palmer did that."

Hell, I thought the fact that I kept Flanagan in the rotation should have told him enough about my confidence in him, but everyone's different. Mike always seemed to me such a confident, self-assured, and relaxed guy. He's also got a wonderful sense of humor. We were going over the Minnesota hitters before one game and Flanagan asked, "Okay, what about 'Clams?'" Nobody knew who he was talking about. "John Castino," Mike said. "Haven't you ever eaten Clams Castino?" He also renamed outfielder Sixto Lezcano "Mordecai Six-Toes Lezcano"—as in the old pitcher Mordecai Three-Finger Brown.

The '77 season was one in which I made two glaring strategic mistakes, the kind of errors that every manager dreads. Before every World Series and before every All-Star Game I have managed, I remember waking up in the middle of the night worrying about allowing one of my players to hit out of turn, or discovering after the fact that the opposing team had batted out of turn. Either would be so embarrassing—and potentially damaging to my club. A manager has so much on his mind during a game, planning for every contingency innings ahead, that he is always in danger of making such errors. That is why, from the beginning of my managing career, I have had everything written down in the dugout, the starting lineup and all reserves, so that I can anticipate opposition moves and be prepared to counter them. But no system is foolproof when you include in it the human factor.

My first mistake occurred in a late-May game in Baltimore against Minnesota. We were losing 2–0 and the Twins had a man on second. Somehow I got ahead of myself and thought the base runner was Dan Ford and that Larry Hisle was the batter. I ordered an intentional walk. After two balls I learned that Ford was the hitter, and we then tried to pitch to him, but walked him unintentionally. Then we had to pitch to the next hitter, Hisle, who singled, making the score 3–0. Singleton's 2-run homer in the ninth left us 1 run short.

Certain writers had been calling me a genius for some time, and when Earl Weaver made that blunder the news went all across the country. The next morning I received a call at home from Billy Martin of the Yankees, who were behind us in the standings. "I just want to congratulate you for the way your team is hanging in there," Martin said. "And by the way, I'm having trouble telling Hisle from Dan Ford. How do you do it?"

I chuckled, but I wasn't all that amused. Later in the season when I saw the replays of the near-fight between Billy and Reggie Jackson in the dugout during a nationally televised game, I was tempted to phone Billy and say, "If you don't want Reggie, I just might be able to find a spot for him on my club. But I'd like to know your secret of how to get along with him." Martin and I have been carrying on that kind of nonsense for years. When we'd beaten the Yankees in two one-run games earlier, Billy had posted a "No interviews" sign on his office. I put up a sign that said, "All Media Welcome."

However, a few days after that mistake in Baltimore we were in Chicago when I again got ahead of myself. We were losing 4-0 and the White Sox batter hit an infield grounder with the bases loaded. I had already decided that if we got the out at first, I would bring in Scotty McGregor to intentionally walk right-handed hitter Jim Essian, giving us a potential out at every base, and have the left-handed McGregor work on left-handed hitter Ralph Garr.

I called for McGregor and went to the mound, where I announced my plan to walk Essian.

"There's no place to put him," Brooks Robinson said, giving me a strange look.

I surveyed the bases and saw they were already loaded. Then it all came back to me: We had not gone to first on the infield grounder but had made the force at home plate. I'd gotten so caught up in my planning that I had not let the facts register.

"What's the matter with me?" I said. "Am I losing my mind?"

"Relax, Skip, you're just getting ahead of yourself," Brooks said.

Then the absurdity of the situation—taking out a right-handed pitcher and bringing in a lefty to pitch to a right-handed hitter— hit me and I started laughing. Rick and Brooks started laughing. By the time Scotty reached the mound, the three of us were almost hysterical.

"What's going on?" McGregor asked. "Aren't we down by four runs?"

"Don't worry about it," I told him. "Just do your job the best you can. Pitch Essian down and in, and maybe we'll get out of this."

McGregor threw a beautiful curveball that broke down on the inside corner of the plate . . . and Essian doubled, the ball scattering chalk on the left-field foul line and clearing the bases. Those three runs negated our subsequent four runs.

After the loss, which was our third in a row though we were still in first place by a game, I called a team meeting. I explained both mistakes, telling the players they were much like when they tried to do too much or became overanxious in a ball game.

"But don't give up on me," I said, "because I'm not about to give up on you guys. I made those mistakes and I haven't made a lot of them in ten years and I'm not gonna be making many in the future—you can count on that. And remember one thing. When you wake up tomorrow you're still gonna be in first place. You just keep playing the way you have been and you'll stay there, I guarantee it."

"It was a good meeting," Mark Belanger later told the writers. "We're all going to make mistakes. You might question Earl sometimes about strategy, but he's not going to make many mental errors. I can't ever remember anything like this happening before."

I went over the circumstances in my mind that night, because if you don't learn from your mistakes you are sure to make them again. I realized that the key to the Chicago mistake was my overanxious desire to get McGregor into the game. That stemmed from a feeling that if we held down the Sox, we could come back in that game and beat them. I'd forgotten a lesson I had learned years before: There are times when you are getting beaten that you simply have to take your lumps in the interest of having all your players ready to win the close games to follow. This doesn't mean you ever give up in any ball game; we've come back from too many 9- and 10-run deficits. But it is pointless to use up so many of your weapons to win one game that your guns are empty in subsequent contests.

I didn't dwell on my mistakes any more than I dwell on those committed by players. A few days later, after winning the first two games of a series in Kansas City, we lost 14–13 in 10 innings. Brooks Robinson, a player-coach in this his final season, was also involved with a toy company, and he had a nifty remote-controlled car that sold for about $60. We set up an elaborate race course in the clubhouse at Memorial Stadium and those of us who got there early every day would take turns timing our runs through the course.

We decided to take the car on the road with us and try it out on the carpet in Kansas City. The first thing Brooks did was send it off from our dugout when a Royal coach was hitting pregame fungos to the outfield. I've forgotten who the coach was, but I'll never forget the expression on his face when, after hitting a ball, he reached down for another one and saw that little car circling his feet.

Then Brooks brought the car back and we stuck a note on the roof and sent the car wheeling over to Royals manager Whitey Herzog. I knew he was facing the same problem I was after that 14–13 game the night before. The note said, "What are we going to do for relievers today?" Whitey took off the note and laughed.

We were 14–3 through the first half of July and regained first place. Then my old friend Billy Hunter, who'd left us to become the Texas manager in June, beat us two games to drop us a half game back. But Oriole fans were turning out in greater numbers than in any season since 1966, and they showed more enthusiasm than I ever recalled.

After Rick Dempsey's left hand was broken by a Don Gullett fastball we brought up catcher Dave Criscione as a backup from Rochester. Dave was a 5-foot, 8-inch tall journeyman catcher who was sipping his one cup of coffee in the majors. But three days after his wife gave birth to their first child, Dave got to play the second game of a doubleheader at home. Dave singled in the fourth and Oriole fans gave him a standing ovation. He singled in the sixth and received another standing O. In the eighth Dave sacrificed what proved to be the winning run to third, and fans gave him still another wild ovation.

The following night I pinch hit for regular catcher Dave Skaggs and Dave Criscione replaced him. With one out in the eleventh inning, Dave hit a game-winning home run to put us two games in front in the standings. The noise from the stands was deafening. I can imagine what joy Dave, after over seven years in the minors, must have felt. I could relate to the short journeyman, and to this day wish that I could have made the major leagues as a player for even one month as he did.

When Dempsey returned to duty on August 21, Brooks Robinson went on the voluntary retired list and thereafter was exclusively a coach. It was inevitable, as was the "Thanks, Brooks" Day on Sunday, September 18, at which a record regular-season crowd of 51,798 people showed up to pay tribute to the most beloved Oriole player ever. The franchise began in 1954 and eighteen-year-old Brooks made his first appearance in an Oriole uniform a year later. He had been an Oriole for most of the twenty-two years since.

The ceremonies honoring Brooks, which were orchestrated by our fine public relations director Bob Brown, were the most moving and emotionally charged I have ever witnessed in baseball. They must have compared with the farewell Babe Ruth received in New York. Brooks rode into and around the stadium in, appropriately, a 1955 Cadillac. Then Brooks and his wife, Connie, and their families sat in the infield while dignitaries and friends spoke for almost ninety minutes.

I spent hours writing a speech on a lined yellow pad, trying to express some of my feelings about this man who had won sixteen successive Gold Gloves as the league's outstanding fielder at third base. A man who had played in eighteen consecutive All-Star games and had been the Most Valuable Player in the American League, in the World Series, and in the All-Star Game. His records occupy over three pages in the Oriole Press Guide, and they are odes to longevity and skill.

But when it came time for me to take the microphone, I was so choked up and had so much moisture in my eyes that I couldn't read what I had written. I threw away the yellow sheet and just said whatever came into my mind, and I don't know if it was intelligent or even coherent, but it was from the heart. I talked about the generosity of Brooks Robinson toward a manager nobody knew because I had been a bush leaguer all my life until I was given the opportunity to manage the Baltimore Orioles. I spoke about how I had wondered the first time I gave Brooks the "take" sign if he would obey and how he did so, and how I never had to worry about Brooks Robinson from that time on because he was a ballplayer who always tried to do the right thing and almost always managed to. And I thanked Brooks for saving my job several times over the years, then I closed saying, "Thank you, Brooks, thank you one million times."

Doug DeCinces ran out of the dugout and tore up third base, which he then presented to Brooks . . . and I don't think I've ever heard a louder explosion of noise from Baltimore fans.

Standing there looking at Brooks holding the base with that wonderful smile on his face and the crowd going wild in the background and all of the love and warmth permeating the stadium . . . I thought, *I'd like to be like Brooks Robinson. The guys who never said no to anybody, the ones that everybody loves because they deserve to be loved, those are my heroes.*

We were still in the pennant race till the last weekend of the season. We went into Boston tied with the Red Sox. To win we needed a sweep of the three games coupled with three Yankee losses to Detroit. The Red Sox eliminated us in game one of the series and we eliminated them in game two. The final game was rained out and we finished tied for second with a 97–64 record.

I had received word that I was going to be named American League Manager of the Year by the AP, and I called a team meeting and told everyone, "If I win any awards, it'll be because of you guys and what you've done this season, not because of me." I did win the award and also the much more meaningful—all the managers vote—*Sporting News* Major League Manager of the Year Award. But, as I've said before, awards don't mean much when you don't win on the ball field.

Although we didn't make the play-offs, we ended the season on a happy note in Boston, thanks to Rick Dempsey. He is a born showman, perhaps because his parents, George T. Dempsey and the former June Archer, were vaudeville performers. His dad also appeared in the musical *Song of Norway* on Broadway in the late '40s. A couple of times Rick had put on shows for fans during rain delays in Baltimore. Our PR director entitled them "Baseball Soliloquy in Pantomime," and on the final day of the '77 season Rick gave his greatest performance ever.

It was raining that Sunday afternoon. After shagging balls in the outfield, Rick began playing with the Red Sox fans, underhanding balls into the stands like a softball pitcher. That drew cheers. But he didn't release every ball, halting his motion and evoking, "Ooooh"s. Then he moved to another section of the stands in right field, held up a ball, cupped his other hand to an ear, and waited for the crowd's response before throwing the ball into the section that cheered the loudest. He repeated this, moving from section to section.

When he'd given away every ball in the outfield, Rick came into the dugout and grabbed a ball bag. He dragged it out to right field as if it weighed a ton, and the fans cheered him every step of the way. He finally stopped, feigning exhaustion. He wiped his brow and raised the bag into the air to thunderous cheers. Then, with great effort, he dramatically turned the heavy bag upside down . . . and two balls fell out. The fans went crazy and he tossed the balls to them.

By then the drizzle had become a downpour and the tarp was rolled onto the infield. Rick came into the dugout and his teammates wanted him to continue. "C'mon, Rick," they said, "give them your Baseball-in-the-Rain act!"

"No, I've done enough today."

"No way—you gotta do your rain act," his teammates insisted.

So Rick stepped out of the dugout and began leading fans in that area in song. "In the good old summer time," he sang and they joined in, then the organist picked it up. All the players started singing, too, and someone got on the phone and had the words put up on the message board. Rick went out to the mound and began leading the entire stadium in song as the message board became a Follow-the-Bouncing-Ball board.

Next Rick came in and took off his shoes, then hopped right back out on the puddled infield tarp. He began skating around barefooted and the organist broke into "The Skater's Waltz."

Dempsey's grand finale was the best. He came into the dugout and stuffed towels around his belly inside his shirt. Then he grabbed a bat and took little mincing steps to home plate like Babe Ruth. He stepped in lefty and dramatically pointed his bat to center field. Fans were screaming and howling and the Oriole players were hollering, "Hit one, Babe! You promised little Johnny in the hospital!"

Rick took a mighty swing and froze, his legs twisted into an X, the bat dangling from his right hand, his eyes watching the trajectory of the ball rising over the center-field fence. Then he did an exaggerated Babe Ruth home-run trot around the bases and slid into the huge puddle at home plate, spraying water almost to the stands. Rick rose, tipped his cap, and held it up as he minced into the dugout. Those fans responded the way an audience does when it has seen a brilliant pantomimist perform. Rick Dempsey is that, and a good man to have on your ball club.

Toward the end of the 1977 season Hank Peters had offered me
a new contract and I agreed to return if all my coaches were also
rehired. I did this every year and then the individuals negotiated
their own deals.

I wondered how long I'd be able to keep George Bamberger,
who was wanted by teams all over the league. I knew George
had been talking to Walter Youse, with whom we were both
very friendly. Walter had left the Orioles' organization for the
Angels some years before. Since then he had said to me many
times, "Why don't you quit Baltimore and come on out to sunny
California. Year-round golf and a ball club that doesn't mind
spending money for players."

I didn't know if Walter had talked like that with George, but I
suspected he had one night when Hank Peters took me and all
the coaches out to dinner. During the evening, Hank took
George aside privately to find out what kind of '78 salary he was
looking for.

Later Hank confided to me, "Earl, I know you want George
back and I do too. But he threw a figure at me . . . well, I hate to
say this—we just can't afford to pay a coach that kind of money.
I'm sorry."

This was in Boston on the season's final weekend and when I
got to the park the following day I presumed George was going
to hold out for the salary he wanted or possibly become manager
of the Angels. George had turned down managing jobs before,

but I felt maybe he now had a hankering to run his own ball club.

George was already at the park when I arrived and I walked up to him, shook his hand, and said, "It was nice having you around, George. I appreciate all you've done and wish you the best of luck."

I went into my office to get dressed and ten minutes later Jimmy Frey came running in. "Hey, Earl," he said, "George is packing his gear!"

"What do you mean?" I asked.

"He says he didn't like what you said to him."

"Well I can't do nothing about that," I said. I was a little annoyed, after all these years together, that George couldn't tell me himself if I'd said something that offended him. I certainly didn't think I'd done anything wrong.

George left and flew home to Baltimore.

When we got home after the final series, George had already met with Hank Peters again. He'd said that the high salary figure he'd mentioned previously had merely been where he thought he'd start. Then George had told Hank what would realistically satisfy him, and Hank said that was within the Oriole means.

So Hank called me in with Bamberger and said to me, "George says he'll sign with us now. You want him, don't you, Earl?"

"Of course I want George," I said.

Then I asked him to come into my office and I said, "Look, I don't understand what I said that offended you, George. I meant what I said when I wished you all the best. But if I hurt your feelings, I'm sorry."

We went out and had a couple of beers to celebrate. I was delighted to have the best pitching coach in baseball still with me. But I didn't have him for long. In January, George Bamberger signed a multi-year contract to manage the Milwaukee Brewers. Here, as I got the story from George, is how this came about:

Our old friend Harry Dalton, who had left the Angels to become the Brewers' GM, phoned Bamberger and asked, "How would you like to be our manager?"

"Harry, I wouldn't," George said.

"What do you mean? Why not?"

"I don't want to be a manager at this stage of my life," said George, who was fifty-two and liked living in the Baltimore area. "I'm happy being a pitching coach, and they're paying me damn good money now."

"Why don't you fly out here at our expense," Harry said. "I'll show you around and we'll talk. I know there's not much to do in Baltimore in the winter time. It'll be a free vacation."

"Harry, you can't pay me enough money to make me become a manager."

"Well, just come out for a visit, George, and we'll see."

So George flew out to Milwaukee. He was escorted into Dalton's office and Harry immediately offered a two-year contract and stated a figure well below the unspoken number in Bamberger's mind. That was what George had expected.

He rose from his chair and said, "It was a nice plane ride out here, but forget it."

"Wait a minute, George," Harry said. "Sit down." He upped the salary considerably.

"Well, that sounds a little better," George said.

"Hey, I know you're settled in Baltimore, George, and that your wife may not want to be here all summer. But I'll see that Wilma has carte blanche to fly in here any time on the ball club. Whenever she's here, all your hotel and living expenses will be taken care of by us."

"That's pretty good, Harry. Throw that in the deal."

"Fine," Harry said. "Just sign this."

"Hold it!" George said. "We haven't settled on a salary figure yet."

Dalton came up again, but George was still not satisfied. So Harry offered another enticement. "How about an attendance clause, George?"

"What's that?"

Dalton explained that George would receive $10,000 for every 100,000 fans over the previous year's total attendance of something like 1.3 million. "It could be a very good bonus for you," Harry said.

"That sounds good, Harry. Throw that in there."

Dalton made a note, then slid the contract and a pen over to Bamberger.

George slid them back and said, "We still haven't settled on salary, Harry!"

As a first-year manager Bamberger got his salary up to what may have been a record for a first-year manager. After all my negotiations with Harry Dalton, going all the way back to the minor leagues and into the majors, I have to say that I was very proud of George Bamberger, and I couldn't have been happier for him.

And Harry Dalton got his manager, who turned out to be the perfect man for Milwaukee. It was no surprise when he improved the Brewer pitching staff tremendously, but he also did a great all-around managing job. The Brewers, 67–95 before George, won 93 games in '78—and the attendance increased some 300,000.

But losing the game's top pitching coach put me in a hole. Our fine minor-league pitching instructor, Ray Miller, had signed on with Billy Hunter's Texas Rangers. I had some people in mind whom I felt could do the job, but when Hank Peters asked if I'd like to have Miller I said, "Yeah, if you can work it out. He knows the organization and the way we do things. And Ray's already worked with Flanagan, McGregor, Dennis Martinez, and our other young prospects."

I'll be darned if Peters didn't get permission to talk to Miller and signed him as our pitching coach. Ray stepped right in behind a man who had coached eighteen twenty-game winners in ten years and performed admirably.

Ironically, some five weeks before Bamberger signed with Milwaukee I thought maybe I'd be managing the Brewers in '78. That thought occurred at the winter meetings in Hawaii when I offered my resignation to Hank Peters after he had made a big trade without informing me. Although I didn't want to give up the Orioles job, I felt I could get one with Harry Dalton in Milwaukee.

This was the situation: We had let Ross Grimsley go as a free agent because Dennis Martinez had to move into the rotation. We also had to make room for Scott McGregor, so we decided to trade Rudy May. Our prime need was a short reliever and a right-handed hitter. We had been talking for days about possibly acquiring Gene Garber, the Phils reliever, or Enrique Romo from Seattle. When neither of those deals worked out, the talk turned to Montreal and a deal for relievers Don Stanhouse and Joe Kerrigan, plus minor-league outfielder Gary Roenicke, who had hit .321 in the American Association.

I got on the phone with the scout who had signed Roenicke to try and check out his potential. The scout, whom I respected, said Roenicke had as much power as Joe Rudi. Not bad, though Roenicke might be a year away from the major leagues. Jimmy Russo swore by the Montreal relief pitchers, particularly Stanhouse, and Russo is as fine a scout as there is anywhere.

But as we sat around in Peters' suite Russo kept whispering in Hank's ear, which annoyed me. The only people present other than myself were Tommy Giordano, the director of scouting, farm director Clyde Kluttz, and Bill Werle, one of our special-assignment scouts. Why was Russo whispering? I wondered.

He finally got under my skin and I announced that I was going to the managers' reception at the Topps suite. I said I'd call by five o'clock to see how the trade was going. If something broke, I told Russo to call me at Topps.

I went down there and had a couple of drinks with Mariner manager Darrell Johnson. At 4:30 I phoned Russo and asked, "Is anything popping?"

"Nothing," Russo said. "You can come up if you want to."

"Thanks," I said. I finished my drink and walked out of the Topps room at 5 P.M. and ran into a writer.

"How do you like the Oriole trade?" he asked me.

"What trade?" I asked, and he told me the deal with Montreal had gone through. He also said we'd traded pitcher Mike Parrott to the Mariners for outfielder Carlos Lopez. I was furious that I hadn't been informed, that I'd found out about the trades from a writer, and that I hadn't been able to call Rudy May before he too would hear about his new address from the media. Rudy had only won thirty-three games for us in the last two years. He deserved better treatment—as did I, damnit!

I stormed into Hank Peters' suite in the midst of a press conference in which the trades had been announced and were now being discussed. I chewed out Russo for not telling me to come right up when the trades were imminent and then for not reaching me before the press conference. Peters ushered me out on the balcony and placated me somewhat when he told me they had phoned the Topps suite and had also sent Bill Werle down looking for me. But I could not see how they had failed to locate me. I offered my resignation.

But the following morning I met with Hank Peters for two hours and he said, "It was all just a lack of communication, Earl. You've been in Baltimore ten years, you've got a house, you just bought a house in Miami. You've got the world by the rear end—why give it up?"

I said, "You're right, Hank." Actually, I couldn't resign if I'd wanted to because technically I had yet to sign my three-year contract. My lawyers were still working on the langauge in some clauses. But I did have a verbal agreement, and I never break my word. I told the press, "Legally I can still sign with anybody that makes me an offer, but when you've worked for an organization for twenty-two years you have to trust it. One thing that really bugged me was the thought that we'd traded Rudy May without informing him. Hank told me he had called Rudy. The whole thing was simply a misunderstanding."

That afternoon I got back together with Jimmy Russo, even though I still felt he could have found me if he'd tried hard enough. But I did like hearing him say Don Stanhouse would be one of the best relievers in the American League. As usual, Russo proved to be right.

Joe Kerrigan was another good relief pitcher. Unfortunately he became a victim of numbers, winning three games and saving three in '78 but not getting enough work to excel thereafter. As for Gary Roenicke, after spending much of '78 with Rochester he made the Orioles a year later and hit twenty-five home runs in under four hundred at-bats.

Going into spring training in 1978 I told the press, "We're not a contender—we're a winner. Maybe this is the year everybody gets to know our names. You'd think after ninety-seven wins last season that somebody would know us."

We won eight of our final nine exhibition games—then lost eleven of our first sixteen in the regular season. During this period we split a pair in New York, and in game one some members of the media reported that Billy Martin and I were feuding, which was nonsense. We were just trying to win ball games. But when a Rich Gossage fastball sailed over the head of Rick Dempsey, I hollered at Thurman Munson, "Hey, tell Gossage to stop that stuff! That's not the way we play ball, Munson. You been wearing us out for eight years and we ain't thrown at you yet, so knock off the crap." Umpire Joe Brinkman summoned Martin to the plate and the incident ended.

The next day a writer went to Martin, who reportedly said, "The umpire warned me because Weaver told him to. Brinkman said Weaver hollered that if he didn't warn me, they were going to hit Munson because Thurman had called for that pitch."

The writer came to me at the batting cage and asked if I'd threatened to have my pitcher throw at Munson. "Munson thinks I did," I said, because I'd sent one of the Baltimore writers to ask him and I could see how Thurman could have misinterpreted what I'd hollered. As for the umpire, I said, "He knows nothing."

Then Billy came over and I said, "If you listen to umpires you're stupider than I thought. I called to Munson to go out and tell Gossage to cut that stuff out. Dempsey got a broken hand [from being hit by Yankee pitcher Don Gullett] last year, remember?"

"Sure," Billy said. "You have to protect your players."

Writers are always exaggerating the words between Billy Martin and me. We just enjoy ribbing one another. Some years ago we had a midget, Don Ross, who entertained the crowds sweeping the bases in Baltimore. Billy Martin said, "If I were Weaver I'd draw the line at having to sweep the bases between innings."

"I'd rather be small of stature," I replied, "than a mental midget."

I can't recall all of Billy's funny lines at my expense, but when writers asked me a couple of years back if we were going to resume our tomato-growing contest, I said, "Martin can't keep a job long enough to grow a tomato. But Billy's the smartest manager ever to lose four jobs."

In the early '70s I had an embarrassing run-in with a Maryland state trooper while driving home one night. It was bad enough when the acne-faced officer gave me a DWI (driving while intoxicated) after I'd had only a few drinks, but he also roughed me up. I angrily called him "crater face" and, in trying to enter his car as instructed, unhinged the door.

Billy Martin had a caricaturist draw a likeness of Martin in uniform sticking his head out of a police car, which a caricature of Weaver was kicking. Billy sent the drawing to me framed in glass and it hangs in my den.

That winter Jim Palmer began all of his banquet speeches by saying, "I'd like to apologize for Earl Weaver not being here tonight, but the Maryland State Police are conducting a driver's education class."

A little laughter never hurts in a tension-filled baseball season, and Martin and I could always laugh at ourselves.

But injuries, a dearth of quality depth, and a paucity of hitting through the season's first ten weeks put a damper on our laughter in '78. Doug DeCinces broke his nose in Florida and got off to a terrible start at the plate, as did Rich Dauer. Rich's average was well below .200 through May. I experimented with DeCinces at second and Eddie Murray at third in the hopes of getting more run production by playing Lee May at first. Our defense suffered and the hitting didn't improve, so I reverted to our original infield.

Kenny Singleton had undergone surgery on his right elbow in the off-season. Doctors removed bone chips and transplanted a nerve, and it took Kenny all season to regain the strength in his right arm. Normally he made strong, accurate throws from right field and accumulated nine or ten assists per season. In '78 Kenny had one assist. He did come on to lead us in hitting with a .293 average and he had 20 homers and 81 RBIs.

But Singleton, while a good outfielder who can handle anything he gets to, is not fleet. And when Al Bumbry broke his ankle in May and was lost for most of the season, our outfield defense went down. Bumbry's tremendous speed allowed him to cover center and well into right field, too. His replacement, Larry Harlow, was a disappointment. Pat Kelly, who split time in left field with Carlos Lopez, had his problems on defense, too, particularly, it seemed, when Jim Palmer was pitching. At least Palmer thought so.

In September, Palmer had a 1–0 lead in the eighth inning of a game against Cleveland. He was going for his twentieth victory. Jim Norris of the Indians looped a flyball down the left-field line and Kelly ran a long way for it. Only a player with his speed would have gotten there, but Pat couldn't hold the ball. Palmer then took himself out of the game saying he had a sore elbow. Jim also said, "Don't we have an outfielder here who can *catch* the ball?" Later he added, "It's frustrating to throw flyballs and have them drop for doubles."

Norris' hit had been scored a double because that's what it was. Had Kelly held the ball after that long run, it would have been a helluva catch.

The Indians rallied to win that game 2–1. But Palmer went on to win 21. Mike Flanagan won 19, Dennis Martinez 16, and Scott McGregor 15 as all three of our young pitchers came through. Don Stanhouse won 6 games and saved 24 out of the bullpen.

Despite their slow starts, Dauer and DeCinces found their strokes in June and never lost them. Rich hit over .280 through the season's last four months to finish at .264. DeCinces looked like Frank Robinson for some three months, finishing with 28 home runs, 37 doubles (a .526 slugging percentage), 80 RBIs, and a .286 batting average. We were the only team in the league to have four batters with 20 or more home runs as DeCinces, Singleton, Murray (27), and May (25) combined for 100.

Yet too many of our big hits came with the bases empty. We ranked tenth in runs scored with 659. That was the primary reason why, for only the second time in my eleven years in Baltimore, we finished below second place. The Yankees, Red Sox, and Brewers all won 93 games or more. We won 90 and finished fourth.

But we were going to do better than that the following year. Our young pitchers would improve and our outfield would benefit from the return of Bumbry and the addition of Gary Roenicke. We'd called him up for the last month of the season, and I liked his bat (.364, three homers) and his glove.

We were also going to sign our first "money" free agent, the young veteran Steve Stone, to give us starter insurance in '79. Stone hadn't been an overpowering pitcher in seven years in the big leagues, but I felt sure he could win for us. And I felt that outfielder John Lowenstein, whom we were going to purchase from Texas, would be an asset to the Orioles, too. He was a solid defensive performer who could even fill in at third or first. Lowenstein batted left-handed and had a nice swing. And you have to say he is consistent at the plate. John once batted .342 in three out of four seasons.

I liked everything about the Orioles in the spring of 1979—particularly our re-emergence as a ball club that would have in regular attendance my Albert Schweitzer: Dr. Longball. When we played an exhibition game against the Yankees in mid-March, I told Reggie Jackson, "I bet we hit more home runs than you guys this year."

Reggie, who likes to project ahead, thought a moment and said, "You might be right, Skip."

I often engage Reggie in pregame palaver because he likes to talk as much as I do. After he'd taken batting practice, Reggie returned to our dugout and heard me talking to writers about him. "I just told these fellows that you were the best free-agent pickup the Yankees ever made," I said. "But with the kind of ability you have, your career statistics should be a whole lot better than they are."

"What do you mean, Skip?" he asked.

"I mean you're very good in tough situations. Put the game or the season on the line and you concentrate and bear down as well as anybody I've ever seen. That's when you're at your best and why they call you 'Mr. October,' right?"

"I think that's the only way to play the game," Reggie said.

"But if you played every inning of every game that way, there's no telling what you'd accomplish. But you don't do it, do you?"

"No, I guess not," Reggie said. "It's awfully tough to concen trate like that through a long season, especially when you know some of it doesn't mean anything."

"Well you're in good company," I said. "Most guys can't do it. In fact, the only players who did it on our club since I've been here were Brooks and Frank Robinson, and they're both sure Hall of Famers."

"They did it all right," Reggie said. "Why do you think they were able to?"

"For different reasons," I said. "Brooks just loved the game so much he was always in it. There would be days in August when we either had a big lead or were out of it and the game didn't mean anything. I'd tell myself to rest him. But by the time Brooks got his uniform on he was like a sixteen-year-old who couldn't wait to get on the field. There was no way you could keep him out.

"With Frank it was because he was such an intense competitor and had so much pride. Every time he got on the field he wanted to be the best. I don't care whether it was the first inning or the last, whether it meant anything or not, he concentrated as hard as he could.

"Now you don't set goals for yourself, Reggie. You wait for the right spot and try to produce the big play, the big hit, and you're good at it. I don't mean that you don't bear down at other times, but you move up a notch or two in certain situations. A lot of guys do."

Reggie nodded and I lit a cigarette. "I think Eddie Murray will be that way," I continued. "Put the winning run on in the ninth inning and Eddie moves way up. If you guys would be able to concentrate like that all the time, what do you think your stats would look like? You'd probably hit .340, Reggie, and with your power the home runs and RBIs would go up with it."

"Who else do you think plays like that?" Reggie asked.

"Well I don't see all the players," I said, "but you'd have to say Carl Yastrzemski and Pete Rose, for sure. Like Brooks and Frank, you're talking about Hall of Famers. Once you have the ability, maybe that's what sets them apart."

What set the Orioles apart in 1979 was the all-around ability we had assembled on our twenty-five-man roster. The goal we set every year—trying to put together a unit that would include a

man who could fill every conceivable role at any time all season
—had been reached. I felt we had our best team since the '71
season.

"The Orioles are amazing," I overheard coach Frank Robinson
tell a writer. "A lot of clubs sit down at the end of spring training, pick the twenty-five best athletes, and head north. Here they
sit down and look for the right mix, and they do it in detail like
no other ball club I've ever seen. It's not just the best athletes or
the best starting nine. It's who can do the best job of sitting on
the bench for a week, then go up and get a hit? Who can steal a
base as a pinch runner in the late innings? Who can play more
than one position if someone gets injured? Nobody in baseball
can put all those elements together better than Earl Weaver because nobody can judge baseball talent as well as he can."

Pitcher Steve Stone—with whom I exchanged some loud words
over his lack of concentration on the mound early in the season—
later told another writer, "If Earl wants you on his team, it's because he's so sure of his own judgment of your ability. You know
he's the best evaluator of talent in the majors, so his confidence
rubs off on you."

We got off to our usual slow start, losing eight of our first
eleven games. But we lost only eight more out of our next fifty-
nine games and were in first place to stay by July 1.

John Lowenstein, who had been around for years with other
organizations that did not place as much value on their twentieth through twenty-fifth players as the Orioles do, said, "This is
a kind of dream for any player. We are playing so well and everyone is contributing."

I always try to give all my players enough playing time to
keep them fresh, and I didn't have to try hard this season. We
had a lot of injuries. Jim Palmer went two months between wins
due to tendinitis in his elbow. Scott McGregor, also suffering
from tendinitis, appeared in only three games through the first
seven weeks of the schedule. A bad back sidelined Doug De-
Cinces for thirty-three games. Lee May missed twenty-two
games with a pulled calf muscle. Mark Belanger sat out twenty-
nine games after breaking a finger. Reliever Tim Stoddard tore a
muscle under his right armpit and pitched only one third of an
inning in eleven weeks. Gary Roenicke was hit in the face by a

pitch and twenty-five stitches were needed to close the wound in his upper lip. He missed eight games.

John Lowenstein suffered a severely sprained ankle running into the left-center-field wall trying to flag down a double. He went on the fifteen-day disabled list August 9, but he couldn't play in the outfield again until the final week of the season. "Steiner," as he's called, brings a very positive attitude to baseball. His heads-up play won us a game the following season in a most unorthodox way. Steiner's pinch single tied the score against the A's and sent Al Bumbry to third. When right fielder Tony Armas threw toward the plate, Lowenstein headed for second to encourage a cutoff play that might allow Bumbry to score. It did. First baseman Jeff Newman made the cutoff and threw toward second. The ball hit Lowenstein in the back of the head and caromed into center field as Bumbry mosied home.

But Lowenstein was stunned and a stretcher was hustled out to him. He was carried toward the dugout seemingly unconscious as the fans applauded in sympathy. Suddenly Steiner sat upright and threw both arms into the air. We all roared. "I planned it on the way to the dugout," Steiner later admitted. "After all, we *were* on TV."

That loose, yet winning attitude permeated the entire team in '79. The players developed some amusing rituals that they practiced daily. Ten minutes before every game, Don Stanhouse would let out a God-awful scream. In the dugout Lee May would start a mock-argument with a teammate, and they would holler at and curse one another until everyone else laughed. Then Lee would move from player to player saying, "Be my pal-ly. By my pal-ly." He encouraged everyone, and all the Orioles pulled for one another. As Steve Stone said, "This is a 'we' team, not an 'I' team."

The pregame ritual concluded with Kenny Singleton leading a locomotive cheer as Al Bumbry stepped into the batter's box to lead off the game. Everybody would join in and you could just *feel* the enthusiasm and spirit.

Another enjoyable ritual was the weekly "Sons of Earl Weaver" rankings. Some of the players had been mockingly referring to themselves as "The illegitimate sons of Earl Weaver." Then Singleton, and I think Dempsey and Dauer, started rating each player one through twenty-five, with the top-ranked player being my "favorite" Son of the Week. If a player had a bad week on the field or got hollered at on the bench or was called into the office, he would be moved down. Nobody wanted to be the favorite son, and since Singleton was in charge, he made sure he was never No. 1. Poor Eddie Murray was probably No. 1 more than anyone else.

At week's end Dempsey would stand up—in the bus if we were on the road or in the clubhouse if we were home—and dramatically announce the new ratings like the host of the old "Hit Parade" program, reading off the chart: "And this week, for his performance against Minnesota, Eddie Murray moves up from No. 3 to No. 1 on the Son of the Week charts." Everyone would cheer. Then he'd run down the list of people whose position had changed. "Rick Dempsey, who had a shouting match with Earl Weaver this week, moves down from No. 19 to No. 24." Everyone would boo. When Dempsey was finished, the chart would be posted in the clubhouse. It was very funny and did for morale what the Kangaroo Court had done in '69. When a group of guys spends eight months together, they should make the time as enjoyable as possible.

The wildest scenes in our clubhouse often centered around Don Stanhouse's cubicle after he'd had a good outing. As he won seven games for us and saved twenty-one, there were numerous scenes. Don had two stuffed monkeys and two stuffed frogs in his locker and he'd share his postgame beer with them, pouring the brew in their mouths. "When I celebrate," he'd say, "I want *everybody* drinking with me."

Mike Flanagan nicknamed him "Stan the Man Unusual" or Stan-U for short. When Don asked him why, Mike said, "Because, Stan, you *are unusual.*" Don said, "Gee, I really didn't think anyone had noticed." I think he was an introvert who worked extra hard at being an extrovert.

I called him Don "Full-Pack" Stanhouse. He took so much time between pitches, that's how much I smoked waiting for him to get us out of a jam. In fact, Don took so much time between each pitch that often our infielders would holler, "Throw the ball, Stan! Throw the damn ball!"

The game was usually on the line when he came in, and I'd

get nervous, step down into the runway, and light up while he took his warm-up pitches. I'd take a drag, then cup the cigarette behind my back and move up on the step. I'd watch him take the sign, toe the rubber, go into his stretch, look left and right checking the runners—then step off the damn rubber! I'd move back into the runway and take two quick puffs, step on the butt and hurry back to see him go through his routine and finally throw a pitch. Ball one! I'd light up again, puff, move back—and Stanhouse would step off the rubber again!

He drove me nuts, but taking so much time between pitches must've driven batters nuts, too. "Full-Pack" was an excellent short-relief pitcher. And left-hander Tippy Martinez became equally effective, plus he could give us two innings one night and still go six the next night if necessary. Tippy won ten games out of the bullpen.

One of my biggest thrills in '79 was seeing Al Bumbry fully recovered from the severe leg and ankle injuries he'd suffered the previous year. Al is an amazing person. He never played baseball until his senior year of college, but he hit so well we signed him. And two months into his first season of pro ball he was called into the Army as an ROTC second lieutenant. He was soon sent to Vietnam as a combat platoon leader. He won a Bronze Star and was promoted to first lieutenant. But Al is far prouder of the fact that in eleven months of combat, he never lost one of his men.

You think a manager doesn't respect that kind of performance? I wasn't in favor of the Vietnam War, which was useless, a total waste of the lives of so many young Americans. I didn't want to see my son Michael have to go over there and possibly be killed or wounded for nothing. So what Al Bumbry had done for his country made baseball seem a little bit insignificant.

But Al came home, hit about .340 in two seasons in the minors, and earned a job with the Orioles in '73, when he won Rookie of the Year honors. The only problem was that Al was a very poor outfielder. He had great speed and could go get the ball—if he could read it off the bat. We told him to go out and shag flyballs every day, and he's still doing that after nine years in Baltimore. Al worked as hard as any player I've ever had. He made himself into a good center fielder through 100 percent dedication. It took him three or four years to become a regular, and I know he kept thinking, though he didn't say it, "Earl will always find stats that show somebody else can hit left-handers better." But, again, Al learned to hang in there tough against left-handed pitchers. In '79 he actually hit for a higher average (.288) against left-handers than against right-handers (.284). He set career highs in games (148), at-bats (569), runs (80), and RBIs (49), while leading the club in steals with 37. And he made numerous spectacular defensive plays.

With Roenicke or Lowenstein in left field, we had our best defensive play there in all my years in Baltimore. Our infield defense again led the league. Belanger suffered through a season-long slump (.167) and young Kiko Garcia stepped in and did a creditable fielding job while batting .247 with 9 triples. He appeared to be our shortstop of the future.

We were still anything but a great hitting team and, in fact, finished eleventh in the league in batting average (.261). But we had 181 home runs to place third in that category and win my bet with Reggie Jackson. Singleton led us in homers with 35, followed by Murray and, surprisingly, Roenicke with 25 apiece. Equally surprising was the fact that Rich Dauer tied Murray for the Oriole lead in game-winning RBIs (14).

Pitching kept us in the games, and the long ball often won them for us. Mike Flanagan was our lone 20-game winner, his 23–9 record earning him the Cy Young Award. I thought early that Dennis Martinez might have a shot at it. After losing his first 2 decisions he won 10 in a row. But then he went 5–14 to finish 15–16, the only losing record on the staff. His inability to hold runners on first and his own fielding cost him a number of those games. Runners got a big jump on him and stole every time he threw a slow curve. So he stopped throwing the slow curveball and the hitters knew they could expect fastballs with runners on.

But Scotty McGregor, after going 0–2 and sitting out six weeks with tendinitis, compiled a 13–4 record the rest of the way. He and Flanagan are two fantastic people. No matter how angry they might have gotten with me at times, they held their tongues. I think they are both intelligent enough to realize that whatever I did, right or wrong, the intent was in the best interest of everybody on the team. Scotty and Mike both have inner peace within themselves; they know how to handle the whole world.

Sammy Stewart was another young pitcher who had an excellent year, winning all 3 games he started and 5 more in long relief. A big, good-natured right-hander from North Carolina, Sammy had all the pitches but had some trouble controlling his hard slider, a wicked pitch when it was in the strike zone. I kept after him about this all season. I remember how excited Sammy was in mid-August when his wife, Peggy, gave birth to their first child. Sammy came running into the dugout to spread the news about his son. While everyone congratulated him, I said, "Tell the kid to get his slider over the plate."

Naturally, Palmer and I could not get through a season—even so joyous a one as this—without a little contretemps. The first occurred on Father's Day when we were in Minnesota. A story appeared in a Minneapolis newspaper headlined: "Jim Palmer Wants Out of Baltimore." In it he said he wanted to go elsewhere so he could make more money—"I'm going to aggravate them so much they'll have to trade me." Well I was aggravated for a couple of reasons. The timing of the story seemed to me ridiculous when we had won 9 of our last 11 games and had the best record in the league. Secondly, the piece replayed all of the arguments between Palmer and myself over all the years and included many of the misquotes and other inaccurate information.

When I got to the ball park I taped the clipping over Palmer's locker and wrote on it: "Happy Father's Day. Now grow up." I told the writers it was time Palmer started acting his age. "I wish they would give the man a raise. He's done a lot for me. But he's also given me all these gray hairs. He says he wants to broadcast the World Series, fine. But he's going to have to broadcast games two, three, five, and six—because he'll be pitching games one, four, and seven for us."

I felt Palmer should have been more mature than to give such an interview. But when he reached the ball park he told me he hadn't replayed the old arguments to the writer, who must have gleaned them from file stories. When I heard this I felt like I'd spoken out too soon. I should have talked to Jim first.

Although injuries reduced Palmer's starts to 22, he finished with a 10–6 record and the second-best ERA (3.29) on the club. He was still the leader of our pitching staff as far as I was concerned, the veteran who knew how to win the big games under pressure.

We clinched the pennant on September 22 and four days later at our last home game of the season, in which we beat the Tigers 13–2, we began chanting the O-R-I-O-L-E-S cheer that the Baltimore fans had been giving us all season long. They had been unbelievably supportive and had broken the attendance record we'd set in 1970 by almost 300,000, as 1,596,922 people turned out to see us at Memorial Stadium. Then our bullpen and the announcers in the radio booth picked up the cheer. At game's end we all rushed out on the field and cheered the fans. Even the players who had gone into the clubhouse early and were half dressed or already in civilian clothes raced out and joined us in thanking those great folks.

Shortly thereafter, once we knew we'd be playing the California Angels, I announced my rotation for the play-offs. We would start Palmer, Flanagan, Dennis Martinez, and, if necessary, McGregor and Palmer again. I wanted Palmer for his experience —this would be his sixth play-off, and no pitcher had ever worked in more—and because he was a right-hander. The Angels lineup was predominantly right-handed.

Palmer came to me and said Flanagan, who *had* been our top pitcher all season, should start the play-off opener. He seemed to think that passing up Mike would hurt his feelings, though Flanagan didn't care. I explained to Palmer my reasons for opening the series with him, but he kept insisting that Flanagan should start. A shouting match ensued.

"If you don't start the first game, you don't pitch in the play-offs!" I said angrily. "Because the only reason for you not to pitch in the opener is if you have an injury. And if you have an injury, we'll have to put you on the disabled list."

Palmer demanded we have a meeting with Hank Peters, who immediately told him, "What you're doing is trying to manage the ball club, Jim."

"That's exactly what I told him," I chimed in.

"No I'm not," Palmer said. "I've had arm problems and back

problems this season, as you know. And I'm not sure I could come back and pitch the fifth game if the series goes that far."

"Let's not worry about the fifth game until we've won the first," I said. "In five previous play-offs, how many times have we gone five—only once."

"Jim, your thoughts are not illogical," Peters said. "But we pay Earl to manage the club and he's got other ideas. You've got to respect his judgment."

"Hey, I'll open the series, if that's what you want," Palmer said. "But if we go to five games and lose," he pointed at me, "it's his fault."

Palmer had a 2–0 record against California that season, having given up only 2 earned runs. Lifetime, he was 21–8 vs. the Angels.

He threw nine strong innings against the Angels in the first play-off game, giving up 3 runs. I brought in Stanhouse, who held the score at 3–3 in the tenth. In the bottom of the inning DeCinces singled and with two out Bumbry walked. I sent up John Lowenstein to pinch hit against right-hander John Montague. That season Steiner had gone 2-for-2 against Montague, when he had been a Mariner, with 1 home run and 2 RBIs. I was down in the runway cupping a cigarette when, on an 0–2 pitch, Steiner sliced a line drive deep into the left-field seats. John Lowenstein had hit 11 homers during the season, and none was bigger than that one.

In game two we scored 9 runs in the first 3 innings, paced by Eddie Murray's three-run homer and Kiko Garcia's 2 RBIs. Flanagan, who retired 15 in a row in one stretch, left in the eighth with 2 on, none out, and a 9–3 lead. Two more runs scored after Stanhouse relieved, and in the ninth it really got hairy. I literally smoked a pack of cigarettes watching Don get 6 outs among the 12 men he faced, all the while fearing the game was going up in smoke. Stanhouse walked a man, then got a force-out. He gave up a double, then got a ground-out. The next hitter singled, and suddenly our lead had shrunk to 1 run.

It was horrible. I couldn't bring myself to yank Stanhouse because every hitter that stepped up was a guy he'd handled all season. I kept telling myself: *I've seen him do this before, I've got to stay with him now. He's got good stuff. He had 21 saves this season, damnit!*

The next hitter singled. *Well, there are runners on second and third; with Don Baylor coming up we might as well walk him and pitch to Brian Downing. He was the third-leading hitter in the league, but I'd seen the catcher take a foul tip off his thumb earlier. That couldn't help his swing. If Downing drives in the tying run, though, Stanhouse has to come out.*

Downing hit the ball to DeCinces, who tagged the runner headed for third—with both hands clutching the ball. We had won, 9–8.

I was still so wired afterward that when writers asked why I had left Stanhouse in so long, about all I could say was, "That's what I wanted to do. That's what I felt I had to do."

Jim Palmer said, "Earl was so nervous he couldn't speak the words to take out Stanhouse."

We had game three, in California, won 3–2 in the last of the ninth. But Al Bumbry made an error on a ball that ended the game. It was a low liner and Al raced a long way in to get there as the ball drove into his glove. Then it popped out and the Angels went on to score twice. It was a tough loss for Stanhouse and even tougher on Dennis Martinez, who had pitched well for eight innings. But errors are part of the game, and no one could fault Bumbry's effort on the play.

Scotty McGregor pitched a 6-hit shutout in the deciding game. His only troublesome inning was the fourth, when the Angels loaded the bases with one out. Then Doug DeCinces made a play at third that was reminiscent of Brooks Robinson, diving to his right to grab a screaming one-hopper. He hooked the bag with his foot and rifled the ball to first for a double play.

For the first time since 1971, the Baltimore Orioles—whom many people referred to as "the no-name O's"—were the American League champions!

Our opponents in the World Series would be the Pittsburgh Pirates, who had a team batting average of .281—including their pitchers! They had no outs in their first eight positions in the lineup. We would be at a disadvantage because it was an odd year. In odd years the designated hitter cannot be used in the World Series. The DH had been an important part of our thinking when we put together the Orioles in the spring. Now our pitchers, who had not swung a bat all season, would bat, and Lee May, Benny Ayala, and Terry Crowley would be pinch hitters. I'd had my pitchers taking batting practice for a week, and three of them could swing the bat pretty good—Palmer, Flanagan, and McGregor. Scotty, who hits from both sides of the plate, had outhit George Brett on their high school team.

I had one more pinch hitter than the Pirates, who carried ten pitchers to our nine. In the National League teams often pinch hit for pitchers in the sixth inning when they're down by two runs. We don't do that in the AL because of the DH.

Despite the Pirates' formidable lineup, though, we had hit 33 more homers than they had, and I firmly believed our pitching staff was superior.

The Series opener in Baltimore was delayed one day by rain. The next morning Baltimore had its earliest snowfall ever, which turned to rain. It was still drizzling when the game started and the temperature was a cool 41 degrees. The conditions resulted in some very sloppy play, as each team committed three errors. First-inning miscues helped us score 3 runs on 2 hits and 2 walks. Then DeCinces hit a 2-run homer to run our lead to 5–0 off Pirate starter Bruce Kison, one of our '71 Series nemeses. But four subsequent Pirate pitchers held us to 3 hits and no runs the rest of the way. Mike Flanagan went the distance and stranded 10 runners to win, 5–4, a helluvan effort.

We should have won the second game as well. Palmer gave up only 2 runs in 7 innings, and Eddie Murray drove in a pair for us with a home run and a double. After Tippy Martinez checked Pittsburgh in the eighth, our first 2 batters got on in the bottom of the inning. With one out Lowenstein stepped in against reliever Don Robinson and the Pirates decided we were going to bunt, which did not say a lot for their scouting reports on us. Robinson threw a fastball on the outside corner to the left-hand-hitting Steiner, who tried to slice it to left. The ball would have shot through the hole between short and third . . . except that third baseman Bill Madlock had charged to play a bunt and shortstop Tim Foli shot to his right to cover the base. The ball hopped right to Foli, who started a double play to end our threat. But if the Pirates hadn't defensed against a bunt, Steiner's hard grounder would have been into left field and scored one run if not two. The Pirates reached Stanhouse for a run in the ninth and won, 3–2.

Rain fell for the third straight game, during game three in Pittsburgh, and play was stopped for sixty-seven minutes with us trailing 3–2. I felt Benny Ayala, though a defensive liability in left, was my best bet in left to hit Pirate starter John Candelaria. Benny had come through with a 2-run homer. And after the rain delay Scotty McGregor permitted only one other run to earn a complete-game victory. Kiko Garcia had 4 hits and 4 RBIs as we won, 8–4.

We were down 6–3 entering the eighth inning of game four (in which the Pirates would amass 17 hits!) when Garcia and Singleton both hit safely. After Murray forced Singy, DeCinces walked, and I knew Kent Tekulve would be the reliever coming in. I'd pinch hit Lee May early and save my left-handed hitters for the sidearming right-hander. Lowenstein pinch hit a double off Tekulve to drive in Garcia and Murray. Billy Smith pinch hit for Dauer and was intentionally passed. Terry Crowley pinch hit for catcher Dave Skaggs and doubled home DeCinces and Lowenstein. Six runs scored. I couldn't complain about our bench. That was our fourth pinch hit in five attempts.

After that 9–6 victory, which Timmy Stoddard won in relief, any number of writers were talking about Earl Weaver as the Series MVP. That was the silliest thing I'd ever heard. I hadn't made one of those hits. Besides, the award was for the Most Valuable *Player*.

"They ought to make the MVP prize a 25-man bus instead of a car," I said. "Then everybody on my squad could use it. They all deserve it if we win this thing, which we should leading three games to one."

But we managed only 6 hits and 1 run in game five, losing 7–1.

In game six Candelaria and Tekulve combined for the first Series shutout since 1975 as the Pirates won, 4–0.

In the deciding game Dauer's home run put us ahead for five innings, then Willie Stargell—whose eighth-inning single had driven in the winning run against us in '71—broke McGregor's shutout with a 2-run homer. Those were all the runs Pittsburgh needed. I couldn't believe it, but we had lost the World Series again.

"Well," I told the press sadly, "we started the season 3-and-8 and finished it 0-and-3. In between we were the best team in baseball. But we'll be back next year."

I sure did feel like shit, though, at that moment.

We opened the 1980 season in Chicago and won 5–3. A White Sox pitcher screwed up a bunt that cost them a run, and Mark Belanger made one of his routinely astonishing defensive plays that killed a rally. With a man on first a White Sox batter drilled an extra-base hit into left center. The runner was rounding third when Al Bumbry threw in the ball to Belanger, who appeared to have no chance; the runner was safe all the way. But Mark, his back to home, whirled and fired the ball to Rick Dempsey, who was blocking the plate and holding his glove six inches off the ground. He didn't have to move it an inch. The ball sailed into the pocket the instant that runner's shoe slid into the glove. Bang, bang—you're out.

That night I went on Harry Caray's radio show, an hour program in which fans call in. Well, I'd been voted the '79 Manager of the Year by my peers in the *Sporting News* poll, and a number of stories had appeared in which I was called "a genius" again. Some people who called in said similar things. "I watched the game today, Harry, and we were beaten by another typical Earl Weaver team. They execute all the fundamentals perfectly. Here we have the same old White Sox. Why can't the White Sox teach their players like Weaver teaches the Orioles? Why can't they get an Earl Weaver?"

I said, "The White Sox don't need an Earl Weaver. If you want a shortstop to execute the way Mark Belanger does—you better trade for Belanger. Every major-league shortstop knows to take the throw from the outfield, turn, and relay home. But Belanger is the only man in the world who can make that play you saw today. And I don't want no credit for teaching him fundamentals because fundamentals don't make that play. That takes God-given ability, which is why Mark Belanger's been making that kind of play for me for fifteen years. The only credit I want is for being smart enough to play Belanger when he's hitting .189."

As I've said, though, for years I'd been looking for someone to replace Mark, someone who could play decent shortstop and give us more offense. Kiko Garcia had beaten out Belanger in the spring until he hurt his back. I was just waiting for him to recover and resume his starting role. In '79 Kiko had played more at short than Mark. Garcia had shown a lot more offense, with 34 of his 100 hits having gone for extra bases. Kiko had also batted .400 in the World Series, with 8 hits and 6 RBIs in 6 games. He would have been the Series MVP had it ended in four games.

But when the season opened Garcia couldn't shake the muscular problems in his lower back, even though he denied he was hurting. I could see he wasn't taking his normal swing and he wasn't beating out the infield choppers that had been hits the year before.

"Kiko, are you all right?" I asked him.

"Yeah," he said. "I'm okay."

Then I'd play him and see balls that he used to get to with ease shoot right past him. And Kiko, who had been a pretty good base stealer in '79, was getting thrown out by two steps in '80.

"Kiko, you're not supposed to go unless you've got a good jump," I'd say.

"I had a good jump," he insisted.

Kiko figured the hell with the pain, that he could put up with it and he would do it all the next day if he just kept playing. He refused to accept the fact that the mind does not allow you to do everything you want to do when you're in pain. "I'm all right," he kept saying.

Finally, in late May, we decided to put him on the disabled list for fifteen days. He returned to the active list in June and put together six solid weeks at the plate, batting .284. In his subsequent 130 at-bats covering 53 games, Kiko batted only .146 to finish at .199. When your hitting shortstop doesn't hit, you go back to your super-fielder. Belanger batted .279 through the season's final 56 games to finish at .228—his best average since 1976. Kiko totaled over 40 more plate appearances than Mark, so I gave the youngster his opportunity. But he just couldn't seize it.

Yet the non-starting or split-time role gnawed at Kiko Garcia. At least three times I had him in my office and explained, "Mark Belanger is the best defensive shortstop in baseball. As long as your batting average isn't higher than his, then Mark is gonna start most ball games. Those are the facts. You must beat him out and you have the opportunity to do so every time you get in the lineup. But it's up to you to produce."

Kiko was unhappy with the situation and continued to be into the spring of '81. His attitude did not aid his performance. We traded him to the Houston Astros in March. All you can do with a discontented player is move him elsewhere, because when the discontent affects him on the ball field he's not going to help your club or himself. If Kiko Garcia ever accepts his role as a player who comes off the bench and who starts against pitchers he can hit, he'll be an asset to any club.

But a manager always has individuals who feel they are not getting enough playing time, particularly young guys who have never played regularly. The main reason why we traded Merv Rettenmund after the '73 season was because he was discontented. He came in and said he wanted to go to a team where he would get a chance to play regularly. He said we weren't getting the most out of his ability. But after batting 321 times for us in '73, he moved to Cincinnati and went to bat only 208 times; his average fell to .216. Like a number of other players who wanted to go elsewhere and did so, Rettenmund would have been better off staying with us. He later told me that when he was sent to the Angels, where he became a coach. I used him against the pitchers he had success with.

Terry Crowley came in to complain that same winter Rettenmund did. "Earl, I've got to have a chance to play regularly," he said. "I've got to have a chance to make some money."

I tried to tell Terry he might be better off with us, but you can't convince a guy who's twenty-six or twenty-seven. I understood how he felt. I'd used him sparingly at first base and in the outfield. He was our left-handed pinch hitter and sometimes DH. He had 11 homers in '73, but he wanted to leave. So we sold Crowley to Texas, which sold him to Cincinnati, which traded him to Atlanta a couple of years later. He was released early in the '76 season. We immediately signed him to a Rochester contract because I'd always liked Terry's bat, and two months later we called him up. He's been our best pinch hitter the last few years. Terry Crowley is very happy with his role these days.

José Morales is the right-handed version of Terry. We signed Morales as a free agent before the '81 season, and he's another veteran who is happy in his work. José and Terry both have over 90 career pinch hits. I doubt that any team has ever had such a duo.

But as you need a variety of skills to contend, you can't make up your ball club entirely with guys who are going to be happy in reserve roles or splitting time. John Lowenstein—who would hit .311 for us in 1980—knows he'll see a lot of action, and I think he's satisfied. Rick Dempsey wants to play every day, bar none, and so does Dan Graham. I tell Dempsey that rather than get annoyed, he'd be better off emulating Lowenstein. Steiner sits on the bench thinking about what he can do when he *does* get into the game. He's always thinking and he's always ready.

It's a tribute to the astute baseball judgment that prevails throughout the Baltimore organization that allowed us to acquire a ballplayer of John Lowenstein's ability for the $20,000 waiver price. The trade for Dan Graham is another tribute. He was with Toledo in the Twins' system and Minnesota was demoting him from their Triple-A roster when we traded for Graham, and Dan batted .278 and hit 15 home runs for us in 1980. The Orioles have always had keen judgment, which is why they've compiled the best record in the major leagues since they were formed in 1954.

I firmly believe that I could assemble a group of scouts—people I've worked with—who in two years could put together an expansion team that would play well over .500 ball in its first season as a major-league ball club. If I could get Billy Hunter and George Staller and some other people I worked with in the minors, I could set up a network that would scout every player in the country, and we'd find enough good ones to win the pennant in three or four years. There is plenty of talent in the minor leagues and among the last three or four players on the major-league rosters. Look what shortstop Bill Almon, whom the Mets didn't want, has done with the White Sox . . . what reliever Kevin Saucier, whom the Rangers didn't want, has done with the Tigers . . . what outfielder Leon Roberts did when he finally got a chance in Seattle and what he's continuing to do in Texas.

Instead of selecting guys who may be good in three or four years, I'd take individuals who could play right away. Guys who may be as slow as Kenny Singleton, but who can hit the ball out of the park. Guys who can play defense and still know how to get on base by bunting for a hit or whatever. Guys who can do one thing *very* well even if they are limited in other areas.

The Orioles came close to winning again in 1980, even though our pitching declined to third in the league (3.64 ERA). Palmer's nagging back problems and an atrophied muscle behind Flanagan's left shoulder limited them to 16 victories apiece. McGregor won 20 for the first time, losing only 8, and Stone went 25–7 and won the Cy Young Award. As I already referred to Flanagan as "Cy Young," I had to call Stone "Cy Present." Palmer, of course, was "Cy Past" and McGregor was "Cy Future." Dennis Martinez was "Cy Future Future," but tendinitis knocked him out for seven weeks and he ended up 6–4.

We still won 100 games, only two less than we had in '79, but the Yankees won 103. We weren't eliminated until the day before the season ended. Going into the final days I had some fun with George Steinbrenner, telling the press: "If the Yankees lose it, George Steinbrenner will build a boat, go to the middle of the Atlantic Ocean, and pull the plug. It would be the biggest fold in baseball history."

"Tell Earl Weaver he can kiss my grits," Steinbrenner shot back through the press. "We're not going to fold. I'll tell you who folded. The Orioles when they were ahead 3–1 in last year's World Series. And this year they got a half-game out and couldn't overtake us."

I laughed. The Yankees had a four-game lead with only three

games to play and we had seven left, but it's always fun to stir up George. He just might say something that could bug his players.

We swept four from the Red Sox in Boston—an Oriole first—and lost only one of our final seven games. But we just couldn't gain on the Yankees, and that was to their credit. It's a shame they folded in the play-offs to my old golfing partner Jimmy Frey and the Royals.

Our problem in 1980 was the old Oriole bugaboo, a bad start. We didn't get over .500 until June. From then on we had the best record in the majors, 72–32, which is .692 ball. In the heat of August and September when a lot of make-up games are played, our deep depth, as I call it, pays off annually. Through 1980, we had played over .660 ball in September/October ever since I'd managed the Orioles.

But a team that's built on pitching is going to suffer most early in the season when there are invariably a bunch of postponements due to rain and cold weather. The result of this is that your pitchers don't get enough work, and you can't settle your rotation until late May or early June.

Once our offense got going in 1980, we set club records for hits (1,523), runs (805), and batting average (.273) in a season, yet we ranked no higher than fifth in the league in any of those categories. The most peculiar thing was that we hit 25 fewer homers than in '79, but scored 48 more runs. Roenicke's fractured wrist and DeCinces' lower back ailments combined with Lee May's abrupt loss of power to explain our homer drop.

As usual we made use of all our players, substituting for regulars whenever it was to our advantage to do so. And as usual the regulars didn't like this, but they never will.

I remember when I began using a pinch runner for Kenny Singleton late in ball games in which we had a lead. Kenny is one of the real gentlemen of the game, an even-tempered man who never gets upset. But when I sent in Tom Shopay to run for Kenny after a late-inning single, Singleton said, "What the heck are you doing, Earl? I've got a chance to score a hundred runs this season."

"Kenny, you know as well as I do that Shopay's got a better chance than you of beating a double play," I said. "Besides, you just signed a long-term contract, you ain't gonna make any more money."

"It's not money," he said. "It's pride, Earl. Pride."

I never care about players' bruised pride or what they might say about me for bruising it. When all is said and done, all I want anyone to say about me is, "Earl Weaver—he sure was a good sore loser."

AFTERWORD

Earl Weaver did not look like a man whose ball club had been victimized by the silly season that baseball 1981 had become. He wasn't bitter when I met him in New York with only 10 games remaining on the burglarized schedule and the Oriole prospects of qualifying for the mini-play-offs appearing to be grim. Weaver refused to concede anything, even though the Orioles trailed Detroit by 3 games, Boston by 2½, and Milwaukee by 1½, and had no games left with either the Red Sox or Brewers. Baltimore would finish the season with 4 games in New York, 3 in Detroit, and 3 at home against the Yankees.

But Earl was realistic in assessing his ball club's chances. "If Boston goes 5-and-5, we have to go 8-and-2 to make the mini-play-offs," he said in the visiting manager's office at Yankee Stadium. "That ain't so good when we don't even get to play two of the contenders. We may have to win all our games." He ran a hand through his silvery hair and smiled. "But, hell, we've won eleven straight games twice this season, so we can do it."

Yet Weaver had every right to be angry. For the team owners who had forced the strike that knocked fifty games off the schedule had also stolen the strength of the Orioles. As usual the ball club had been built on pitching and "deep depth," which normally provided the Orioles with a distinct advantage in the stretch run of a 162-game season. But in the silly season the less-deep opponents had not been run down. They had not stumbled and gasped in the heat of August because the missing June and July games had taken no toll. No team in either league had been hurt as badly as Baltimore by the seven-week strike.

Nevertheless, Earl Weaver was not about to rail against the fates over which he had no control. "I was actually for the split season initially," he said, and laughed mirthlessly. "I thought it would help attendance throughout baseball, except for the teams that had been assured of being in the play-offs. But our GM, Hank Peters, had it pegged from the start, which was why Baltimore voted against the format the owners presented. Hank said that when we resumed play again in August it would look like April and May to the fans. They checked the standings in mid-August and saw the teams with 3-and-2 or 4-and-1 records, and they were confused. By the time the race had developed and should have been interesting to the fans, they knew the season was almost over and didn't care. Attendance is down all over the league. The worst thing in Baltimore was when the fans realized they had to root for the Yankees because they were already in the play-offs. When Baltimore fans couldn't root *against* the Yankees, there went baseball."

Phil Pepe, who writes for the *Daily News*, came striding into the office with a huge smile on his face. "Got my ten dollars, Earl?" he said. Pepe had bet that Columbus, the Yankee farm club, would finish ten games ahead of Rochester in the International League. Columbus had ended up nineteen games ahead of the Orioles' top farm team.

"Right here," Earl said, handing over a $10 bill. "That bleeping Steinbrenner loads up against our Rochester club. Of course, we had so much trouble up here that I defeated my own bet. I kept taking Rochester's best players—Steve Luebber, Cal Ripken, Jr., and Jeff Schneider."

A half dozen writers now convened in Weaver's office and a discussion ensued about the previous night's fight between Reggie Jackson of the Yankees and Indians' pitcher John Denny. Jackson alleged that Denny had thrown at him, and after the game George Steinbrenner said the Yankees were going to start suing pitchers who threw at their batters.

"Well I don't believe in throwing at anyone," Weaver said. "If a pitcher can't get guys out without throwing at them, get rid of him. If he has to hit batters, send him to jail. Seems like George and I agree on everything." He laughed.

Dick Young, the veteran columnist for the New York *Daily*

News, said, "Batters never ran out to the mound when pitchers still batted in the American League."

"Hey, guys still run out to the mound in the National League," Weaver said. "They always did. Hell, Joe Adcock not only chased Reuben Gomez off the mound but all the way into the clubhouse with a bat. If you got a hothead, you're gonna have a fight.

"But you still got guys like Bobby Grich and Don Baylor who get hit all the time and don't give a shit. We broke Grich's hand early this year and we weren't throwing at him. We hit as many guys as any team, but it's not intentional. The other night in Detroit, Sammy Stewart hit Lynn Jones right in the bleeping neck. It was a 100 percent accident. But I thought Jones was dead—until he got up and ran to first. We hit Carlton Fisk twice in one game, for chrissake, because we know where we're going with him."

Earl rose from behind his desk and pushed a wastebasket out to an empty space on the floor. "Fisk's elbow hangs over the plate," Earl assumed a batter's stance with his left elbow protruding over the home-plate wastebasket, "and the object is to aim at his elbow. Jam him right in here," he drew an imaginary line under the elbow, "and Fisk ain't gonna hit the ball. The pitch's almost a strike."

"That Denny really looks like he's throwing at guys at times," a writer said.

"He will throw at guys," said Jimmy Russo, the Oriole superscout who had been following the Yankees in preparation for this series.

Under terms of the strike settlement negotiated by Marvin Miller, the players were to share 60 percent of the gate receipts from the first three games of the mini-play-offs that had been added. The managers and coaches would not share in the gate receipts. But Oakland manager Billy Martin had said, "If me and my coaches don't get paid, we won't be there. Let Marvin Miller manage."

"What do you think of Billy's threat not to manage in the mini-play-offs if he and his coaches don't get paid?" Dick Young asked Weaver.

"Well, if you have to work and don't get nothing for it . . .

that ain't so good," Earl said. "But we did get paid during the strike and the players didn't."

"Yeah, but the coaches don't make that much," Young said.

"Is Billy talking about an additional five days' pay or a share of the play-off money?" Earl said. "I've already told Hank Peters that if we get into the play-offs I don't want additional pay. My feeling is that the players—who went without pay during the strike while managers and coaches got paid—should get the play-off money. I do feel bad for the coaches because they do an awful lot of work. But this was predetermined in the settlement, so we couldn't do anything about it."

"That's because Marvin Miller made the agreement with [owners' negotiator] Ray Grebey, and the coaches had no representation," Young said. He is among the most widely read sportswriters in the nation, his columns appearing in both the *Daily News* and *The Sporting News*, and he invariably champions the owners over the players.

"Marvin Miller only does what the players tell him to," Earl said.

"Wait a minute," Young said.

"We are not members of the association," Earl said. "Marvin Miller has no negotiation rights for the coaches or managers."

"The point is he ignores them!" Young said.

"Well let's go back three years," Earl said. "Marvin Miller sent around to all the coaches and managers in baseball a bulletin that said we [the Major League Players Association] would like to include you in the basic agreement and have you become voting members of the organization. At that time, we [the Orioles coaches and Weaver] went to Hank Peters, and I said I didn't see any reason why we shouldn't go into the organization and get a vote. We voted to, but the vast majority of managers and coaches in baseball did not. Only about 30 percent wanted to join the MLPA."

Dick Young said nothing more before leaving. But a couple of days later he wrote in his column: "The outrageous part of Miller's disregard for managers and coaches is that these men pay dues to the players' association, yet are not permitted to sit in on clubhouse meetings when players take votes." Young did not acknowledge the fact that managers and coaches paid dues to the MLPA because they chose to, and that they had no voting rights because the majority of them had chosen not to accept that opportunity when it was offered to them, as Weaver had pointed out. I now fully understood when Earl says that certain writers refuse to print the facts that vary from their views.

Earl went over the Yankee hitters with his catchers and Jim Palmer, then sat in the dugout during batting practice. Jimmy Russo sat next to him and said, "Marvin Miller should have to answer to all the part-time scouts who had to pull their kids out of college this fall because of the strike."

"Miller didn't cause the strike—the owners did," Earl said. "They thought they could break the union. The owners didn't have to let those part-time scouts go, either."

Henry Hecht of the New York *Post* came by and asked Weaver for his MVP pick. "Ricky Henderson [Oakland], I guess," Earl said. "But if we win it, Eddie Murray should be the MVP. He's had more RBIs than anyone in either league in the second half—42 in 40 games. He's leading the league in RBIs. I always like those guys who drive in the runs because they win ball games."

The RBI men win games when their own pitchers hold down the opposition. That was Jim Palmer's assignment in the first game of the New York series. Palmer's early-season problems with his arm, shoulder, and back had resumed in the second half and he had left some games early, leading some of his teammates to mumble questions about his courage. The feeling seemed to be that other Oriole pitchers were less reluctant than Palmer to pitch with pain. Most major-league pitchers who sustain lengthy careers have to learn to pitch while experiencing varied amounts of pain. But Weaver stayed with his veteran, and Palmer had come through in several recent outings, including his last start, a five-hit victory over Milwaukee.

He was even stronger against the Yankees—"Vintage Palmer," Weaver called it—but he gave Earl a scare in the fourth inning. "My back spasm's coming back," Palmer told Weaver in the dugout.

"*What* back spasm?" Earl said, shocked.

"I had it on the bus coming up."

"Well, is that it for tonight?"

"I don't know, Earl. I'll go out and see."

Weaver got Steve Stone up in the bullpen, but he wasn't needed. Palmer went all the way, giving up only four hits and a lone run as Baltimore won, 5-1.

The writers, reflecting on Palmer's problems over the year and his 7-8 record, tried to press Weaver to comment on his decline. "Eventually there will come a point where he just can't do it anymore," said balding Henry Hecht of the *Post*.

"That'll be a long time from now," Earl said. "You won't have no hair left then, Henry. Palmer's coming back. I think he's gonna be pitching with a little more pain from this point on in his career. But as long as he can pitch to the spots he wants to and get the breaking-balls over, he's gonna be in control out there."

When the writers dispersed, Oriole radio broadcaster Tom Marr came in as Earl stepped into the shower. "Well, Rick Dempsey's got to be happy tonight—2-for-4," Tom said to me. "He's only hitting .212 and he's always worrying, but Rick is some tough catcher. A few nights ago he got hit in the back of the head with a bat. The hitter swung all the way around and Rick needed five stitches. The next night he played and jammed his ankle running to first base."

"It's all green and purple right now," Earl said, coming out of the shower and drying off.

"I saw him in the clubhouse before the next game against Detroit and I said, 'You're not gonna play on that?'" Marr continued. "Dempsey limped over to his locker and said, 'My ankle's not bothering me. I can run, I just can't walk.' Then he saw he wasn't in the lineup and got angry!"

"Well don't the SOB know that two nights in a row he made the last out swinging like this?" Weaver said, bending from the waist and swinging like a man underwater. "Dempsey gave me a funny look and then sulked."

"He asked for the stats on the Detroit pitcher," Marr said, laughing, "and I said there aren't any on this pitcher. He's a rookie we've never faced!"

"Dempsey didn't know that kid was right-handed," Earl said, laughing.

"The organizational meetings [in which the Oriole management discussed plans for 1982] early this week worried him," Marr said. "He asked me, 'Are they in there talking about how disappointed they are in the catchers this year? Do they want to get rid of me now?'

"I said, 'You're paranoid, Rick. You're a great catcher. I don't think they're going to get rid of you.'"

"Well, I'll tell you this," Earl said. "We're looking for something better."

"You're always looking for something better," Marr said.

"Yeah, and it's not hard to find when somebody's hitting .212."

"But it is hard to find a catcher as good defensively as Dempsey."

Weaver nodded. "That's for sure."

On the drive from Yankee Stadium to the Sheraton Hotel where the Orioles were staying, Earl mused, almost to himself, "If we'da beat Detroit two more games this season, we'd change places with them and everybody would be looking up at us now. Then everyone would be asking, 'What makes you so good?'

"We let a game against Chicago get away," he said to me. "I took out Palmer in the eighth leading 4–2. Tim Stoddard came in and went whiff, whiff, whiff. In the ninth he got the first guy. Walked Tony Bernazard on a questionable call. A bloop double down the left-field line. Got the second out. Then Ron LeFleur blooped one over second and tied the score. They scored two more to go ahead 6–4. But Eddie Murray hit a 2-run homer in the ninth and then we loaded the bases with only one out. We didn't score again, and the White Sox did. If we had won that one and two more from Detroit, we'd be walking away with the pennant."

At the Sheraton, Earl went directly to the bar, as he does after all road games. He ordered two gin and tonics, saying, "Might as well celebrate!" Then he began talking about his recent arrest in Baltimore for driving while intoxicated, an offense for which he had last been cited in 1973. "I go out to dinner with Marianna every Sunday night that we're home," he said, "and they only caught me twice in fourteen years."

"You know, he went on the radio and told the whole story on his show!" Marr said. "And he was nice enough to mention that I was there with my wife, who is a Baltimore cop!"

"The only thing that I regret about the incident was that I was too dumb to call a cab and not get behind the wheel," Earl said. "I really don't want to jeopardize my life or anyone else's. It is a serious offense and I know I shouldn't be driving after an evening of celebrating. The truth of the matter is that I usually don't. Marianna drives home 90 percent of the time, and has done so ever since the 1973 arrest. I'll lose my license for a month or two."

Scott McGregor pitched the second game in New York, against Tommy John. They are both underpowering, left-handed con men. Neither throws over 82 mph, but each "has his last pitch working for him," according to Weaver. They set up hitters, McGregor with a slow curveball and a slick change-up, John with a sinker and a slider. Then they'll come in with high fastballs, often right into a batter's power . . . when he can't make use of it.

McGregor had compiled a 44–18 record since 1979, including an 11–4 mark this season, and he had pitched 1–0 victories over the Yankees in each of the previous two seasons. But the 1–0 shutout he threw this night was as fine a game as he'd ever completed in the majors. He gave up only 4 hits and he struck out 11 batters. He threw just 93 pitches—a remarkably low total when at least 33 went into the strikeouts.

"Scotty went out in the ninth saying he wanted to get them on three pitches," Earl said afterward. "In other words, they're gonna get things to hit—but he ain't gonna allow the winning run to home plate. Good pitchers like Scotty and John make it look easy."

"Those guys weren't pitchers tonight," Russo said. "They were artists—in, out, down, up. Phew! I need a drink."

"Wait a second, Russo!" Earl said as the writers streamed in. "I want to tell these guys we won because of your great scouting. Russo tells me John can't get off the mound that well, and he's right. We won the game tonight when he couldn't throw out Bumbry's topper. [Doug DeCinces had walked before Al Bumbry's swinging bunt, then Rich Dauer had driven in the run with a single.] I put the bunt on with two out because the third baseman was back and I thought Bumbry might beat it out."

"Scotty threw only twenty balls all night," Russo said.

"He was exceptional," Earl said. "But as good as everything looks tonight, it all boils down to the same thing. We got to keep winning."

The Orioles had now drawn to within one and a half games of Detroit and Boston, tied for first, and within a half game of third-place Milwaukee.

In game three of the series Mike Flanagan, who had not fully regained his rhythm since his return from arm trouble, was relieved after 4⅓ innings, trailing 3–2. Tippy Martinez gave up only 1 hit over the next 4 innings, as home runs by Gary Roenicke and José Morales sent the Orioles ahead 4–3. But Tippy walked Rick Cerone leading off the ninth—the last thing a pitcher wants to do. Bobby Brown sacrificed Cerone to second, and Weaver brought in Steve Stone to work on Willie Randolph, who is not a good curveball hitter. Stone broke off a curve and Randolph pounded it into the ground toward third for what should have been out number two. But Doug DeCinces could not come up with the ball.

Weaver called for Tim Stoddard. Earl knew the Yankees would send up the left-hand-hitting Bobby Murcer, and he wanted the hard-throwing Stoddard to face him. Unfortunately, Stoddard couldn't control his smoke. He ran the count to 3-and-1, then came in with a fastball out over the plate. Murcer hit it into the bleachers. Yankees 6, Orioles 4.

In his office, Earl Weaver was ashen, even his tan had been drained away by Murcer's blow. He had the look of a man I had once seen carry his bleeding son into an emergency room after an auto accident. Where Earl's voice was usually loud and full of confidence, he answered most of the writers' questions in a low, stunned voice.

"What were Murcer's stats against Stone and Stoddard?" a writer asked, wondering why Weaver had not left in Stone.

"Murcer was 3-for-5 off Stone and 1-for-3 off Stoddard," Earl said. "Aw, shit! I pulled Tippy to bring in the best breaking-ball in the league against Randolph, who was 1-for-12 against Stone. You got your book. You know what you want to do, and you got a guy in the bullpen who can do it. Stone got Randolph to hit the groundball, and we missed it. We get that out and we can walk Murcer, but you can't walk the tying run over to third. I had no more options."

"You just figured you'd rather have Stoddard than Stone against Murcer," writer Ken Nigro said.

"That was my choice, that's why I did it," Earl said. "That's what I wanted to do. There ain't no other answer."

"You preferred the fastball pitcher?" Nigro asked.

"Well, Murcer's gonna know that he'll likely see curves from Stone if he stays in. But when he goes 3-and-1 with Stoddard, he *knows* he's gonna get a fastball. That was the thing to avoid . . . going 3-and-1. Christ!"

"Is Murcer a curveball or a fastball hitter?" someone else asked.

"Murcer's a both-ball hitter. You got to throw him a pitch he ain't looking for. Shit, what hurt most was the lead-off walk in the ninth. Well, we'll never know what Tippy would have done if I'd left him in. And we'll never know what Stone would've done if I'd left him in."

The Oriole trainer abruptly ushered in a doctor to examine Weaver's right bicep. That shoulder had been troubling him ever since it had been separated in that 1957 dugout fight in the minor leagues. The muscles in the arm had atrophied and, working out with a five-pound dumbbell in an effort to strengthen the muscles, Weaver had recently felt something pop. The bicep appeared to be twice its normal size.

"You've ruptured the lower tendon," the doctor told him, "and it just rolled down your arm."

"Will it affect my golf swing?" Earl asked, simulating a swing.

"No. You'll lose a little strength in that arm, but otherwise it shouldn't bother you."

"As long as I can play golf, I won't worry about it," Earl said. "Thanks, doc."

The writers left and Earl turned toward Jimmy Russo, who looked disconsolate, seated in the corner. Earl asked him if it had appeared from the stands, where Russo had been charting pitches, as if Stoddard had been throwing hard. Russo shrugged. "He threw the ball pretty good," Russo said without enthusiasm. He walked into the clubhouse with his head down.

Earl showered and the color had returned to his face when he emerged, but his voice was filled with emotion and regret as he confided to me, "Christ, I feel like I let the guys down. They know Stoddard's had some arm problems. They know he's given up a couple recently . . ."

Russo came back into the office and Earl said, "Well, as much as we wanted the SOB tonight, we're still very much alive."

Dennis Martinez, whose 14–4 record and seemingly tireless arm had made him Weaver's 1981 Cy Young Award candidate, lost to the Yankees the next afternoon, 5–2. Yet the Orioles bounced back on Tuesday in Detroit, winning 7–3 as Murray doubled and homered to drive in 4 runs. But the following night the O's were crushed, 14–0, and eliminated from the race. As Weaver had said, they could not afford to lose more than two of their final ten games. And the one they'd let get away in New York had sounded the knell on the Oriole play-off hopes.

The next game, played on a cold, damp night in Detroit, was one in which a less proud team might have capitulated. Instead, the little shortstop Lenn Sakata hit 2 home runs and the Orioles took a 4–0 lead. The Tigers, fighting to stay in first place, came back to tie the score in the bottom of the ninth. But Tim Stoddard shut them down for 1⅓ innings, and the O's, refusing to give in, won in 10 to knock the Tigers out of the league lead.

The Orioles also won two of their final three games against the Yankees. Scotty McGregor pitched another shutout to raise his record to 13–5, and Mike Flanagan combined with Stoddard for a 5–2 victory. Eddie Murray hit his twenty-second home run in the last game to tie him for the league lead and also earn him the RBI leadership with 78.

"We did everything we could think of," Weaver said, "but the season was just too darn short."

The Orioles finished fourth in the second-half standings, two games behind Milwaukee. If the won-lost records for the entire season had applied to the final standings, Milwaukee (62–47) would still have been first, with Baltimore (59–46) in second place one game behind. But the split-season format seemed totally ludicrous in retrospect. After all, the team with the best overall record in baseball, Cincinnati, did not even make the mini-play-offs. Yet a team with a sub-.500 record, Kansas City (50–53), made the AL West play-offs. The format devised by the owners was neither equitable nor rational. What else is new from baseball's upper echelons? Edward Bennett Williams, principal owner of the Orioles, has said that baseball's hierarchy could "foul up a two-car funeral," and that was resoundingly demonstrated in 1981.

Earl Weaver had a solution to baseball's leaderless leadership problem: "What baseball needs most right now is a Commissioner who is paid by both the owners *and* the players," he said. "Because only then will the Commissioner make unbiased decisions. As long as he's paid solely by the owners—who have the right to fire him—his decisions are always going to benefit his employers. In the late sixties when I was trying to obtain my pension benefits, the Commissioner tried to squelch them to save the owners money. But if we ever have a Commissioner who is paid by both the owners and the players, his decisions will be made with the best interests of the game at heart. It's a great game, and it can only grow stronger, more popular, and more profitable for everyone in the profession if we have impartial leadership at the top.

"If half of Bowie Kuhn's salary was being paid by the players, he would have stepped into the owners-players deadlock well before the strike deadline and said, 'Let's get together, fellas. A strike will only hurt everyone and it could seriously damage our profession.'"

Kuhn did not step in, and everyone lost. The question now is how much long-range damage was done to a growing industry before the strike that was premeditated by a relatively small group of owners. Will the taint of the silly season of 1981 carry over to 1982 or beyond in the eyes of baseball fans? Baseball is a sport steeped in an almost sacrosanct tradition, and that tradition was mutilated by the silly season.

"I think the fans will come back," Earl Weaver said, "and I feel we need an impartial Commissioner who would assure everyone of stability in the game. I also think it might be a good thing to have a Commissioner who once had worn the uniform on the ball field. Anyone who has given most of his life to baseball would never permit it to be mistreated again. I have had the uniform on for thirty-five years, and I know I could walk into a meeting with Marvin Miller and any group of owners, listen to both sides of any issues, and get a settlement in a matter of days. Maybe hours. You give an impartial man who knows and loves baseball the final word—and he will insist on quick and just resolutions of all disputes. The man doesn't have to be a genius to do the right thing for the game."

Even before the season ended, at the Orioles' organizational meeting, Weaver began thinking about how to improve the ball club for 1982. A look at the stat sheet indicated that the O's had to come up with more offensive punch at both the catcher and left-field positions. Gary Roenicke had hit for average, but left field is a power position. And the man who had hit 25 home runs in '79 had virtually lost his longball stroke in '81. Rick Dempsey and Dan Graham had driven in 93 runs while splitting the catching chores in '80, but their run production had been less than one quarter that in '81. The Orioles would undoubtedly attempt to bolster those positions through trades over the winter. Weaver would have other options as well if Cal Ripken, Jr., slugged up to expectations in the spring.

"He just didn't hit when we brought him up, but he will," Earl said. "I couldn't give Cal much of a chance because we were running out of games. But he showed us he can play either third base or shortstop. He's got good hands, and if he could hit 25 home runs up here, Ripken could be another Roy Smalley—only better defensively.

"Now Ripken doesn't have the range at short of Lenn Sakata, and Lenn doesn't have Mark Belanger's range, but very few shortstops do. Sakata has excellent hands and he hit very well in the second half of '81, including 5 home runs in only about 40 games. So if Lenn's our shortstop and Ripken hits, Cal could play third." It seemed likely he would after DeCinces was traded to California for outfielder Dan Ford.

Earl Weaver was looking forward to what could be his final season as the Oriole manager. He will make that decision during the 1982 All-Star break when he meets with his financial advisors and projects his income for the years ahead from his salary, savings, investments, and baseball pension.

"Once I retire, I don't want to come back," he said. "But I do want to go out a winner."

The only future job that interests him would involve doing some baseball commentary on television. Earl enjoyed commenting on the 1980 play-offs and World Series for CBS-TV's weekend "Sportsworld." I can't imagine a more enlightening and entertaining commentator on baseball than Earl Weaver.

"I think my experience in the game would allow me to say some things that others don't necessarily see," Earl said. "Of course, I have to admit that Maury Wills proved as a broadcaster that experience on the field doesn't always result in insights. I remember a game he broadcast when the team that was losing by several runs got men on first and second in the seventh inning. Wills said, 'They might sacrifice.' I said to myself, 'Well, Maury, I doubt that you'll ever manage in the big leagues.' I guess the folks in Seattle weren't listening.

"But, hell, I'm continually amazed at the number of intelligent people who don't listen. I still believe in the words on that sign I hung in the Baltimore clubhouse the day I took over the Orioles: 'It's what you learn after you know it all that counts.' You learn by listening and observing, and you never stop. Billy Martin, who had played Shooty Babitt at second base for some fifty games before he realized the youngster couldn't handle the position, came over to me during our last series with Oakland. It had taken Billy some time to make up his mind on Babitt, but now he was rather firm. 'Earl,' he said, 'if you ever see Shooty Babitt playing second base for me again, I want you to shooty me.' He learned.

"Managers are always learning," Earl Weaver concluded, "and mostly we learn from our mistakes. That's why I keep a list of my mistakes at home for reference. I used to carry the list around in my pants pocket, but I finally had to stop. It gave me a limp."

EARL WEAVER'S MANAGERIAL RECORD

YEAR	CLUB	LEAGUE	W	L	PCT.	POSITION
1956	Knoxville	South Atlantic	10	24	.294	8
1957	Fitzgerald	Georgia-Florida	65	74	.468	4
1958	Dublin	Georgia-Florida	72	56	.563	3
1959	Aberdeen	Northern	69	55	.556	2
1960	Fox Cities	Three-I	82	56	.594	1
1961	Fox Cities	Three-I	67	62	.519	4
1962	Elmira	Eastern	72	68	.514	2
1963	Elmira	Eastern	76	64	.543	2
1964	Elmira	Eastern	82	58	.586	1
1965	Elmira	Eastern	83	55	.601	2
1966	Rochester	International	83	64	.565	1
1967	Rochester	International	80	61	.567	2
1968	Baltimore	American	48	34	.585	2
1969	Baltimore	American	109	53	.673	1
1970	Baltimore	American	108	54	.667	1
1971	Baltimore	American	101	57	.639	1
1972	Baltimore	American	80	74	.519	3
1973	Baltimore	American	97	65	.599	1
1974	Baltimore	American	91	71	.562	1
1975	Baltimore	American	90	69	.566	2
1976	Baltimore	American	88	74	.543	2
1977	Baltimore	American	97	64	.602	2-T
1978	Baltimore	American	90	71	.559	4
1979	Baltimore	American	102	57	.642	1
1980	Baltimore	American	100	62	.617	2
1981	Baltimore	American	59	46	.564	2
Major League Totals			1,260	851	.597